AUTOBIOGRAPHY

OF AN

ORDINARY MAN

with odds and ends to match.

CONTENTS

OATMEAL AND PRESBYTERIANISM

In the life of a man in any station who has lived three
score years may be found incidents and passages worth
noting, and carrying instruction to such as see them and
regard them rightly.   Not from any elevated position
the writer occupies, nor from any superior qualifications
that he possesses, does he propose relating some of his
experiences in life, but for reasons as above indicated.

So to begin he will aim at giving a faint picture of his
Maternal Granny.   Beyond Grandfathers and Grandmothers,
of his ancestors the writer knows nothing beyond this,
that they claimed descent from Adam and Eve and certain
later forebears who, it is said, came over with valiant con-
querors: presumedly hungry.
                         Bell Reid, as known to her grand-
son resided in Banff.   She was a little spare woman of
three score years and ten; and to use her own words she
was "peer as th' Kirk moose."   Kind friends gave her a
four pound loaf once a week, which "sometimes laisted tull
th'ine o'th'ook, sometimes no."   She was at times "verra
dowie", but never a complainer; without effort she was contented.   A wiry little woman she had been in her time.
On one occasion she tramped forty-four miles in a day to
visit a married son in Aberdeen; returning in like manner.
Granny was fond of a smoke, though not able to buy much tobacco.   Perhaps she thought, if smoking was good for men
it could not be bad for women.   She was also fond of
her Bible, and often read in it with Matthew Henry's com-

ments.   Working as a stocking knitter and bobbin winder
she had long hours, though at times short enough, with
small wages and hard lines, but no grumbles, at least that
were heard by her grandson.   One consolation she said,
she had; with little, or next to no money, no one could
steal from her.   In extreme poverty Granny was not wretched; she was a Christian woman; she was a member of a
Christian Church, John Murcher her minister, she was respectable and respected.   She wore a white skull cap and an
old faded red mantle, but "didna fash hir heed aboot bein
oot o' th'fashon".   Contented in mind with a little dry
humour, conservative in her ways, and matter of fact was
Granny.   Hearing that Sir A.B. had got a kiss of the Queen's
hand, Granny quietly remarked that she supposed, that Mr.C.
D. would also be "gettin a kiss o'hir fit, or hir hip, or
something.   "Sandy" said the neighbour spoken to "Isna
yer Granny a funnie boddie?"   Granny often mislaid her
"specs", not unlike some other Grannies, we may suppose; "I'm
sure I dinna ken whaur they are; yae see I wus goupin ou'r
the winda (on the third story) an'gyn tha've fa'in aff ma
nose, I may bid gweed day tae them."   My old Granny knelt
down and prayed in silence before retiring to her nightly
rest, enjoining her grandson to do the same; as she put it,
"say his gweed words".   His, poor boy, were soon said; but
he remained on his knees till Granny rose from hers.   One
night she seemed to forget the loonie's presence as he
heard her in an audible whisper say "O LORD LET ME NOT DIE
UNPARDONED; O LORD LET ME NOT DIE UNPREPARED."   (I think
it is owing to our English Bible that Scotch folk seldom
pray in the vernacular.)   Unknown to dear old Granny her

her words have often been repeated since, and will likely be repeated again. Granny at times shewed herself a droll old woman. On one occasion her grandson came to see her, he being in such a hard up condition for decent shoes, that she had some difficulty in taking him to the Kirk service with her. She got over the difficulty however, although the boy of eight years of age did not take very kindly to the arrangement. One of Granny's "auld bauchels" was hung on the toes of his one foot, the heel of the "bauchel" projecting behind. What remained of an old shoe of his own was placed on the other foot, while on Sandy's head was balanced an old hat of his uncle's, not quite half the boy's height, but fitting him tolerably well, at least regarding length, for "the loon had a lang heed." To the Kirk I went with Granny, but with grave misgivings anent my general appearance: for I noticed that the folk were looking at me, perhaps laughing. Granny was seemingly thinking about other things. Granny is now long since dead, but in memory continues to speak. Fearing God she was polished in poverty, and had had her own share of sorrows. She might quietly smile, but I never heard her laugh, nor saw her weep; I never heard her speak loudly, nor in anger, nor complaining. As a child I liked my Granny's kind, couthy quiet voice; and as a man I hold her memory dear. Perhaps I am more indebted to Granny than I know. Just a little more about Granny. She was poor but did not fail to see, that in being poor there were certain advantages. "Yae see, laudie, if it waur kent that I had a five poun note i'ma kist, an ull gaetit man micht cum in an' murder me, an' tak the note. Bit fin it's kent that affen I hinna

five bawbees tae ca'ma ain, syne I can sleep in peace, nae
worth robbin." Happy old woman, who could thus extract
consolation from what is often regarded as the worst of
evils.

O, the lullaby of the sea on the shingly beach between Banff and Macduff as listened to by the dreamy little soul from the rickety "e'most flat o'the e'most hoose
Vricht's Clos,"Banff, while leaning over the window sill.
These days are gone , and for ever. O, the overawing sensation when the boundless blue waters came into view on
my not infrequent visits to see Granny. O, science, so
called, what terrible havoc hast thou made with the glorious visions of things unknown: glorious while un-fathomab-
le, pleasing beyond expression, while mysterious deeper than
all our powers of conception.

Now, about my paternal Grandfa-
ther. He was a weaver, a blanket weaver, a poor man with a
wife and family, in the early years of the nineteenth century, contempary with Waterloo, and died about 1840. That
so far; much more than that I do not know concerning him;
having never seen him so as to recollect him; though I understand, he once saw me when an infant. My Father and Uncle, however, spoke of my Grandfather in my presence, and one
thing I heard worth remembering. As an orthodox Presbyterian and good Christian he had a strict regard for Sabbath observence. If a neighbour or acquaintance called
on my Grandfather on Sabbath, he received them courteously,
and enquired as to their general welfare, but not much more
in that direction. Very soon he would open the Family Bible and without any apology or frefatory remarks begin to

read a portion for general edification: with more courage than some of his descendants, whom we know, possess.
On these occasions the visitor would, as a rule, "slip a-
wa"before Grandfather had read much.   My cousin, who
had seen him described him as "a gai keen auld man".
An old female acquaintance spoke of him as"bit a sober
boddie", (not very big nor robust).   Oatmeal, of but
poor quality I fear, potatoes and greens, and not much of
them, in these sad and "sair" years before and after Waterloo, would tell hard on the poor man's bone and muscle.

My first sorrow--- Aunty Bell, my father's sister, was a
good young woman, a farm servant.   She suffered from
cancer in the breast and died after a second operation.
She was"bonny"in my childish eyes, and when I heard of
her death I wept loud and long.   My Mother said "Aunty
had gaen tae Heaven". and gradually my tears dried up.
But still I see her fair face and happy smile through
the vista of sixty years.   Perhaps now, rather than
look back, it were better to look forward.

My Father was
successively a herd laddie, a ploughman, and a day labourer.   His parents being too poor to send him to school,
in childhood, except for a very short time, he then only
learned to read a little; but putting himself to school
when a young ploughman, he learned to write and cypher
in a fair way.   He also helped his Father, so far as
his scanty means permitted.   My Father's wages as a
ploughman might average from ten to fifteen pounds a
year, food and lodgings additional.   My Father was married to my Mother when he was about thirty-three years of
age

age.   By that time he had saved some fifty or sixty ,
pounds and in tended to rent a croft when, and if, circumstances permitted.   Circumstances never did permit. My
Mother was prostrated by a serious illness soon after
marriage, from which she never wholly recovered.   My Mo-
lived till attaining forty nine years of age, being some
twelve years younger than my Father.   As a labourer my
Father's wages were on an average eight or nine shillings a week.   Ten shillings a week in summer, often less
but never more; in winter , during short days and inclem-
ent weather, six or seven shillings a week would be too
often the amount of his wages.   So, with a sickly wife
and three children he and my mother had a "sair stauchel"
to make ends meet.   He spent three "bawbees" now and again on snuff, his only luxury.   As for beer or whiskey
he could not afford to be other than an abstainer, nor
wished to be.   My Father was a kind husband, an anxious
parent, an intelligent man, humourous in his way, a devout
orthodox Presbyterian, a trembling and God fearing Christian, with a very sensitive conscience.   His troubles and
fears were that he might not be able to pay his way, train
his children aright, and by God's mercy in the Christ Jesus reach Heaven at last.   My Father's intolerance of
his children's faults was perhaps a fault in himself.   I
remember being home on a visit when about seventeen years
old, my Father being then off work through sickness.   He
coming with me a short distance as I started again from
home, took me by the hand to say "Good bye" and halted; then
the tears stood in his eyes as with a faltering voice he
earnestly said "O, Sawnie man dae the richt geet." a word in
season

season never forgotten. In my early days my Father sang
songs and whistled tunes while dandling me on his knees.
So long as in good health his poverty did not make him unhappy nor cause him to grumble; his home, thanks to my Mother was always clean and comfortable. My Father and his
family were most regular attenders at the Kirk, and never
wanted decent clothes to go in. At the disruption he gave
his penny weekly to the Sustentaion Fund, and a penny or
"bawbee"was regularly dropped into the collecting ladle of
those days. Our house was a single apartment on the
ground, with a low roofed attic, or "laft"where two of the
family slept. The annual rent was, I think, two pounds. A
small plot of ground behind the house sufficed to grow a
few vegetables, and flowers of which my Father was very
fond; the ground went with the house. One thing which dis-
turbed my Father in his later days was that perhaps he had
given too much time to his flowers in the summer evenings
when he ought, he thought, to have been indoors instructing
his children. In this there was perhaps, a little morbid-
ness; children may at times be too much instructed, even in
good things. Regard should be given to the patience and
capacity of children.

My Mother, Granny's daughter, suffered
much bodily pains in her life. She was a simple, unedu-
cated, but intelligent and well meaning woman. My Mother's
parting advice to her boy was, "Pray, Sandie, without fail,
and without ceasing." My Mother though very poor was
very cleanly; much ailing but not complaining; often smil-
ing, sometimes heartily laughing, but sometimes weeping with
a "sair hairt".

This poor man, my Father, for many years be-

fore his death in bad health, with his poor sickly wife,
often unable to procure more than keep soul and body together, under more favourable circumstances might have
lived till old age.   But my Father died when fifty-three,
and my Mother when forty-nine, my Mother surviving my Father seven years.   They got their portion however. They
never went without a meal, nor wanted Church going clothes.
They never ate a pauper's crust, nor failed to pay their
debts.   And yet I may confidently say, that my Fathers'
earnings, all the year round, did not exceed eight shillings)
a week.   With this my parents put me and my brother and
sister to school, paid fees and bought books, but with an
"awfu tuave".   With the schooling we got, though by no
means first class, my brother and I have filled responsible,
and to us even lucrative situations; now enjoying all the
comforts and luxuries that we need or desire.   But for
our conscientious and devoted Father and Mother would it,
or could it have been so?   Assuredly not.   Without the
schooling given to us, in virtue of no compulsory clause,
except possibly one inserted in their hearts at their children's baptism, we must have followed pretty closely the
"Poortith cauld" of our respected Parents.   But it must not
be forgotten that we, the children of these parents, received an education in addition to the public school: a schooling which money cannot buy, nor mere influence procure. One
lesson which I was taught in my youth was "waste not" it
was a part of our home religion to carefully gather and
eat the crumbs lying on the table after a meal.   To allow
the smallest portion of eatable food to go to waste was
regarded as a sin.   Another lesson was, ask counsel and
guidance in all things from God in prayer.

Calvinism I was taught in its severest aspects. I mention this to shew that Calvinism, so called, and the most rigid scrupulousness in religion and morals in my Father went hand in hand. However, I do not think that this was at all peculiar to my Father. I continue a Calvinist, not merely because my Father was one, but rather because I cannot see my way to be anything else. I try to act as if all well doing depends entirely on my own exertions; but pray as if all my well doing depends alone on God's good blessing. Calvinism was then, and even now is, to my mind a fearful and appalling system of truth. In my boyhood the question often arose in my mind, "Am I among the chosen number?" The only satisfactory, if satisfactory, answer I have ever got is, "Work out your own salvation with fear and trembling; for it is God that worketh in you" &c. With a free Gospel pardon offered to me, and to all who hear it proclaimed, difficulties in the matter should vanish. If I think that I have got the "white stone" stone" spoken of in Revelations, the less I say about it the better. However unreasonable and unkind it may appear, those who know me refuse to know me by anything but my works and general conduct. Of this I do not complain, nor should any one. Calvinism is taught in the Shorter Catechism; from it the doctrine might be excised, but it would remain true all the same. In such facts as follow Calvinism is permanently involved. I am a native of Scotland, with all the advantages to body and soul which that fact implies. Another man has been born in Central Africa, and reared a cannibal. Whom have I to thank for the difference? Certainly not myself, my Father, nor another, except to a very limited extent.

Parenthetically about my Father when a "loonie" about
five or six years of age.   A little baby brother, George,
was given him to nurse for a little.   The baby was frac-
tious.   "Bit" said little Sandy "fat wulla say tull'm? "O, "
replied his Mother "jist say Geordie, peer folla". (poor
fellow).   "Geordie, peer folla" warbled out the juvenile
nurse and stopped; with what success in quieting his junior brother I was not informed.

In my Father's family, it
may be asked, how were we fed in those days, the forties.
Well, oatmeal porridge with a little skimmed milk for
breakfast; for dinner potatoes and salt, seldom much more;
sometimes it might be oatcakes with skimmed or butter
milk; for supper boiled greens with "kail brose" (oatmeal
stirred in the boiling water in which the greens had
been boiled, with salt.)   On certain occasions we might
have broth consisting of vegetables boiled in water and
salt but no flesh meat (bar'fit broth).   On Sundays as
an extra, a little butter to our oatcakes, and a fish lug
with a cup of rather mild tea.   All the same as a rule
we were happy children.   If we got but few nice things
out of the pastry shop, we could always without charge
stand outside the window and look in at them without any
risk of disordering our stomachs.

When a "hird laudie" I
built many castles in the air.   What a pleasure these
castles gave; nor am I aware of any harm done to me by
the building of them.   The creation of a second world
in one's mind gives a double happiness, and as a rule
gives more pleasure than the grim reality.   Happy "hird
laudie" dream away, the reality will slowly, and let us

hope not unkindly, reveal itself in course. What science and art are to riper years, sources of enjoyments, creative imagination is to youth. One of the highest enjoyments of Eternity will be, I conceive, a youthful imagination, a magical halo enswathing the simplest of God's works; and existence itself the exuberant joy of a healthy childhood.

When at cattle herding my work began at six:o'clock in the morning, and with an interval of several hours at mid-day, when I had to do odd jobs as directed, my herding continued till eight in the evening and for seven days in the week. Only in exceptionally bad weather were the cattle brought into shelter during grazing hours. Highly respectable farmers I served, and the herd laudie was cared for in the true orthodox fashion. Poor fare; somewhat tasteless, oatmeal cakes with skimmed milk, potatoes and greens. As a rule, no butter, no eggs, no flesh meat, no instruction, no Church, no personal looking after, though at times sadly in want of it. My Mother washed my shirts and stockings, but she resided miles away. Like other boys however I got through. I remember my Mother who had come to see me on one occasion when my jacket was much out of repair, proposing to return and repair it, when the laudie suggested that she should bring a "cloot" large enough to cover the entire garment, but I do not remember that she did it. Mother had much to do at home.

With "hird laudies" as with many other matters, it is not so much what many well meaning people do, as what they neglect to do. In all stations of life this seems to be the practice, more or less, a shirking

of responsibilities

of responsibilities that cannot with propriety be shirked.
My experience of farm life revealed few good or elevating
influences beyond what I might carry with me from my Father's home, or from good books; not very numerous in a
farm/kitchen or bothie.   The farmer left all his servants
young and old, to hang as they grew.   The same with the
Parish Minister and Elders, so far as my experience went.
Song singing in the evenings and idle hours was the servants chief enjoyment, generally love songs, sometimes lewd
Songs.

          Burns' songs were sung in our hearing, and certain of
his poems read; Hallow'een, Tam o'Shanter, The Jolly Beggars,
often enough, and oftener than the Cottar's Saturday Night.
Holy Willie's Prayer, An Epistle to a Tailor, and such like
were the greatest favourites; and generally speaking, Burns,
at least among the young folk, seemed to be valued and rel-
ished more for the sake of the bad parts of his writings
than for the rest.   I am not insensible to the genius of
Robert Burns, his marvellous powers and deep insight, his
exuberance of animal spirits, his keen sense of the ridic-
ulous, his hatred of sham, cant, and hypocrisy as seen in other people, and of such native goodness as he was said to
possess.   At the same time I would be false to my convictions if I did not state my opinion, that among the rural
population of the district where I moved, the writings of
Robert Burns ♦♦♦, were, and are, productive of much more evil
than good.   Feeling that Burns is good company, or at least
not bad, the tendency among his readers is undoubtedly to
copy Burns' faults, while giving his virtues, such as they
are, the go by.   I am no admirer of Burns, a clever man but
utterly Godless and profane, far too much given to casting

ridicule on sacred things, and very smart at making sin
and vile practices to be regarded, by the young and inexperienced, as only trifling indiscretions, more to be
laughed at than shunned and detested.

As a boy I read a
good deal, and almost invariably what came first to hand.
I read penny chap books; they were still the current literature in country districts in my boyhood, not of much
account perhaps, but much better than none to reading boys.
I must have possessed "dourness" to a reasonable extent.
In the gloomy autumn evenings the farm servants fond of
singing, or listening to singers, were at times very persistent in urging others to sing, whether willing or not.
I cannot forget how dogged I was in refusing to sing on
such occasions when not inclined to do so. Whether the
same doggedness remains in me as an old man I really cannot say. It is good sometimes to be "dour", if one can
manage to be so without shewing it: but regarding himself
to be in the right. "Dourness" for its own sake cannot
be commended.

When I was a boy, and tramping along a coun-
try road on one occasion, I fell to sauntering and musing,
and as I looked at my breast and legs said "Me- ma- sel,
Ma sel- ma sel, and so on, when such a strange sensation
came over me, as if startled at my own existence, that fear
caused me to shake off the feeling. Twice I experiment-
ed with similar sensations. I felt so frightened at a
sensation which I cannot describe that thereafter I never
dared to repeat it; nor would I advise any one to try it.
Evidently the creature is formed to look out. To try to
look inside one's self, except to the extent of finding a

companion, often safe and laudable, is a risky proceeding and may unhinge the mind.

I am not much of a naturalist, but when herding I observed a few things somewhat out of the common rut in my experience. I tended a cow that was very fond of trout; her name was Tibby. Tibby would hurry from the far end of the field on hearing my cry, "a troot tae Tibby" and devour the dainty morsel. She would stand behind an angler, in mute expectation as to what from the burn might turn up. One day I found a big black snail in the act of eating off the head of a young bird in its nest. I had seen a snail eating clover, but was not prepared to find one carnivorous. Birds that I had often heard, but did not with certainty see while a boy, were the corncraik, the cuckoo, and the "bull in the bog" (bittern). In later years I have frequently seen two of them, but not the bittern. The bog where it formerly bellowed is now cultivated land. The first time that I could with certainty say, that I saw the cuckoo $$$ was in crossing a moor among the heather. I was startled by its cry as it flew over my head. I did not expect to see or to hear it in such a place. I have seen four rainbows simultaneously in the sky, but only once. I saw a small and very pretty crescent in the sky, shortly before or after sunset, in the summer of 1846. I was puzzled at the time concerning the "bonnie wee mean", but now suppose I must have seen Venus or Mercury under favourable conditions.

When a boy I was a great talker to myself, am so still at times. Capital company; by no means always associated with lunacy

lunacy, as some people suppose.   O, what enjoyment, at least
for a time, in absolute solitude; that is alone so far as
our fellows are concerned, and yet not alone, not alone.

Old
farmer "Rosie" was at one time my employer, a little grey
haired man eighty-two years of age.   He had never had a
day's sickness, irreligious and profane, and always whistling,   He was quick tempered, but his ebullitions did not
last long.   He did not like to see his boy using the
stick too freely among his cattle, and seldom or never used
it himself.   One evening he was assisting me to drive the
beasts home, up a brae where they were much enamoured of
the sweet grass that grew by the wayside.   Rosie "hished",
Rosie "hied", trotted from one side of the road to the other; till fairly losing patience he burst out, "Hech sic
deevils tae ca", when the "hird laudie"lost his gravity in
a "sniccar".   Rosie died in a year or two after,"gathered
to his fathers", whatever that may mean.

In my early days I
suffered much in winter from chillblains on my fingers.
They seem to be constitutional.   I know of no certain
cure except genial weatherand perhaps active finger exercise with protection from cold and damp.   I have found
benefit from rubbing the parts affected, with a mixture of
rum and salt.

One day among the lea grass I found a small
bird's nest.   There were in it, if I remember aright,
three young birds and an egg.   From day to day I took a
look at them.   When taking what proved to be my last
look, I found not the little birds, nor merely an empty
nest, but the mark of a cow's hoof which had come right

down upon the nestlings, crushing them to a jelly. Can any one say, why such an arrangement? Explain satisfactorily, and many other things as inexplicable, might be seen through. "Even so, Father" is all we can say, meantime.

At Brae Farm lived a calf, where it first saw the light. After four or five months it was sold and removed to another farm, two or three miles distant, as the crow flies. It was double that distance by the roundabout road leading through a country town, which the calf had travelled when leaving home. The calf was, or very soon became home sick: shown by its continuous lowing. One day finding its way out of the park where it had been placed to graze, it started for its old home. But with an instinct, wisdom, or folly, call it what we may, it did not go back by the good macadamised road, the public highway, the only road it had ever travelled, but started through a plantation, down through fields into a roadless low lying ground, swam a flooded burn at the risk of its life, getting out all right on the side next its old home. Then the calf making a mistake turned to the right instead of the left on the road it had reached, but where it had never been before. Then on reaching the main highway at the junction, it discovered it was wrong, wheeled to the left and was speedily at its old quarters by the direct road, though it had the choice of another.

The farmer was busy repairing a window, but could not see his way to overcome a difficulty that stood in his way. The laudie was standing by and suggested to his master a way in which the thing could be done. "Ye'r richt, laudie",

said the farmer, "They shud be hanged that hae nae invention, and they shud be hanged that hae ou'er mony."

Johnny
and the horse were at the stable door; the horse heading
in, and Johnny heading out.   Johnny had the horse's hind
foot between his legs and was trying to pick something
from about the shoe.   The horse becoming tired of having
its leg in a cramped position, without any warning stretched it out, sending Johnny at equal speed right into the
dung pit, head foremost into the soft contents but not much,
if at all, hurt.   The onlookers laughed heartily; but why
should they laugh?

I am not a fisher; I never caught a fish.
But I remember an old gentleman wading knee deep in the
Deveron, having hooked a goodly sized fish, salmon I understood, and seeming anxious to land it.   Addressing me he
requested me to stand by in readiness to hold his rod
while with the "clip" he would lift the fish out of the water.   The old man had shortened the line, the salmon was
close at hand, and wriggling into a small pool at our feet
might have been lifted with the hand.   But the fisher evidently lost his head; he threw down his rod, adjusted his
"clip" and went for the fish, that seemed to be clear of
the hook.   With the "clip" the fisher lifted his prey a-
bout a yard from the ground, when somehow the "varmint" gave
itself a sudden turn, got clear of the weapon, and falling
into the water was instantaneously lost to view; leaving
the boy looking on with indifference, but the old man la-
menting, "o, the clip, the nasty clip, it yielded; and a fine
fish it was too, the nasty clip, the nasty clip, O, dear O."
Amateur anglers may take a lesson.

In old Johnny C's school, the Parish School and he was
"Reverend", I spent several winters, herding in summer;
there things went on in a use and wont manner. A Bible
lesson at 9 a.m. began the day's work.   By and by a reading and spelling, or geographical lesson was followed by
writing from copies and getting our quill pens mended.
Then arithmetic in some stage and in a leisurely fashion.
Not an inconsiderable part of our time was spent in playing at "X and O" on our slates, telling stories to one another, and placing crooked pins where our companions might
sit upon them for brief periods.   Such pins were yclept
"John Oggs"; they were ingeniously bent so that they, the
"Johns", sat quite steadily with the points straight up.
Boys and girls sat promiscuously, and "sic fun".   In these
merry days a boy could sit hours on end doing nothing beyond amusing himself and his companions.   Not the least
part of the fun was to see old Johnny whipping to the best
of his ability a boy who all the while was giving his fellows abundant laughter by his grimaces and pretended sufferings.   We were jolly boys; no dictation, no science, no
cramming, no hard inspections, or sore heads from overwork
was our lot.   And yet we were good scholars; at least the
ministers at our annual examinations always said so.   Then,
"auld Johnny", Reverend he was, and had grown very Reverend,
was always ready to give asked for assistance.   He had
been an able man in his day, but was long past his best.

My

Father died when about fifty-four years of age.   He had
been for a number of years in poor health.   His lungs
were affected, consumption I suppose, but he continued to
work at his daily toil.   One cold day in December my Fa-

ther was brought home in a farmer's cart, lying among straw and evidently very ill. He was laid in bed, suffering from acute pneumonia, and died in a few days. I need not detail the struggles of a poor widow in poor health, with two dependent children; I had by this time left home for good. Suffice it to say, that with some assistance from kind friends my Mother managed to get along without Parochial relief.

ii

The question may here suggest itself, Is it possible by any Government measure to alleviate, apart from pauperism, the condition of the very poor? and more especially where poverty is not the result of their own ill doing. The question in these days is much thought over, as such proposals as old age pensions, "fair wages", and the relation of Capital to labour plainly enough indicate. I have thought over the matter, knowing well what it is to be poor; and that, without poverty being attributable to evil conduct or imprudence, and have arrived at this opinion. To raise the very poor and place them in comfortable circumstances is impossible without their own self exertion, patient perseverance, prudence, strict temperance, frugality, and correct moral character. While saying this we do not forget that circumstances may occur over which a man may have no control; ill health, loss of savings, and such like. But the best way to provide against such contingencies and old age is by friendly societies or Post Office Insurances.. My Father lived in trying times. Our country had not recovered from the Peninsular and French wars, and suffered much from what we regard as a combination of crime and stupidity,

i.e. Protection.　Industries that cannot support themselves by competion are worthless and deserve to go down.
A betterment to the working classes that required neither
self denial nor ordinary prudence would not be any blessing to them; while to the country at large it would be a
standing evil.　Since the repeal of the corn laws our
country has partaken of a prosperity and trade expansion
undreamed of before that event.　The working classes of
to-day can earn , in not a few cases, as much in a day as my
Father could earn in a week.　But on the other hand, we
can at present see in our large towns a wretchedness to
which I in my Father's single apartment was an utter stranger.

　　It is not small houses, nor small wages, nor the greed
of the Capitalist, that makes the so much to be deplored
dirt, rags, and general vile conditions in many of our lanes
and closes; but the low moral tone and imprudence of the
inhabitants.　No doubt, those who can should teach the
lapsed, but what if the lapsed do not want to be taught? No
doubt they should be assisted in their distress, and to
some extent they are; but too often it is heartless and
thankless work; not infrequently serving to perpetuate the
evils that effort is trying to cure.　It is not the man
who scatters money in charitable doles who is the real benefactor to working men, nor he who pays wages in excess of
what he can rightly afford, having regard to the work done.
He is the benefactor who gives employment, paying a wage
that leaves a profit to himself, tending to secure perman-
ency, and to provide for his employees a certain, if small,
income, as much better than none at all.　It is a thing of

every day occurrence to find working men going idle, not
because they cannot find work, but because they cannot
get what they would like in the way of wages.   High wages should be sought after, but any wage should be accepted rather than go idle. It should always be to an employer's advantage to give good wages to a good workman.
Certainly it will pay him better to give good wages, if he
can afford them, and thus keep his business going, than by
refusing current wages bring his industry to a standstill.
Good workmen can live by competition as employers have to
do.   Incompetent workmen always aim at monopoly.

There
are evils in the world among all classes, rich and poor, for
which there seems to be no practical remedy.   We hear of
of the evils connected with riches, and obloquy is thrown
at rich men, as if they were the authors of all the evils
that exist in the world, and could, if so inclined, put all
things right.   We regard rich men and Capitalists as the
real benefactors of society, and that in spite of themselves
when they do not deserve any credit for good intentions in
the matter.   Love of money! Who does not love it?   As an-
swering all things we cannot but love it.   Only is money
an evil when it leads to bad conduct, overreaching and crime.
Burglars and thieves are lovers of money.   Political agi-
tators and seekers after place and power, however poor, are
yet lovers of money.   And perhaps not a few who enveigh
bitterly against the rich, but too clearly indicate that
their own love of money is at the bottom of their animosity
to such as have more money than themselves.

Unions among
working men with a view to procuring higher wages, may in

certain cases do good, if good it can be called, but there
are many drawbacks connected with them; and if a benefit
to the young and vigorous, certainly to the old and less
vigorous they are often an evil.   I know of no tyrrany
among employers at all to be compared with the tyrrany of
workmen to those, their fellows, not connected with their
Union.   But while men are what they are, things, it is to
be feared, must remain as they are.

Much has been said, and
continues to be said anent the elevation of the lower
strata of society in recommending, "better houses, better
surroundings, and not till these are obtained can we expect better men and women."   But in speaking so is there
not apparent, a putting the cart before the horse?   Give
a palace to some folk, and in a short time they will turn
it into a pig's sty.   I have known one poor sickly woman,
and I believe there are not few but many such, who with
her husband and several children resided in a single apartment, who could and did keep it as clean and wholesome
as any good house needs be, except on washing days, she
having no washing house; and why not?   When I see, as I do
see, big strong women, dirty and untidy, seated in the street
gutter or door step doing nothing but wasting their time,
no wonder if their houses be found nasty smelling, filthy,
and little short of being abominable.   But this is not
the fault of the house, nor of its surroundings; the fault
lies entirely with the inmates.   How to mend matters one
cannot well say, but to ignore facts would be foolish.   To
shut up drinking shops and put an end to the sale of intoxicants might do much in the right direction, but that, it is
to be feared, would not do everything.   No matter how poor

men and women may be water is cheap and decent clothing
not expensive.   The poor may keep their persons and
houses fairly clean, and live respectably, God fearing and
Church attending; that is if they feel so inclined.   In
a state of nature the so called lower animals oan keep
their abodes clean and comfortable, and why not man?   No
improved dwellings nor pleasant surroundings will do much
for people so long as they are inclined otherwise.

                                                  John
Crow was an acquaintance of ours, and rough spun.   William
Fox was also an acquaintance, but much more refined.   In
conversation one day, John to William, "I say Willie, dae ye
ken what kine o'a place Heaven is?"   "H'm, I'm afraid I do
not, John."   "Weel, Willie, I'll tell yae what kine o'a place
I wud like it tae be an'me in it; jist a place whar I wud
hae plenty o'bread an'cheese tae eat, beer tae drink, an'a
pipe an'tobacco tae smoke."   Willie is long since dead;
what became of John I know not.

                          But returning to my own life
and experiences: when about fifteen years of age I became
much indebted to an uncle who got me placed with a drapery
firm in Aberdeen, on the understanding that I would repay
him whatever outlay he might expend on my behalf, when in a
condition to do so.   He was eventually repaid, and otherwise assisted till he died at the age of seventy-seven.
He was known to me as a packman, paying for a hawker's license   He was never married, but had done his part in the
way of assisting his poor relations, and knew well what poverty and hard times meant.   Almost always on the tramp
with his pack on his back, he was an intelligent little man
thrifty, honest, and truthful.   He was a member of the Free

Church in Banff, attending the stated Communions, though
seldom at that Church at other times.   He was well versed
in Church history, a reader of his Bible, and very intolerant of extravagance.   My Uncle may have had faults, but
if so they were not seen by me.

In the Granite City the
chief of the firm that employed me was about five feet in
height, not quite so much in girth, with a round, red, fat, $$$$
face and bald head.   He was an old Navy man, had been in
youth a weaver, but was pressed into H. M. service.   He
was present at the battles of Martinique, Gaudaloupe, and,
St. Domingo: I read these names on his medal, awarded to
him about 1850, through Col. Fordyce M.P., I think.   So the
quondam weaver and sailor was now draper and manufacturer,
Free Church Elder, and Town Councillor.   He was crusty and
good tempered by turns, an anxious old man, his, in every
sense, better half had died shortly before I came.   He had
two rather wayward sons; one day I overheard one of them
giving expression to the wish, that father might break his
leg on a journey not approved by the young man.

As a draper
I was sometimes trained by the old man.   Take what follows
as a sample, no customers being at the time in the shop.   In
a nautical drawl, "Find something to do; no ingenuity in
you; you'll never make a merchant."   Poor me, on next occasion trying to mend matters I pull down certain pieces of
cloth from a shelf, with a view to tidying up a bit.   "What
are you taking these things down for? Put them back again,
and do something useful."   With a view to do "something
useful" on another occasion I go to the back shop, so called,
trying to keep out of the old man's way. (He was about

seventy years of age.) "Can't you stop in the front shop
here and wait on customers?and so on.   Bad boys,perhaps,
and not much wonder.   Bad a good many things, and not
much surprising.   One thing I can well remember,viz.the
very heavy parcels I had occasionally to carry on my head,
as if intended to break my neck.   The evil,I am afraid,
is still imposed on many not overly strong,nor much complaining boys.

          When I had been nearly four years thus
trained and initiated into the mysteries of selling flan-
nel and sewing thread,my Father died.   By the influence
of a friend I obtained a situation in Limerick,and went
there hoping to be able thereby to assist my Mother with
my younger brother and sister.   I was able to do so, and
thus save them from that much disliked bugbear,the Parish.

Rather curious, the drapery business as carried on in the
name of Arnott, Cannock & Co. Limerick.   The Irish are
Irish, however, and that makes considerable difference.Make,
or compel the customer, by hook or by crook, to buy what
they ask for, provided you have got it to sell; if not,
then persuade the customer to buy something else.   But
allow the customer to go without buying, and not unlikely
the shopman would have to walk after her; almost to a certainty if another smart young man gets hold of the customer and sells after the first has received the "swap".
High pressure, rather, but in Limerick business was business.
I don't think that in Scotland Irish methods would work; I
mean the methods adopted in dealing with the lower, or least
intelligent among the Irish, by far the larger number. The
more intelligent and higher classes in Ireland were not so

easily managed; but it was important in a good "hand" to measure the customer and act accordingly.

One day a simple, but well to do country girl came into the warehouse proposing to buy a cloak, provided she could get one to her mind. Dan(the hand) shewed her a cloak, price thirty-five shillings, but somehow it did not please. A number of other cloaks were shewn at various prices, but in spite of all Dan's persuasive powers the young woman was likely to give him the "swap", in other words leave without buying. Leaving Daniel "clane bate" the girl started for the door, but Dan was equal to the occasion. Quickly lifting the first shewn thirty-five shillings cloak, with his scissors he cut a slit some six inches long in the back of it. Hurrying after the young woman who was then almost at the door, he tapped her on the shoulder, and requesting her to return for a minute said he had found a "bargain". A bargain was the very thing for the Nationality. "This cloak" said Dan "is a little damaged, can be easily mended, the correct price is fifty rhillings, I will let you have it for thirty-seven shillings and sixpence." Done, the money paid, and every body satisfied. Smart hand was Dan.

A woman wanted three yards of shirting stripe and was shewn a piece at fivepence the yard. It did not please; the first article shewn seldom does. I, standing by, am quietly requested to cut off three yards of said fivepenny cloth, round the corner, unseen by the customer who was looking at another piece. They were cut off. "Will you buy a reniment?" says Martin. "Shaw" says Biddy. "This" says Martin "is three yards of sixpenny cloth which you may have for one shilling and fourpence." The cloth is at once bought and paid for, the seller getting the extra penny paid for the cloth in the form of a premium, called a "tinge" in drapery parlance.

A respectable looking lady required some twenty-four yards of fine long cloth (its technical name). This being a rather large purchase she, the lady, had evidently made up her mind to obtain a reduction from the regular price. Altogether out of the question, was the ruling practice in the warehouse. The lady was shewn the finest in stock, sevenpence halfpenny per yard; also some other pieces at sixpence the yard. "This sevenpence halfpenny one will do" said Madam "but seeing that I am taking so much, you must let me have it for sixpence halfpenny." From this position the salesman could not budge her ladyship. If the lady gave the young man the swap, the consequences to him might be serious, but accede to the lady's request he could not. Added to all this the young man had a conscience, a somewhat rare commodity in these parts. He wished to avoid positive lying and also downright cheating, but he had met a Tartar. At the same time he must sell without reduction. He managed thus. Shuffling the cards, in other words the pieces of cloth on the counter, he was able to smuggle the sevenpence halfpenny one out of the way, and out of sight, while the lady's attention was diverted by a remark of her companion. Turning round and again addressing the salesman, but now laying her hand on a piece of sixpenny cloth, which she evidently thought was the sevenpence halfpenny one, she said in rather a decided tone, "You must let me have this for sixpence halfpenny." With quite an innocent look the

young man referred the matter to his superior, who being
agreeable, twenty-five yards were sold at a halfpenny
more per yard than it had at first been offered for.
"What could I do" said the Christian young man to himself, "she would not buy the cloth for sixpence; it would
have been rude in me to refuse sixpence halfpenny." In
spite of one's better nature ladies sometimes have to be
managed.

To cut a piece in two, selling one half of the
piece at fivepence halfpenny per yard, and the other at
sixpence, was a common practice. To sell articles, such
as crinolines, costing the same money, and in all respects
similar, at one shilling, one and twopence, and one and four
pence, was regarded as quite correct. In certain cases a
woman would pay one and fourpence readily enough when the
same article at a shilling would have been rejected.

"Ting-
ing" has been referred to. It means a premium of a penny, twopence, or a larger sum paid on the sale of an artti-
cle, or yard of cloth, of old fashion or inferior quality,
to the salesman who manages to dispose of the goods: bads
perhaps they should be called. In certain departments
"smart hands" could by "tinges" earn from five to six shillings per week, in addition to their regular salaries. I
have seen a piece of inferior calico that was not selling,
quickly got rid of in this fashion. Said the manager, the
buyer for the department, "Here Murphy, cut this piece into
six yard lengths, tight. Cut them each five yards and
seven eighths; put tickets upon them and mark them six
yards, and I'll tinge them for you." Paul carried out the
instructions faithfully enough. Our buyer said that Mur-

phy and O'Brien would either of them, "hang his father for a penny." The short lengths were duly ticketed and marked six yards"; it was fivepence halfpenny cloth per yard, but now priced two shillings and tenpence. The extra penny was for Murphy, or for whoever might sell the bargain. Sold they were very soon. Simple customers were persuaded to buy the cloth, probably as worth sevenpence the yard, and think that they had made a very, an extra good bargain. A

A peculiarity among the poorer classes in Ireland was a seeming want of any reliance on their own capacity to judge. They would frequently, if not always, consult any neighbour or stranger standing by, in regard to quality and price, before they could decide to purchase.

Brokers in the drapery business were, or are, as I subsequently found out, not peculiar to Limerick. The Broker acts, or did act, as a sort of guide to the purchaser, and might be a creditor. In any case there is an understanding between the broker and the salesman, for their mutual benefit. The salesman charges an extra price more or less above the usual charge; the broker persuades the customer to buy, and the profits are divided between the two worthies. I found this done in Glasgow also, in a house bearing the highest reputation for fair dealing. Some young men might try to deal justly and honestly in such matters, but they were not regarded as "smart hands", and one young man, we knew, was discharged for his pious scruples. The Manager was an office bearer, and the young man a member in the same Free Church. Business is business.

But let us go back to Limerick. One morning a young woman, from the country seemingly, came into the warehouse at an early hour and alone. She requested to be shewn some dress stuff with a view to purchase. To the chagrin of the department chief and his assistant she, the young woman, was clearly going to give the "swap" an intolerable insult and lowering of status to a couple of crack hands, as our two salesmen regarded themselves to be. After much coaxing, scolding, bullying, and threatening to give her in charge to the Police, for coming to steal, as they averred, a not uncommon occurrence, it was all to no purpose. Then the second in command seizing Mary by the back of the neck, started with her to the door at a good round trot, over twenty, yards or more, right to the two or three exit steps, down which the girl rather hurriedly strode, finally sitting down on the pavement with her feet in or near the gutter. I do not think that she was much injured, at least I heard no more of the matter, and the maiden was fat. Jim Brian was the principal actor in this episode. He was in every way a bad fellow. I have known him to be in the beer shop and theatre with others of his own sort, when his wife was lying seriously ill. She was a beautiful young woman, but before I left the city she drowned her two children in a wash tub, and cut her own throat.

In Limerick, in the fifties, the ordinary style of dress among poor women was a blue cloak or mantle in the country, and on the woman's back a creel or basket covered with the cloak, all purchases being put therein: sometimes a child and other things savoury with the rest. A woman as described stood by the counter, to buy, if suitable, a yard or two of blue cotton cloth. The young man who attended to her considered himself competent and intended to sell. The woman was hard to please, she had been shewn a number of pieces without result, and at length turned to go away. This roused Michael's wrath, and seizing hold of the edge of the basket on the woman's back, and wheeling her round shouted, "Arrah can't you stand by the counter and see the goods?" "What did you come in for, to humbug us?" Then with a handy bit of the cloth rolled on a stick he gave the woman a hearty dig in the side. "Look at this, will this suit you?" Again and again the woman tried to get away, but was as often in a similar manner pulled back again and scolded. I was standing by, but forget how the transaction ended.

A quiet looking country lad came to the merino counter. Paul stepped forward to serve him. The lad wanted so many yards of drab merino: over twenty as I remember. Must be the same shade and quality as a small bit he handed to Paul. Paul found a piece of merino pretty near the colour and quality of the pattern, but the exact thing Paul could not find, and the messenger was inexorable, "exactly the same or not at all." "Give me the pattern, and I'll try again." said Paul, and this time he succeeded. Dropping the real pattern on the floor he, quietly and quickly, clipped a similiar bit off the most likely cloth, and sold the quantity required off that piece.

To give an idea of cheapness as existing in all departments, grey cotton cloth (calico) was always sold at cost price or below it. Customers could judge concerning its value. On many other articles where ignorance existed in the buyer, a large, if not extravagant profit could be obtained.

I presume that in some other mercantile establishments
there exist practices akin to the drapery ones current
in my Limerick experiences.   In Scotland I find it a
very common practice, when inquiring for an article which
the shopman does not happen to have, to be told that such
an article is not made, or cannot be procured, when it
would be much better to say simply that he, the shopman
has not got it.   Recently I went in search of a New
Testament in extra large print and was repeatedly told
that such a New Testament could not be obtained, it was
not printed.   I found one however, by applying at the
right quarter.

There were in this Limerick warehouse a
number of Scotchmen but mostly of little credit to our
country.   Scotchmen of Christian character and standing
will be respected and make their influence felt for good
wherever they go, and there were a number of such in Limerick in my time.   But others of my countrymen I met
there were as bad as any in debauchery.   As a rule they
were more intelligent, and without the vindictiveness of
the Irish, but not holier men.   William Henderson, a Scotchman, was the only man in Ireland, who knowing my general
character, tried to induce me into a beer shop.   "Come on,
I'll not ask you to take beer or whiskey; take a class of
lemonade."   I looked at him, "though he knew me better
than suppose that I would enter such a place,"so William
had to give in.   Strange the eagerness of some men of
bad habits to induce others to do as they themselves do.
However young men are not tempted very much except when
they are willing to be tempted; or desire to do wrong and
blame the temptation.   Tempters, male or female, can estim-

ate pretty fairly as to who are willing and who are not. They do not spend much time on the latter, while little time needs to be spent on the former: at least our experience leads us to say so.   Scotchmen of bad character, unlike the Irish, I found made no pretence to goodness in any way.   In religion they were simply nothing.   They were bad, pretended to be nothing else, and were clearly decided to take the consequences, be what they may.

It was during the Crimean war when Sandie Shaw drew my attention to the following fact.   Night by night as the Freeman's Journal was laid on the Library table, it was the Scotchmen who eagerly scanned its contents for the latest war news, an Alma, or an Inkerman.   Natives paid little or no attention, though thousands of their countrymen were at the seat of war, and departures of daily occurrence.

Some seventy men and boys were employed in the warehouse, mostly resident, and with a few exceptions, a filthy lying, and dishonest lot of libertines these young and old gentlemen were. God made the family, the Devil made the Barracks.

Our food was bread and butter with tea to breakfast.   Our dinner was beef or mutton with potatoes.   No extras, but fish or eggs with milk and bread and butter on Fridays and other fast days, for the Roman Catholics, the majority.   An hour or two after dinner tea was served the same as breakfast; no supper.   One evil connected with my barrack life in Limerick was that I had little or no choice as to my bedfellow.   There were six or eight beds in each room, two sleepers in each bed.   I might have, and at times had, to

sleep with a companion who was suffering from loathsome
disease, or with a drunkard, though not always, nor very
often drunk.   I remember Michael Benson who after being
present at some considerable eating and drinking function, laid himself down by my side in a most undesirable
condition.   After considerable noise and tossing about
Michael wanted a drink.   The lights were extinguished,
and water not easily got at; I refused to go in search of
it.   However, Pat Hailly came to the rescue and volunteer-
ed to water Mike.   "But what will I bring it in"? said
Pat. "O, bring it in a basin, Pat."   Said basins were by
no means very clean, and on occasions were devoted to more
questionable purposes than washing hands and faces.   "All
right"says Pat. "Mind and rinse it, Pat."says Michael. By
and by Pat returned in the dark; "Here it is, Michael, here's
the basin, drink now."   "I've got it, Pat, all right."
Michael set to, he had evidently been thirsty, and in the
middle of his draught gurgled out, "Did you rinse it, Pat?"
"Yes, Michael, I rinsed it three times."after which assurance, Mike resumed his drink, and thereafter fell asleep.
Very disagreeable to me were such experiences, but they
were in the bargain, I suppose.

            Learning to swim one morning
in the Shannon, while cautiously stepping backwards, I slipped into a hole and sank overhead into the river.   Being
able to swim a little, to the best of my ability I struck
out, and getting into shallower water managed my way into
the bank.   I got a fright.

            In Ireland I was struck with
the jocular indifference with which death was regarded
when occurring to a companion or acquaintance.   I was nev-

er present at a wake, but my companions'conversation led
me to understand, that the general conduct at such meetings did not differ much from what might have been expected at a wedding; general riot and merry making. Again, to
eat beef or mutton on a Friday appeared to be regarded as
a deadly sin; but to lie, to steal, profanity and drunkenness, were looked upon as trifling offences. Still these
people, young and old, posed as good Catholics, and so good
Christians.

There was much commotion in the streets of Limerick, and on the Shannon, one bright Sunday afternoon.
Boat racing, I could gather, from passing remarks, and "Father
O'Brien's boat"the favourite. Sabbath in saying, or performing masses, from early morn till noon, was to that extent
observed by the priests. One hour at mass, so far as I
could learn, began and ended all individual observance.

In
my experience, I could not say that I ever met with a strict-
ly truthful, or honest Roman Catholic Irishman, that is judging from his conversation and practice. Lies, dishonesty,
and license were somehow regarded as venial, and as sins easily got rid of. A religion which regards sin of any kind
as a trifling matter, or inculcates that its consequences
can be easily evaded, cannot make a good, prosperous, or happy
people. I left Ireland without regret, except for the condition of its people. I had spent three years of my life
in the Green Isle, but could not make up my mind to settle
down there.

It was during my residence in Limerick that some
well intentioned people in the larger island arranged for
one hundred ministers, or preachers, invading Ireland, and

thereby converting the natives from Roman Catholicism, or
at least enlightening them in an evangelical way. I understand, the scheme was highly disapproved of by the Protestants in Ireland, the promoters were urged not to proceed with it, but to a certain extent it went on. I remember very well on leaving our evening service in Bedford
Street Chapel on Sunday about eight o'clock, seeing an im-
mense crowd in front of Cruise's Hotel. There was much
noise and excitement, and a priest gesticulating and addressing the people, while cheer upon cheer followed his words
that I was not in aposition to make out. At first I was
ignorant as to the cause of the tumult. On inquiry I was
informed that it was owing to an attempt at public preaching in the streets by some of our missionary friends, newly
arrived. The preachers seemed to have narrowly escaped
with their lives. A deliberate attempt was made to throw
one of them over the bridge into the Shannon. Only by
the assistance of the constables and a few active Protestants
ants were the men got into Cruise's Hotel, and smuggled a-
way, I understood by a back door. Next morning, the Magis-
trates were appealed to for protection, but said, they could
give none. With much difficulty the preachers got to the
Railway Station followed by a motley crowd of men, women, and
children hooting, and throwing after the strangers such miss-
les as came readiest to hand. I have since thought, were
a hundred priests to come to Scotland on a similar errand,
would they have a similar reception? I think not. They
might be argued with, perhaps laughed at, but on the whole I
think, we would be glad to see them.

       Regarding the drapery
business in Ireland and elsewhere this question has been

put in my hearing, "Is it not possible to be a good salesman, and yet truthful and honest in dealing with customers?"
Perfectly possible, say in a Glasgow wholesale warehouse,
where the customer cannot be cheated, and lying would be
useless.   There the buyer knows too well what he wants,
and what he should pay for it.   The same answer may be
given regarding the retail tradewhen plain every day materials are being disposed of to intelligent and self re-
liant customers.   But when females and fashions have to
be manipulated, a successful salesman requires an elastic
conscience and an ample stock of mental reservation.   In
most fashionable shops there is always a lot of old stock
to be disposed of, and an eagerness on the part of the ven-
dors to dispose of it.   Among the first questions a woman
is likely to ask concerning fashions are, "How long have
you had it?"   "Is it this season's style?"   If the salesman tells a suitable lie to the lady, the article may be
sold at once; but if he tell the truth about the old thing,
it never will be sold except at half its value.   No doubt,
much of the blame lies at the buyer's door; she does not
it may be, know well what she wants, nor why she wants it.
A buyer should always know exactly what she does want, without having recourse to the wisdom of the seller, or to his
advice.   Ladies at times, in a manner compel the shopman
to cheat tem or tell them lies.   Fancy straw bonnets were
much in fashion at one time.   They were in some cases very
elaborately got up, and were expensive.   Says Fred to me,
"You see that lady; she has just bought one of our most expensive bonnets.   She was most particular in asking if we
had another like it?   I knew very well she did not want
another like it.   Of course I said, "Very sorry, we had not."

Had I said "Yes" she would have certainly gone without buying.

"Prigging", or seeking to buy at the price first asked , is an old practice, and one seldom resorted to nowadays.   Such buyers come, orcame, to be known by sales-men who put on as much extra price at first as they thought would suffice for abatement to secure a sale. In doing so they might sell at a higher figure than a per-son, not a "prigger" could have bought the article for.

Over-charging was termed "shaving", and invariably resorted to when a broker was in the company.   Buyers should know not only what they want but, if possible, how much they should pay for it.   If a buyer is ignorant no pretension to a knowledge not possessed should be made: better trust the salesman and be guided by him.   But in any case do not haggle and worry without definite aim.   Remember the salesman must, if he can, sell; lead him not into temptation in the matter of lies.   In some retail warehouses the a-mount of an assistants sales in a given time could be as-certained to a penny; and not a little ill will and envy was occasioned by the eagerness of salesmen to cut one another in the matter of catching customers, and in exceed-each other in the amount of sales.   But apart from that system, the walkers in retail shops are continually keep-ing their eyes on the various assistants, and forming judg-ments as to the qualifications of each in his own depart-ment.

After all, drapers , perhaps, are not worse than many other tradesmen, but my experience tends to say "no better". My chief on one occasion told me plainly, that I "must learn

to stretch my conscience "in the matter of lies. I remember a young man, an old school companion, in the con-
fectionary business relating to me as follows. His employer told him quite sharply, that in selling "seconds" he
must always aver that they were firsts; "and I had to do
it," said Alick, "and now when selling seconds I always
swear that they are firsts." This was in Scotland. In
conclusion re.drapery, these "great sacrifices" and "cheap
sales", for the most part mean very little beyond drawing
attention to the fact, that the advertiser wishes to sell.

I have had some experience in selling American sewing machines, and under the direction of an American agent. Perhaps a few words about the latter will be more instructive or entertaining than about the machines themselves.
"Write," said my employer one day, "to Mr.Hagan, Dublin, and
send him some needles. I should have sent them a month
ago, but forgot all about them. He was very kind to me
when I was over, and I do not wish him to think me careless.
Say in your letter that I told you, on my return, to send
the needles, but that you forgot all about them: and thus
shield me." I listened, nodded, but made no further reply.
I sent the needles, but in the letter used that convenient
pronoun "we" (we forgot); thus saving my own conscience and,
in a way, obeying my employer. This man had a desire to
seem honest and truthful in the event of his death. He
had a dislike to be cursed as a swindler after "shuffling
off this mortal coil", at least he said so. To Mr.A. of
Edinburgh this said seller of sewing machines made some
remarks anent.one of his own employees. "Why, he is a

straight and truthful fellow, won't tell a lie, which is no
doubt very good so far: but when people have to make money (by selling sewing machines) we must say what best
suits the purpose, if we want to go ahead." Now, are not
such ideas curious and instructive? Here was an employer
whose fault with his employee was that he would not on occasion tell lies to customers; at the same time expecting
and wishing the employee to be always true to him, the employer. A more arrant liar than John A. Grant, as I may
call this employer, I never met; but he has gone long since
to his final account, where lies avail not. In the fifties there were Singer sewing machines and Thomas ditto.
In a certain Glasgow factory both machines were in use.
A young mechanic employed in that house, gave it as his opinion that Thomas' (the rival machine) was the better; Singers' no where beside them. My chief, the Singer agent, coming to hear of these words of the machinist, sent for him,
received him courteously, and asked him if he would come
and work in Singers at a larger wage than he received from
his then present employers. The young man readily agreed,
entered the new employ, and was allowed to remain long
enough to ensure that his previous situation was filled up;
then our smart Chief's purpose being served, at the end of
one or two weeks, the praiser of Thomas' Machines, the rivals,
was discharged. The young man looked dumfoundered, but
there was no help for him; he went.

         "Blank smart fellow" said
Grant, my employer, regarding James Arthur of Arthur &Co.
The firm suspended payment when the Western Bank of Scotland failed. However Mr. Arthur was able to convince his
creditors, so it was reported, that the firm's liabilities

amounted to £60,000, while the assets amounted to £80,000,.
"Quite solvent, give the firm time, and all debts will be
paid". But our Yankee's idea was "Blank smart if James
had the money; and blank smart if he had not the money, to
make his creditors believe that he had it: blank smart in
any case.

In selling sewing machines and keeping accounts
I got mixed one day with the latter. John A. on seeing a
wrong entry cursed and swore at me in such a fashion that
I there and then quitted his service, intending to return
to Ireland, and start again as a draper's assistant. Finding to do so was impracticable, I was evidently settling
down on my beam ends. No work, no pay; I had however some
two pounds in hand. To my mother I sent one, retaining
the other to pay my landlady. After that my resolve was
to enlist in the 74th. Highlanders, a Scotch Regt. that wore
trousers. I thought of a kilted corps, but my legs I regarded as not up to the mark for public show.

iii

Does the Almighty hear and answer prayer? A strange question from one who has prayed often, continues to pray, and
has no doubt as to being answered. But there is reason
to believe that many do not pray, and some who regard it as
useless to pray.

In Glasgow I became acquainted with a lady
sufficiently my senior to make friendship in no sense a
danger to either of us; a devoted Christian who by her
counsel, and probably by her prayers, earnestly sought to
help me.

help me.   One evening when I was sad and sore at heart,
Miss S. pointed out to me a story, or belation, in the
Christian Treasury to the following effect.   An old missionary in the far North of America was in his little
station overtaken by an unusually early winter, and starvation for himself and his dependents seemed inevitable.
His only resource was prayer.   He prayed, and far into
the night was supplicating God, when a tap was heard at
the little window.   "Massa, come out quick, dere's fish in
de ribber."   "Nonsense, impossible," said the old man; however he went to see.   A sudden and unlooked for thaw had
broken up the ice, and he saw the fish in dense shoals, and
as if waiting to be caught.   They were caught, and in sufficient numbers to ward off the wolf of starvation for
that entire winter: for in a very short time the frost set in
in again, and so keen as to freeze all the fish caught, so
that they remained quite good till the return of mild
spring weather.   "I wished you to read this" said my kind
friend "I thought it might encourage you to pray, and trust
in God."   Not exactly the sort of comfort I had hoped for
when Miss S. sent for me that evening.   I had rather hoped that some very desirable situation had providentially
turned up in answer to my prayers.   No matter I was pleased
with the story and thought that I also in my distress
would follow in a particular way the example of the old
missionary, and set a day apart for the purpose.   On the
appointed day I remained in my room, reading my Bible and
praying for a considerable part of the forenoon.   Resuming after my dinner, I again earnestly laid, or rather spread
my difficulties before God in Christ's name, when in the
act of rising from my knees I heard a knock at the outer

door.   "Gentleman wants to see you."   It was my recent
employer; he wanted me to return, "thought because I had
not told him to go to Hell that day, I would have returned,&c."   The fact was that Mr. G. wanted to return to
America on a visit, and was prepared to trust me in his
absence.   I was glad to return on much better terms, was
thereafter kindly treated, and actually thought then, and
continue to think still, forty years after, that my prayers
were answered by Him to whom they were addressed.

                                              Though
comfortable enough, for the time being, selling sewing machines at 11 Buchanan St. (now Stewart & Mc. Donald's) I looked
to the future, but could see no further than the then present. Some time before this when knocking about dismal
Glasgow, how dismal to a young man when out of "crib", vain-
ly searching for work, Mr. Tudhope, not a very attractive
looking man, had a short walk and talk with me.   "Your
prospects cannot be darker than mine were at one time" said
Mr. T. "yet in God's good providence mine became brighter
and I am now comfortable and happy."   For conscience sake
Mr. T. had given up a good situation, but in a striking manner was provided with another.   One day under a dark mental cloud, Mr. T. was stepping along a Glasgow street when
he felt a tap on his shoulder.   It was a former employer
who reengaged him; soon after took him into partnership
and made him his successor in business.   "But" said Mr. T.
to me, "Do you not think that teaching would be more to
your mind than the drapery?"   Mr. T. and I were teachers
in the same Sabbath School connected with Union Free Church.
The suggestion was a new one, an idea which bore fruit in
due time.

While still among the machines, one day when leaving for
my lodgings, in my usual course, my eye caught an advert-
isement in the North British Advertiser, accident$$ally,
some may say, though I say "No", and yet very accidentally
so far as my looking for it at the time was concerned.
Had I not observed the advertisement then, it was very un-
likely that I would have noticed it afterwards: it was,
"Wanted, Governor's Assistant for Duke Street Reformatory."
I called on the Governor, made inquiries, feeling my way
through a most dismal November fog.   By and by I was ap-
pointed and entered on my duties, leaving my American
friend on good enough terms.   He subsequently asked me to
return as a something important, but I declined with thanks.

Rather a queer place, the Reformatory, and queer people
there.   Like other assistants, I was treated kindly at
first, but gradually had handed to me a number of wet blan-
kets to wrap around my juvenile enthusiasm: I was then
twenty-five years of age.   To a young man monkishly in-
clined the situation might have suited well enough, but
monkery not being my fort, Duke Street to me was very dull
and depressing.

        Boys' Reformatories.   Well, in Duke Street
boys were taught to read, write, and cypher.   Some learned
a trade and afterwards followed it out; but clearly, many
did neither the one nor the other.   What boys, and girls
too, need most is moral and religious training, and to that
far too little attention was paid: that is of the right
kind, and in the right way.   An Inspector examines, or did
examine, the boys annually in the three R's , sees them at
work and looks over the premises.   But to examine anent

a boys morals, or even religious knowledge, if not impracticable, is at least very difficult.   Sydney Turner did a lit-
le in that way sometimes, recognising its importance and necessity in any true reformation; but then he was a clergyman and singular.   So far as we can gather it is much the
same in other Reformatories and in Industrial Schools.
Without seeking to detract from whatever good has resulted
from both classes of institutions, nor forgetting that connected them, faithful men and women have worked not in vain
in reclaiming juvenile offenders, and in the highest sense
instructing waifs and strays of modern society; yet we may
be allowed to point out various drawbacks that will, more or
less we fear, ever attend the promotion of such work.

Begin
with Directors.   When Sheriff Watson and Dr. Guthrie started their Ragged Schools in Aberdeen and Edinburgh, their
fellow Directors and Helpers were as a rule, men of decided
Christian character, and they would be careful that only
tried Christian men should undertake the work or be appoint-
ed to it.   Now, every school has its Directors, but they are $$
by no means picked men: they are for the most part ordinary
average, and sometimes very ordinary.   To be a member of
Committee in such an institution gives an air of goodness
to certain gentlemen, the only air of goodness they possess.
In our experience we have met such gentlemen.   Then there $$$$
are the Officials in our institutions; like Officials, like
Directors.   Very much, if not everything, depends on the
Superintendent.   Superintendents may be classified thus.
First, the really good, earnest, Christian man, willing to
spend and be spent in aiming to secure the children's high-

.est welfare.   Of such I have met some, but not many.   Sec-
-ond, those whose aim is their own glorification, and comfort
in their situation.   Children under such supervision live
in a place, but not in a home.   Third, those whose qualifications for the work, in any sense, are of little account,
and concerning whom the puzzling thing is, how they came to
hold such positions, or are permitted to continue in them.
But let a Superintendent be the best of men and well qualified in every way, he may be, and often is, sadly handicapped
by those who are set to assist him in his work.   In the
case of schoolmasters, labour masters, or general officials
it seems next to impossible to in our experience, to procure them with the requisite traits of life and character
most needed in training young people from a lower to a
higher level in habits and morale.   An official in such a
school ought to be a man of irreproachable character, and
of consistent Christian profession, good tempered but firm
in treatment, a total abstainer from intoxicating drinks
and tobacco in every form, an intelligent and well informed
man, good mannered with perfect health and easy digestion, a
good looking man with no imperfections nor peculiarities
of manner, patient and persevering, and able to see what is
hopeful in his work as well as what may be discouraging.
He should be a man not indifferent to his salary, but conscientious enough to remember that a servant is for his
work, and that schools are not intended merely to provide
comfortable berths for officials.   It may seem from what
we have said, that we aim at drawing a picture of a perfect
man, a picture of men barely obtainable among the sons of
Adam.   Well, such men are in the world, we cannot doubt, but
in a minority, and so valued.

valued in whatever position they fill that they do not re-
spond readily to advertisements they are not looking for,
and that may never meet their eyes.   Advertisers for servants need not be reminded what a number who are utterly
destitute of the qualifications required for a situation,
will apply with all assurance as to their suitability.
Again and again we have advertised for a man and his wife
to fill by no means difficult positions, but from seventy
to one hundred applications on each occasion, have failed
to find a suitable pair.   Bad tempers, fondness for drink,
and inveterate smoking, are rampant evils among the majority of those classes from whom assistants in Reformatory
and Industrial Schools are drawn.   A higher class of officials in such schools are desirable than Directors can
very well secure or pay, and only inferior men will care to
work under worthless superintendents, where such happen to
be.   Again, a superintendent, man or woman, can and does
love his, or her, own children, individualise them, watch over
and discipline them, in a more or less satisfactory manner.
But when a man is expected to so watch over two or three
hundred of other people's children, he finds difficulty in
even individualising, while to love them as his own, or to
love them at all in any proper sense, he finds it impossible.   Many of the children may be, frequently are, repulsive in various ways, with bad tempers and dirty habits, dis-
gusting in their tastes and vile in their inclinations:
heredity manifesting itself in nasty ways.   To clean the
body and keep clean may be practical and easy, but to clean
the mind, or even the mouth a very different matter.   Pity,
the official may; but that parental love to which the child
may hitherto have been a stranger, a love which only par-

ents can bestow, but which an essential element in mind or soul reformation of a child, is almost, if not alto-gether wanting.   Then, the positive wickedness of some children renders corporal punishment necessary, and often necessary it may be, while the thoughtlessness of most children, and their aptness to do wrong through mere inadvertance, exuberance of spirits and fun, go far to make a Superintendent an ordinary policeman among the children under his care.

There is in these days the popular opinion that flogging children under any circumstances is a mistake, that other methods answer better, and that in any case flogging does no good to the culprit.   Let us consider.   I enjoin my boys to throw no stones.   Over and over they are commanded to throw no stones.   But stones are thrown, windows are broken, and passengers on the streets are endangered, if not injured, and complaints are made by outsiders.   In the play hour the master finds a boy earnestly doing what he can by stone throwing to break the glass in an empty house on the other side of the street, and managing wonderfully well.   What could, or did the master do?   He gave the boy some ten or twelve strokes on the bare hams, and admonished him.   That put an end to stone throwing on that boy's part, and served as a significant warning to his companions, at least for a season: we do not say, for ever.

Dan Fulton was nicknamed "Daft Danny". That did not harm him much had that been all.   But certain boys had an evil habit of tripping Danny up, when they could, and almost every day.   One could see on the poor boy's head big contused lumps caused by the fun, so called, of his

larking companions.   Remonstrances and cautions were about
as effective in stopping the practice as Church sermons
would have been.   The Superintendent could put a stop to
the evil in no way but by administering some sound floggings
to the prominent delinquents.   But further, in such a seemingly simple matter as obtaining silence, when silence was
requisite and had to be enforced, we have found ourselves utterly helpless without an application of the tawse to break
in certain new comers.   We may here mention some other
faults we have had to deal with in the course of a superin-
tendence of one hundred and fifty boys drawn from the lower
strata of town life.   These have been such as these; obscene language, worse than obscene, blasphemous and abominable,
persistent lying, striking and hitting for fun and in earnest,
utter inattention to orders, destruction of half worn clothing, shoes included, with a view to getting a new supply, stealing, from companions mostly, chewing tobacco and smoking. When
spitting tobacco juice could not be safely done on the floor,
then it has been done on the walls and even on the blankets.
For faults such as those mentioned flogging, in our experience,
was the only punishment much cared for; deprivation of food
or liberty, much less so.   Even flogging is more of a restraint than a remedy; possibly more a warning to others
than a reforming agent to the boy concerned.   It is questionable if he who will not be warned and do right for fear
of punishment, will be reformed by its administration.   When
boys quarrel, fight, or use tobacco, it is sometimes better
for a master to be blind, though in reality he sees quite
well.   Our schoolmasters and workmasters almost invariably
smoke and the boys know as much, even when masters are prohib-
ited from using tobacco in the boys presence.

Boys absconding causes sore vexation to a Superintendent.
But why abscond? it may be asked. "One would think
that in a school where children are well fed, comfortably
clothed, and generally well taken care of, there should be
no absconding." Ah, well, some boys will abscond merely
from a love of adventure and freedom, dislike to restraint,
to work, to discipline, and possibly from a want of family
feeling in the institution. Boys will at times run away
after a whipping, especially if undeserved, or if over severe; which may happen, not intentionally, but through some
misunderstanding on the part of the master. In Duke St.
Reformatory a boy was severely flogged for stealing a
pound note which he did not steal; though confessing that
he did, to escape further punishment: forced to assent to
a lie. The real culprit subsequently revealed the truth,
exonerating the boy who suffered the penalty. We have
flogged a boy on the false testimony of companions, given
to save themselves, as we afterwards discovered. On the
whole we think it is better not to see a trespass, than to
make a fuss when there is no reasonable likelihood that
the delinquent will be discovered.

A standing difficulty
is in dealing with inexperienced or stupid assistants, to
get them to see and act wisely, to communicate privately
to their chief anything calling for inquiry before decided action. Not infrequently mistakes are made, and
that is given as a fact which may be only a supposition,
or given from hearsay, which a little patient investigation would have shewn to be without foundation, or to be
of such trifling nature that punishment of any kind would
be inadvisable. And at times, Alas! the Superintendent

may be in a hurry, and finds it easier to punish a boy right
off: not having time nor inclination to listen to a boy's
statement which might be one sided or untrue, or being true
might shew the assistant to be in the wrong.   It is very
awark to find the assistant wrong, and in no way punish him,
while if the boy is wrong, he may not escape.   Frequently
mistakes are made in identifying boys: in uniform they may
be much alike, and patient inquiry may be at a discount.

Absconding, to which allusion has already been made, certainly
means in most cases discontent.   But when it begins it is
apt to become infectious, and very troublesome, more from example and excitement than from any tangible or coherent reason.   If the premises are such that getting away is easy,
but still requiring some planning and scheming, to abscond is
is a constant temptation to a stirring and adventurous boy.
Better to have no enclosing walls than walls that can be
easily climbed.   We have known boys at liberty on a Saturday afternoon from two till six o'clock returning all right
at the latter hour and climbing over the wall before bed
time.   In Duke St. Reformatory certain lads seemed to think,
and talk among themselves, of nothing else than how they
could manage to get away.   When boys escaped in one way,
that door being forthwith shut and guarded, the great thing
was to find out another, and invention never seemed to fail.
On one occasion a number of boys got away by taking the key
of a loft out of a master's pocket as the coat hung on a
nail in the workshop.   They opened the loft door, got out
by a skylight, dropped over the wall and were far away before they were missed.   Another time, it was on a Sunday
evening in winter as the boys came into the play ground

from supper, four boys got over the wall, a regular prison
one, by using a stable claut, catching the wall top and
climbing over by means of the handle. A long form placed against the wall answered the purpose on another occasion. One night an old watchman got himself tied up by
a group of boys, when taking the keys from him they decamp-
ed at their leisure. Descending from a dormitory window
by means of an improvised rope made from torn sheets, a boy
fell and broke his leg. That boy had to remain. On several occasions the premises were ablaze, evidently with a
view to escape.

Taking fits was a method occasionally resort-
ed to by boys, with a view to discharge from the Reformatory;
and so well were these simulated, that even the doctor with
difficulty could say that in certain cases they were not real.
I remember the case of a boy who might have succeeded in permanently injuring himself had he not been checkmated. After not a few methods had been tried without effect, the boy
was informed that with a view to cure him a red hot poker
would be applied to one of his vertebrae on each occasion
he happened to be in a fit. "It would be very sore, but as
we must try and cure him, he must try his best and endure
the pain, complaining as little as possible: it was the doctors orders. The boy listened and nodded, but took no more
fits, at least while under my care.

But then, it is to be re-
membered that Duke St. Reformatory was simply a prison without keeping the boys in cells. The boys were allowed little or no liberty. Their relations were permitted to visit them once in three months, for five minutes in presence
of officials. Under such circumstances reformation was

hardly to be expected.   Doubtless the schooling they received was a benefit to the boys,but any other benefit
was not very apparent.   Further,among lads,many of them
over sixteen years of age,evils existed that could not be
prevented,and that cannot be described. "Duke Street" was
a failure,it no longer exists.   Similar evils may exist
in other Reformatories,but probably not so bad.   As already indicated,the great desiderata in public institutions
for children,and possibly for older people,are family love
and conscientious care taking.   Parental love is always
absent.   Any other love is but a poor substitute,and the
child feels this,though he cannot very intelligently give
expression to it.   The more conscientious and anxious a
Superintendent may be ,the more will he realise the truth
of what we say.   Too often however,Institutions seem to
be for the officials first,for the children,second.   "Only human nature" it may be said,and said truly.   Who of
us is is altogether free of the ailment?

                              Turning to Indus-
trial School work----Archie Campbell was a quiet,good looking,and in no way vicious boy,generally well behaved,but
not very smart at his lessons.   Our schoolmaster was very
anxious for good results,and believed much in whipping.
Archie felt disheartened and "ran away".   I discovered
that he had a brother at farm service several miles away,
and presuming that Archie might be there,I went in search of
of him and descried him in a field with his brother,some
distance off.   Before I could reach the spot Archie saw
me,took to his heels,disappeared over a stone fence into a
corn field,and so was lost to view.   Hurrying to the
fence,I mounted,but nothing could I see of my boy,nor

through the long corn had I any idea what direction he
had taken. Chagrined enough, and vexed exceedingly, after
wandering about a short time I remounted the wall and "drew
my bow at a venture". "Come along out of that, and look
sharp, I have no time to spare." I cried in a rather loud
voice, but without the slightest idea where the boy might
be, or if I would be heard or attended to by him. No matter, Archie thereupon arose from among the corn only a few
yards off and returned with me to school, like a lamb. I
think the schoolmaster saw that he had made a mistake in
his treatment of the boy. Archie gave no more trouble;
he turned out a steady well doing lad, and eventually enlist-
ed in the 93d. Highlanders. The last time I saw him he was
about to sail with his Regiment to the Cape.

Last night, say
my notes, I found John Rigg, an old school boy, standing outside the school premises. "Turned up again like the bad
sixpence", as another reminded me that evening, "What shall
we do with Rigg?" His stepmother had him sent to our
school after his father's death. The boy was then eleven
years of age. Now he must be sixteen or seventeen, though
he looks like twelve or thirteen. He squints with one eye
and has a somewhat sinister cast of countenance. John was
easily enough controlled in school, when under supervision,
but a great delighter in mischief when it could be done
with impunity; he was in his element when any passing disorder occurred in school; but at least on one such occasion
a prompt flogging effectually cooled him. Two and a half
years ago, John's legal time in school expired. Since then
he has been tried in various ways and places. First, in
the local Boys Home, then by turns in three different farms

in Arran. No employer can or will put up with Rigg: what with lying, disobedience, bad language &c. he is said to be an insufferable boy in every way. On several occasions he has been received back into school, giving him so to speak, another trial. His case is provoking. A sound flogging, as occasion might require, I regard as the best thing for John, but then who can rightly be authorised to give it to him? This morning, a party in Arran requests me to send him a "nice boy;" I think I shall send him our young hopeful. I wish the boy may improve, but like too many others who have passed through our hands, vice and crime seems to be his only natural element. Of course John has learned to smoke, and somehow finds tobacco. On Saturday John was sent off with a trust worthy boy to see him on board the steamer for Arran. I gave said boy a shilling to pay John's fare; Arran should be reached by 2 p.m.. In the eveneng John was again at the gate; the Captain had not got the shilling. John had been put ashore, and now told me a story I could not believe; the more so that I found a new cap under John's arm. I "admonished him", and on Monday morning sent him away again: Will he stop?

Yesterday an assistant made a grievous complaint against a boy whom I, perhaps, should have condignly punished on the spot, in accordance with military rule, the assistant being an old soldier. I did not, however, and it was so far well. My ex-serjeant of engineers returned to me in five hours saying that he had reported the wrong boy. It was another boy who was in fault, but the boy who told him, the serjeant, "had made a mistake". Rather difficulty to uphold authority with such men in such cases; and yet this

assistant was, all over, the best we ever had: he was the
tenth.

Our schoolmaster is sorely afflicted these times.
He took a residence far away from his work; some three
miles distant.   He was advised against removing, but had
all arranged, at least in his mind's eye.   "The Railway
runs past the door; can get up and down with no difficul-
ly, fond of long walks, too."   "The Committee of School
would not, or could not, object." though the Superintendent
did., decidedly.   And now poor man, the train will not
stop to suit him, in spite of all his influence with the
Station Master, Superintendent and Directors of the Railway.   In fact, they seem bent on thwarting him and annoying me.   Our Schoolmaster wants to get away half an hour
before his work is done, to catch one train, and wishes to
get away a quarter of an hour earlier to catch another
train.   He does catch a train in the morning when leaving
his residence, but catches it in such a way as to be invariably five or ten minutes late in arriving at school.   Well,
be thankful, never mind, I am not his wife.

We have had troub-
les with other schoolmasters, and not much harm done.   Mr.
Pert passing through our shoemaker's shop saw our Janitor's
shoes about to be repaired; said shoes being large, Pert called them "fish boats".   One of the boys promptly informed
their owner, who highly offended, threatened to throw the Dom-
inie over the stair head; but as he did not, I presume his
temper cooled down.

iv

A bit of a breeze with our Matron the other day.   Some of
our bigger boys are charged with sending "billet doux"to
certain girls.   "Can you shew me one of these letters?"
"No".   "Have you seen any of them, or do you know their contents?"   "No, but, &c."   Shortly thereafter our boys are
lectured to the effect that no letters are to be sent in
future, or "look out": and so we trust the matter is ended.
Reckoning without our host however.   Mrs.Correct returns
to the charge a few hours after, and hands me a sample "billet" containing some boys "haavers", but nothing bad.   The
subscriber is called to task, but explains, that said letter
though written, had not been sent to any girl, but had been
taken from the boy by the schoolmaster and handed to the
Matron.   I felt annoyed and was cross; for now having re-
opened the case , I must punish the boy or not support an
official.   I wriggled out of the coils somehow, but such
events worry.

Grievous complaints this morning from Janitor.
Four boys mounting on as many clothes boxes keep jumping
off them.   I remember that I was once a boy myself, and did
pretty much as these boys do. · Must pretend to be angry,
but cannot be very.   Men in Industrial Schools should have
equable tempers, should never lose their equanimity, and yet
at times seem angry, or at least look severe.

To-day I had to
whip one of our biggest boys for striking a younger and
smaller one.   Quarrelling and fighting is a sad source of
trouble amongst us.   Constant surveillance is the only pre-
ventive, and even that, at times does not prevent.   Said big

boy gave as excuse, that the younger one was "tormenting
him"; in other words , laughing at him, and saying things
not liked by the bigger one.   Very likely, very likely,
but we cannot permit the big to strike the small.   "Do
not be too thin skinned; laughing at you will not, at least
needs not, hurt much."   Gave him six strokes on the bare
hams, as he had been repeatedly warned against his hitting
practices.   He was a boy, or lad almost as tall as myself.
Had he shewn fight I could not have managed him without
assistance, which we both knew was easily obtainable, if
need be.   When boys are really in the wrong and reasoned
with quietly they, as a rule, take punishment submissively.
It is only when they regard themselves as the victims of
passion or dislike that they become revengeful.

                                                    Matron again
complaining.   Certain boys have been looking through the
school windows at the girls.   Matron looked at the boys;
but they did not at once start back, as if frightened, or
found out, but "continued looking."   This latter fact was
the provoking thing.   "Should give the boys severe punishment."   However, I did not punish; I reprimanded them, and
put some marks against their names, for future reference.
Hope that will suffice to cure the heinous offence.   How
often, when myself a youngster, I have looked at girls, I
would not like to say.   How often Matrons, some of them,
have looked at boys, I do not know.   Report has it that one
Matron, whom we know, is very busy looking at, and running after an old boy; but of course that is entirely different.
Another Matron, in our experience, was very indignant at
girls daring to look at boys, or "vice versa".   But nature
is nature, and we should remember.   The dawnings of love in

young people should not be regarded as cardinal sins.   It
may be convenient and prudent sometimes, to pretend blind-
ness to such matters, but with our eyes quite open.

Mrs. Pine,
our sick nurse, is a respectable, good looking woman and very
cleanly, which to us is a strong recommendation.   She is not
unkind to sick children, nor inattentive to orders when ex-
plicitly given.   Still, she appears to think, that boys should
not at any time become sick, or lie in bed.   She rather "fa-
shes" at sick children.   If a patient's feet are cold, she con-
siders that the right way is to let said feet get warm in
their own way and at their own convevience; will have it
that there is nothing wrong when the Superintendent thinks
differently; and is always eager to send convalescents down
stairs, and out into the open.   I have at times to speak rather pointedly to her ladyship, taking care however not to go
too far in my strictures.   We might have a worse servant,
and moreover I must remember, that I am paid to look after every thing and every one.   With perfect officials I could
perhaps, be dispensed with: or may be a more ordinary man, or
even woman, might suffice to fill my place.

Full often one is
bothered in this manner.   He wishes a thing done, and that
something done in a certain way, and in a kindly suggestive
manner points the matter out to the official concerned. But
how often have his kind suggestions been taken so very kindly that no attention has been paid to them until pointedly
and shortly the official has to be told that the thing must
be done.   Pity it should be so; but too often there is no
help for it.   It is unpleasant to one who would like to order in a kindly way, or suggest rather than command.   On the

other hand there are those who anticipate one's wishes;
they take pleasure in assisting.   In engaging assistants
to perform certain duties, which are fully explained to
them before engagement, "O, yes, certainly, "they will agree $$
to all or anything that is, or may be required of them.
But no sooner are they fairly settled down, and secure in
their situations, than an agitation is begun with a view to
alterations giving relief to the grumblers, though thereby
throwing their duties on other officials, or leaving the
work not done.   Few things have caused irritation equal
to that so produced by not a few, male and female, especially
female.

         Years creep on.. I am now in my fifty-sixth year.
Whither I shall die in harness remains to be seen.   Die I
must, but not before God's good time.   In the early days of
my Christian profession I had no fear of death.   At cer-
tain times then, the prospect of death to me would not have
been unwelcome.   Glory, I thought without doubt, would be my
portion, die when I might.   These later days I am not so
confident, not so anxious to be amongst the glorified.   Do
I now fear death?   Not exactly, but somehow I do fear dying.
When I hear of a man dropping down dead, I think or say,
"Blessed are the dead that die in the Lord."and cherish the
hope, or have a secret desire, that in such a manner I may
die.   But however that may be, as my dying son said in writ-
ing not intended for prying eyes, "Dying grace will perhaps
be given for dying hours."   Happy James, we think he found
it so.   Happy wee Jeannie, she died, not knowing what death
was.   With these I look for peace in the future world; with-
out them as Carlyle says "Ah me!" ·I have been reading of
Roman palaces, their grandeur, magnificence, and costliness;

detailed accounts rivalling "Arabian Nights Entertainments",
and pondering over these works have come to the conclusion,
that a mother's kiss to her darling babe is to her worth
more than all the palatial edifices ever reared by the hand
of man; that intelligent love is the keystone of a happy
Universe.   To me, in my fifty-sixth year the love I had, yea
have, to my little daughter, Jeanie, and to my son, James, both gone
gone before me, is an outstanding fact, transcending most other facts in my fleeting existence.   To me, the yearning of
the soul is one of the most certain of all certainties, as
having a reliable foundation, and indicating a great truth,
the immortality of the soul.   The Psalmist has put it, "As
the hart panteth after the water brooks, so panteth my soul
ater thee, O God."

Sanderson was a stout stirring boy, quiet
and submissive, and by no means a bad or troublesome boy, so
far as our experience of him went.   One of his eyes became
inflamed, a case of ordinary opthalmia.   "Remain indoors as
much as possible, leaving off foot ball playing till your be
better", were our instructions to the boy.   Shortly thereafter I saw him at foot ball playing with all his might, and
partially undrest although the day was cold.   I took no
notice so far as reproving the boy was concerned, but watch-
ed the result.   The affected eye became highly inflamed,
and both eyes were making for a bad condition.   I thereupon reproved my protege, reiterated my warnings, pointing out
the consequences of his inattention to my instructions.
Then, though the boy's eyes were getting better, they were by
no means well, yet on the following morning "my dear boy"
was out in the cold and at foot ball again.   I did not repeat my scolding, but the fault repeated, I felt I must flog;

and thereupon did without doubt, reach his heart and intellect, through his hide, the only effective avenue that seemed open to me.   Moral suasion, oral suasion, dorsal suasion,
all seem to affect more or less, the various classes of mankind: but pain, and pain only, we can regard as the universal
policeman, theorise to the contrary as we may.

Last night, a
boy of thirteen, "98", quarrelled with another boy, "57" about
possession of a foot ball.   After a short tussle, both boys
went to supper with their companions.   On returning to the
play ground, "98" stepping behind "57" tripped him and threw
him on his back.   "57" complained to me, and I gave "98"
two strokes with the tawse.   The boy took the punishment
with a bad grace, and shortly after, in my absence, tightened
his cravat around his neck, with the apparent purpose of
strangling himself.   With some difficulty I untied the cravat, took it from him, and promptly repeated his former punishment, but doubling it.   Subsequently, I was told, that after being some time in bed, the boy arose, tore the lining
out of his cap, and set about another attempt to strangle
himself.   I have taken no notice of this to the boy himself, but the Doctor says I should fasten boxing gloves on
the boys hands to prevent suicide.

Two brothers, Alick and
James, entered school together.   James having been spoken
of by the Teacher as "simple", "Simple Simon" became the
boy's nickname.   The other day James complained that he
had got seven marks against his name for looking at Alexander.   Alexander in turn complained that he had got sev-
en marks for looking at James.   The word "simple" had occurred in a reading lesson, and on its being pronounced, in-

nocently enough, Alick, the rogue, looked significantly at James, while James, expecting as much, was in readiness to resent Alick's grinning glance.   Seven marks each from the Schoolmaster, are rather too many for such faults, but order must be maintained.

Another boy, "93", reading in the Bible concerning certain followers of Absalom, that they "went with him in their simplicity", struggled through the verse, till arriving at the formidable word, he thought he had it, and dubbed it "simple Simon" setting the class in a roar, but could not understand why, or where the laughing.######. should come in.

In the matter of nicknames, how come they? Forbidden they are, but suppress them I cannot.   Some fancied resemblance in the boy named seems to originate the nickname, and henceforth it becomes a fixture.   In not a few cases boys answer more readily to their nicknames than to their proper names, and teachers find it more convenient to use the former.   Some boys take so naturally to their nicknames, that to such I have used them without compunction; but others resent them so keenly, and evidently feel the use of them so much, that their use must be forbidden under pains and penalties.   Curious names fall to the lots of certain boys.   Here are a few samples; "Brick" "Sparrow" "Spuds", "Jook-a-pie", "Puddin face", "Toralorarido", "Cove", "Patchy", "Pigeon", "Stumpy", "Jamie the horse", "Samson", "Cuddy", and "Grumph".   It is quite a common occurrence for a boy to complain to me, that "Pigeon" or "Spuds" is calling him names, altogether failing to see the absurdity of his complaint.   Let us think of this, my Christian brother, do we ever act likewise, when in our complaining moods, before men, and before God?

Was the other evening at a meeting of
young men, connected with our Church, and took part in a
discussion.   Working men, engineers, joiners, painters, &c.
have, as a rule, very decided opinions in this direction. Re.
Apprenticeships, "No master should be at liberty to engage
a workman, say as a painter, who has not served an apprenticeship in accordance with the rules of the Painter's Union, said Union defining what "painter" means, and who will
conform to such rules and regulations as the Union of working painters have enacted, or may enact."   I tried my best
to shew these lads, the gross tyranny that might result from
such rules; that like tyrants generally, they were merely
fighting for their own hands; that all such Trades Unionism
is much more a conflict between a Union on the one hand, and
working men outside the Union on the other; that workmen
should remember and act fairly for the general good and liberty of all.   Benefits to one's own class may not benefit
other classes, often the reverse.   The producer has to study
the consumer's wants, and the price he is willing to pay.
The producer needs not try to compel to consume merely on
the ######### ######## producer's account.   Where monopoly
exists the producer may, in a manner, compel or prevent the
consumer, but not otherwise.   Strike?   Yes, if you consider
yourself benefited thereby; work or not work, combine or not
combine, but here I draw the line.   Do not interfere, directly or indirectly, between an employer and his employee.   Let
there be free labour, free trade, in that as in merchandise,
if ours is to remain a free country, and not a country handed
over to Trades Union Tyranny and monopoly.

James Smith was a

very respectable old man, a rope spinner, and had served
sixty years with the same employers.   Having served seven years of an apprenticeship, James considered it would
be hard, and unfair, if a man who had served no apprentice-
ship should be placed alongside of him at the same work
and wages.   By and by James found out that it would suit
him better to attend to a steam engine in the rope work,
and did so attend, although he had never served any apprenticeship to the engineering trade.   I fancy not a few
trade unionists are equally inconsistent as James was; and
have no difficulty in working at times where they can find
work, though not at their own trade, forgetting altogether
about their apprenticeship theory.

V

In St. Giles, Edinburgh, Dr. Dodds has preached a sermon, the
subject being, "What is a Christian?"   "To believe that
the Christ is able to lead us to God, and act accordingly."
So I understand the Doctor as saying.   To believe that
Jesus of Nazareth has been invested with a power, which in
our opinion , belongs to God alone.   But how am I to believe all that the Doctor desiderates regarding Jesus, and
yet not regard Jesus as very God, it baffles me to comprehend.   The Doctor does believe in the Divinity of Christ;
but very charitably, far too charitably we think, says, or
seems to say, that a man may be a true Christian, and yet
not a believer in the Divinity of Jesus.   The Doctor says,
"All the belief that is required to make a man a Christian,
is belief that Christ can unite him to God."   "If a man

believes that with Christ's help he may be transformed
into the likeness of God, he has all the belief that is essential ****** he is a Christian if he believes that
Christ has the will and the power to make him truly a child
of God, and if he acts upon the belief." So says Dr. Dodds.
But we say, if Christ is able to do all this, he cannot be
less than God, and we presume Dr. Dodds would say the same.
But further, the Doctor says, "We must not too hastily conclude, that a belief in Christ's Divinity is essential to
the true Christian; to the mature Christian it is essential
no doubt, ****** I do not understand how any one who thinks
that Christ was merely a man, and that now he lies in his
grave in the lone Syrian town can at the same time trust
him to lift us to fellowship with God." This last sent-
ence is very well said, if that were all; but the Doctor
goes on to say, "If the Unitarian accepts Christ as the perfect revelation of God, ****if he practically makes Christ
his God, are we to grudge him the name of Christian? Certainly not, say we; but then the supposed Unitarian would be
no longer a Unitarian. In all this Dr. Dodds' orthodoxy
may be right, but his logic, as we understand the term, seems
sadly at fault.

The existence of Christianity, its inception
in the first century, proves the fact, the reality of the resurrection of Christ. However much superstition existed
among the Jews and the primal Jewish believers in Christ
and his teachings, said superstition would have led them,
would have inclined them, in an altogether different direction from faith in the resurrection of Jesus of Nazareth.
When Jesus was put to death, neither his disciples nor any
one else, thought for a moment that he would rise again from

the dead. That Jesus had said that he would rise again was well known, but the rulers regarded his words as those of an impostor; while his disciples regarded his words as in some sense symbolical, or a parable; they seem to have forgotten his words, or had paid little attention to them when uttered. The reality of the resurrection was forced upon them. Not one of them seems to have had any idea of such an occurrence before it took place. At first, so little did they apprehend the meaning or intention of the resurrection, that we find them returning to their former occupations; regarding all that had happened concerning Jesus of Nazareth and his death, as a something unexplainable, but in which lay all their highest hopes for ever buried. Had there been no resurrection, there would have been no Christianity. Had there been no faith in the former, there could have been no existence for the latter. Renan admits as much; though refusing to regard the resurrection in any other light than a myth. But the resurrection, itself, without having regard to its purpose and meaning, would have been looked at as of little importance; and consequently would have been speedily forgotten, and the name of Jesus of Nazareth would have sunk into oblivion. It was on the day of Pentecost that the meaning and intent of the resurrection came to be clearly understood and forthwith acted upon. The new light thrown on the minds of Jesus' disciples neither made stronger nor weaker the fact to their faith, that Jesus had risen and ascended into Heaven. But outside the reason and purpose of it, the resurrection would have remained an insolvable riddle; which sinking out of notice would have been soon forgotten. But when the purpose and importance of the resurrection were clearly revealed to the disciples,

we find them in the face of persecution and death maintaining their profession of faith in it, and in him who rose.
There is nothing more striking in our New Testament records than the difference in speech, hopes, and aims of Jesus' disciples, depicted as before and after the resurrection and the outpouring of the Spirit at Pentecost.   Nothing is said of Paul before these events, but in the Acts we are told enough to enable us to see Paul as a Pharisee of the strictest sect, an ardent persecutor, and the last man to be thought of as becoming a Christian, a preacher, and martyr to the new faith.   But evidently Paul was no fool.   He believed in the resurrection, and had means of finding out the truth regarding it, in ways not available to the twelve.   In any case, these first Christians believed that Jesus had risen, founded their faith on this truth, and sealed their testimony, in many instances, with their blood.   No worldly benefits were obtainable, nor could be hoped for, in the firm stand they made.   Their words are not the words of mere fanatics, or enthusiasts in search of earthly goods.   I have faith in these men.   They could, and did, test the truth of the resurrection in ways impossible for men living thereafter.
Concerning the resurrection I am constrained to believe as they believed.   Christianity, as set forth in the New Testament owes its origin to the resurrection of its founder.
Christianity was received, preached, and to some extent organised, before Paul was convinced of its truthfulness; and after his conversion, he was evidently for a long time regarded with suspicion by many of the Jewish Christians.   First, because he had been a persecutor, and second, because of his strong antagonism to the Jewish rites and ceremonies, as in

any

any way essential to salvation. Nevertheless, to the
Christian nowadays, Paul's testimony is of first class importance, as that of an educated man, competent to analyse
current reports; and of a Jewish patriot and enthusiast
whose natural inclinations and bent of mind would have
led him in an entirely different direction: which for a
time they did.

In these days, our old current faith in Biblical inspiration is called in question, and in quarters
where it was least expected. As to the so called "verbal inspiration" of the Bible, I have yet to learn what is
exactly meant by "verbal inspiration", by those who hold
most tenaciously to the doctrine. I firmly hold, that if
God speaks to man in any language, or in any book, it is in
our English Bible. In God's providence it has been given
to us, and to the world,; and I cannot see my way to mending,
far less ending, it as my chart in life and what lies beyond. Jesus of Nazareth, very man, but very God, is my only
hope in life and for Eternity. Pardon for Christ's sake
and regeneration by God's Spirit is my creed. In life
and death I feel constrained to cling to it, and am pleased
to do so. It suits my felt conditions. Deprive me of
this confidence, and I lapse into utter darkness, radicle
and complete. I speak as an intelligent and reasoning
man. Deprive me of the Divine Saviour, and this is what I
fear, more repulsive to me than any fear of Hell, "death an ####
eternal sleep." I shudder at the thought. And yet, why
should I? Standing, as Carlyle says, between two Eternities, the past one is to me a blank, causing me no sorrow, no
regret, no pain. No man weeps because not born a thousand
years ago. A man may, in imagination, look back a little

way, but the backward gaze is very limited, and ends in a
blank.   But there arises not the faintest sigh of regret
that he had no part in the past; he is rather pleased
that he has been a late arrival: call it early, if you will.
But then, looking ahead, what a prospect!   Was there ever
sane man who did not wish to live, to live and explore, to
search and climb, in a word to become a Co-Worker with God,
living eternally?   One difficulty stands in the way of
living eternally, it is this, as appears to me.   In living
for ever, might there not come a time when a man would forget that he was once a poor, weak, dependent, and sinful man?
Might I not forget some things I should remember, and fail
in my attitude before the infinite and eternal one God?
~~Godfmebddjwerbasten $$.~~   I cannot admit my faith as shut-
ting me out from two Eternities; one is past, the other com-
eth, it lies before us, it is at the very door.

In all that I
believe anent Biblical inspiration, and what the Bible reveals
and teaches, the crucial point with me lies in the question,
"Did Jesus of Nazareth rise from the dead?"   If Yes, as I
believe he did, then all the rest relating to the supernat-
ural in his life follows, or is conjoined with the resurrec-
tion, as a matter of course.   Anything said for, or against,
the Old Testament does not affect my position in the least.
On the other hand, could it be shewn that Jesus did not rise
or that no satisfactory evidence existed that he did rise
from the dead, all my faith in evangelical Christianity and
a written revelation would go by the board.   I believe in
inspiration, but logically it is an afterthought.   At least
in dealing with an antagonist to Christianity I cannot ask
my opponent to grant Biblical inspiration as a premiss.   If

he refuses to receive the Bible as the writings of honest
and truthful men with average intelligence, I fear I cannot argue with him.   But if he grant so far, I regard my
position as a sure one: waving altogether the question of
inspiration.

Nowadays, there seems to be few, or no Atheists.
By Atheism we mean, and entire denial of a supreme intelligence to whom the Universe owes its existence.   If there
are any we meet them thus.   I am, I exist, but I am not
self-existent.   I am only a recent arrival.   I can look
back to the edge of time, before which I was not.   I am
intelligent; I can reason, and to some extent comprehend reasoning powers, or intelligence in others.   Seeing that I
amnot self-existent, I must owe my existence to a power outside of myself; and that power must be greater, superior to
myself, must at least be intelligent, a reasoning power.
Without trying to construct a chain of causation, we call
this necessary, self-existent, intelligent power, God.   No
Multiplication, or combination, of non-intelligents can ever become intelligent.   A thousand monkeys are as far
from making one intelligent man as one monkey is, in the
scale of creation; nor can any mere multiplication of
shell fish, birds, or mammals, produce anything to any real
extent differing from themselves, far less produce intelligence.   Non-intelligent existences we must regard as
the work of intelligent power, outside and distinct from
themselves.   In a word, we cannot conceive of intelligence
in man as evolved in any way but in virtue of intelligence
conjoined with power external to man.   We do not pretend
to understand, or in any way comprehend, self-existent Deity,
but none the less we must "nolens volens" believe in the ulti-

mate fact beyond which we cannot go.   Reaching this I so
far feel satisfied, while stopping short would put an end
to all satisfactory reasoning and rational deduction.   To
me the self-existence of God is mystery: utterly beyond
my highest or faintest conceptions.   To God, his existence
is simplicity itself.   Truth, when fairly presented, is always consistent with itself, and understood without difficulty.   The primal truth of God's existence and infinite
power, cannot be fairly presented to the finite mind; but
its truth is not in the least affected thereby.   We may
by and by know more, but never all.

Looking into the New Test-
ament, and without reference to the resurrection of Jesus,
or verbal inspiration, I find these words, "Come unto me, all
ye that labour and are heavy laden, and I will give you
rest, &c."   To me these words go far to close discussion
anent Jesus' claim to Divinity.   These to me are Divine
words proceeding from Divinity.   "These are not the words
of him that hath a devil."   It has been said by some, that
in the gospels no claim has been made by Jesus to be God.
Is it so?   When Napoleon sat in council with his numerous
staff, the discerning eye of an utter stranger would speedily find the Emperor, although by word of mouth no direct
claim to be such was made by the head of the army.   So in
our gospels, "Thy sins be forgiven thee." "He that doth not
take up his cross daily and follow me, cannot be my disciple".
these and such like words indicate the Master, the Christ,
Divinity.   These sentences we have in our Bible, and as witnesses there they remain.

But what about John's gospel? Well,
I have got it in my possession; no matter who wrote it or

compiled it.   Of one thing I feel certain; a large part
of the tract, and more than enough to satisfy me, was uttered by one greater than man, by a greater than angels, by
God as evidenced in Jesus of Nazareth.   In John's gospel ###
one needs not particularise.   Grant the aim at truthfulness in the production, and further argument is not needed
to shew the Divinity of Christ.   But grant, or not grant,
I regard the matter thus. The works of a Milton, a Shake-
peare, or a Burns, prove themselves.   To quarrel over the
name of such an author would be a mere waste of time.   We
have the words, the name is of secondary importance.   Some
say "Bacon, not Shakespeare"; and some say "Not John, but an
other".   Settle these questions as may be, the fourth gospel we have, and as a self evidencing production I mean
with all my heart to keep it.   My religious faith is
grounded in the gospels.   By the light of the central lu-
minary, Jesus, the Christ, I look as far backward, and as far
forward as I can see my way; leaving the rest for God to
reveal, or otherwise, in his good time and way.

                            Went the oth-
er evening to hear a Unitarian minister lecture on Professor Bruce of Glasgow Free Church College.   Among other
things the lecturer said that in Matthew, Mark, and Luke
there is not one word that would lead us to suppose that
Jesus of Nazareth was anything more than a man.   This set
me a searching, examining, and counting; and I found in Matthew over fifty passages, that would lead me to regard Jesus
as more than a mere man; and over thirty passages that imply or assert Divinity in Jesus: about equal numbers in
Luke, and half as many in Mark.   Thus differently do men
read and interpret the synoptical gospels.   While the Unit-

arian in reading finds no evidence of Divinity in Jesus,
another finds these gospels bristling with evidences;
that is while regarding these utterances as the honest
words of honest men. He said some bold things this Unitarian; such as saying how he would characterise God.,
in the event of there being an eternal hell. His words
we do not feel at liberty to quote; but at the time, we
thought, that such presumption and wickedness in utterance
would go far to make the hell he deprecated, a righteous
necessity in God's Universe. My difficulty is not the
punishment of sin , nor its duration, but the existence of
sin. While sin continues, its punishment must continue.
Unitarianism seems to be a system of negations. No clear,
positive teaching, or inculcation of truth seems to belong
to it. A dislike to the idea of everlasting punishment appears to lie at the root of the system: if system it can
fairly be called. The denial of Christ's Divinity is apparently the sole bond of union in the persuasion. This denial comes as a matter of course from them when perusing Christ
's words anent the future punishment of unpardoned sin.

It was
said of Paul "Behold he prayeth." Does this mean that Paul
never prayed before? Perhaps not; but certainly we may in-
fer, that Paul now prayed as he had never prayed before. The
true Christian cannot fail of communion with God. Without
such communion, we much doubt if a man can be a Christian at
all. Is communion with God possible outside a sense of
pardon and reconciliation? Is a true sense of pardon possible, except through Jesus the Christ, the Mediator between
God and man. Men were saved before Christ came; and where
the Christ has not as yet been revealed, we are loathe to re-

gard salvation for the thirsty and seeking soul, if there
are any such in heathendom, as impossible.   But in such a
case, an equivalent to faith in the Christ, the Redeemer,
must be involved in the sinner's attitude before God.
Pardon in virtue of the action of a vicarious daysman must
ever be the portal to reconciliation and communion with
God, for the guilty.   Man cannot clear himself of guilt; if
cleared at all, it must be by another, and that other sinless
and almighty.   Neither can a sinner be cleansed by punishment.   Punishment may deter, it cannot renew; nor is renewal
its intention.   Hence the necessity of a new heart; made
new by an external power.   These conclusions we regard as
logical from premises that all acknowledging moral obliga-
tion, and possible guilt in man, assent to.

I cannot think of
a man becoming God; but I have no difficulty in conceiving
of God as assuming the form and nature of a man.   I can
never think of the Christ, the man, but as having behind the
human form the Divine consciousness: God in the form of a
man.

Is a man's work, life, or exertions, in any way advantage-
ous to God?   Can a man do anything that may not be done
by God without man's agency? that is apart from sinful action.   Can a man in any way contribute to God's happiness?
There is one way, but we cannot think of another.   It is
to love God, and so add to God's happiness, if that may be.
Love, however, involves a great deal, and attention to common
place duties may often go far to prove its existence.

Death has been busy of late ^{vi} among men we have known, more
or less acquainted with.   Provost Leland, turned sixty,
a busy, successful, (if the ownership of ninety thousand
pounds means success) and dogged man is said to have died
of fear that he was dying.   So frightened at death that
he died!   Probably not a singular experience.

David Murch-
ie, eighty-two, a worker to the end, a missionary in home
work, confident of his salvation, a hater of Calvinism, but
generally a lover of good things.   Wise in his generation was David, fond of comfort, fiery in temper, four times
married, (on occasions acknowledged "three times") a little
vain in certain ways, but who is not?   We cannot but hope
that he has gone to the home of the blest.

Fishmonger White,
over fifty, among haddocks successful.   It has been said
of him that rather than sell at less than his imposed
price, he would wickedly destroy large quantities.   Fond
of intoxicants, yea, too much fond, did said fondness prolong
his days?   Has like fondness done so for any man?

Andrew
Sellar, fifty-six, unmarried, very prudent, very careful of
money, beginning as a junior clerk, he eventually attained
a first class position in the same employ.   He left behind him many thousands; so said gossip.   In any case
Andrew took no money with him.   It would be interesting
to have five minutes talk, just now, with our old acquaintance

Adam Johnson, sixty-six, minister of the gospel, and I
think a faithful one, earnest and conscientious, decided in

his convictions and fearless in expressing them.   But to
me his characteristic feature was a halting when he should
have gone on; a refraining in action when one would have
been inclined to ask, Why?   Courageous in words, but in action slow, if not indeed, right about face.   He preached on
Sacremental Monday evening, vigosrously and acceptably, paid
a pastoral visit thereafter, went home about ten o'clock,
then at half past one in the morning was suddenly called
and went.   A good man in a wicked world can be ill spared.
So we judge.George Nailor, clerk, turned sixty, we suppose.

Have known George some thirty years.   Poor man; poor not
so much in what he was as in what he was not.   "The stars
in their courses"fought against George, or at least he
thought so.   He might have done better in life; but of
whom may that not be said?   Independent in his way; would
not work for ninepence if he considered himself entitled
to a shilling.   Some of us have had to work for just what
dexcould manage to get.   George had in early life been under religious impressions, but want of employment had
brought him almost to the Lunatic Asylum.   He was not a
fool exactly, but was far from wise.   He has gone to a
judge who will deal fairly with him.   Some years ago I
met George in a despondent and vicious mood: he wished
$that he were dead".   So far gratified now, poor man; but
similar wishes have not been unknown to ourselves in days
gone by.
        Another neighbour gone, John Mc.Kim, fifty-six.
Death not altogether sudden, I understand, but unexpected so
far.   Have known the man for a long time but was not
drawn to him.   Might nod to him in passing, but had not a

good opinion of him, nor of his boon companions, as known
to me.   Our opinion however will count for nothing in
the world to which Mc.K. has gone.   Had we known how
soon some of these acquaintances were to go, we might
have spoken very seriously to them; and yet we knew they
had to go.   Why should a short time sooner or later,
shut one's mouth, why?   Since the foregoing was written
Mr. Mc.K's minister has spoken very highly of him.   Said
minister's last words in the last sermon he preached in
Mc.K's hearing were, "God speaks, hear, the time is short,
Amen."

The lady referred to on page 41 was an intelligent,
sincere, and devoted Christian woman.   She had unbounded
faith in God, regarding Him as the hearer and answerer of
prayer, through Jesus the Christ.   Of her early life I
knew little.   Her father was a master tradesman; her two
brothers were outside my acquaintance.   Miss J. by teach-
a school of girls managed to support herself and her aged,
widowed Mother.   But through an affection of the head
Miss.J. came to lose her hearing, almost, if not entirely.
Slowly becoming worse and worse, friends, doctors, and prayers seemed to completely fail her.   Dr. Bell, an aurist in
Glasgow, treated Miss. J. for her hearing and spoke kindly
and encouragingly to her.   But one morning Dr. Bell drank
water impregnated with lead, and soon thereafter died.
When Miss J. was informed of Dr. Bell's death she wept like
a child.   Miss J. had many inquiring and sympathising
friends; but no friend could restore hearing.   To teach,
hearing was essential, more especially to teach girls to
play the piano.   To add to these troubles, sore in their
way, one of her brothers, out of employment, through his own

misconduct, cooly enough came to reside with her, availing
himself of this brotherly privilege at his poor sister's
expense.   One friend, we know, believing Miss J. to be
badly off, in as gentle a way as he could, offered to lend
her ten pounds, more or less,   No one was depending on
him at the time, and whether the money was returned or not
to him did not signify much.   Miss J. was very grateful
for the offer, but declined to receive the money, just then.
She had entire faith in God, that her wants would be provided for in answer to her prayers.   Sometimes one may
not see that prayers are in reality being answered when
circumstances point in another direction.   Before this
time Miss J.'s Mother died.   I understand the wreck of a
brother filled the Mother's place.   "My school has dwin-
dled away almost to none, I cannot live without the means
of living, yet these matters give me no trouble.   No matter what becomes of me in time or in eternity, I feel assured that God the Father cannot do wrong.   God knows my
circumstances, and will provide me with what is right in
his eyes.   My faith in God does not falter for a moment;
at all times my heart rises to God the Father."   These
words were not taken down verbatim at the time, but they
may be safely regarded as if they had: such words, in such
circumstances, are not readily forgotten.   Not long after
that interview I called to see Miss J.   I was informed
that she had died, and had been buried a few days before.
On a very cold Sabbath evening, a communion time so far as
I can remember, Miss J. was present at a service in Union
Free Church, Glasgow, caught a severe chill, was laid down
with pneumonia, and died after a few days illness.   She
seemed to have been buried as a pauper, or laid in a paup-

er's grave in Anderston old burying ground.   A few friends
who had known Miss J. in life had her body lifted and removed to Sighthill Cemetery, A small granite obelisk was
placed at head of her grave, near the postern at the North
side of the Cemetery.   God alone knows his own.

On the oth-
er hand, my neighbour, James O'Brien, also gone, kept a spirit
shop, in which shop there was often much noise, bad language,
fighting, and general evil work going on.   Have seen James, $$$
himself, rather drunk on the public street.   Apart from his
being a Roman Catholic, I cannot think of such a man being
called suddenly from his business, as James was, into Heaven.

Have known Peter Smith, painter, these thirty years.   Tall
and of good personal appearance, he had evidently a good op-
inion of himself.   Consequential and fond of convivial
meetings, we understood, was a Deacon in Free St.David's, ex-
ecuted any painting that required to be done on the Church
premises; did it, and was well, too well paid for it, as cer-
tain of the Deacon's Court thought and said.   In my hear-
ing, one who had occasion to know, spoke of Peter as a per-
fect "scamp"; was somewhat inclined to think so myself, but
to Peter I never said so, though in fact cordial enough with
him.   Had I known the day on which he was to die I might-
-but hold---enough.   Peter has gone; in a short time I
must follow.

vii

Two days ago, a boy, "85", came to me saying that our Janitor's

wife, a rather superior English woman, as we had at first
supposed, had sent another boy to say to him, "that he, "85",
was a hoary headed sinner". Thought there had been some
mistake, but asked our lady if she had really said so. "O.
yes, but you know that we are all sinners. I only said it
in fun. The boy should be whipt for telling you." I requested that she would not say the same again, and so con-
cluded.

        To-day (Sabbath), as on some previous occasions, our
pastor, Mr. Lee, sadly complained that his people do not attend his prayer meetings at 8 p, m, on Wednesday evenings:
sore discouragement to him". And as for people in other
congregations, who in like manner do not attend their "earnest minister's prayer meetings, It was disgraceful." We
could not avoid thinking, that people should be lovingly or
attractively drawn, rather than driven in any way to any
meeting.

        Miss Gall has written to me a note requesting me
to "put in a word" on her behalf for a situation now vacant.
I consider Miss Gall to be quite unsuited for said situation, and with no right conscience could recommend her for
it. In a civil note I replied that my influence in that
quarter was "nil", and that I thought a different sort of
person from her would be appointed. Poor woman, a notable
example of the thoughtless cruelty of parents, not rich,
teaching a dependent daughter nothing beyond trifling occupations and playing the piano. How much kinder had Miss
Gall's mother set the girl to scrub floors and wash clothes
rather than make her a so called lady, with a view to an independent gentleman marrying her. But we need not pursue
the subject farther than to say, that MissGall has had not a

few situations given her, but has not been able to retain
one of them.   That she is a burden to herself she may not
see, but such a one is a sore trial to an employer, till he
gets rid of her: not because the woman is anything bad, but
rather because she is nothing good; no head, no hands, a was-
ted life, as we may regard it.   O, that list of negatives,
but what we do by far and away, compared with what we do not,
but should do, or might reasonably be expected to do.
                                                  Kent's
hole, --have been reading an account of it.   We grant premises to avoid the danger of denying facts.   Man has been
a much longer time in the world than our Bible leads us to
suppose.   Sixty thousand, or for that matter sixty millions
of years.   Either way does not disturb me very much, nor
lead me to regard Jesus of Nazareth in any other light than
as Divine, the Saviour of men.   Kent's hole, so far as it
goes, is clearly against man as a mere product of evolution.
And whether God made Adam the first in Eden six thousand
years ago, or six hundred thousand years ago; or another
whom we shall in like manner call Adam, in another garden, or
in totally different circumstances, does not in our opinion
materially alter the issue.   Millions left without a true
knowledge of God, for say a hundred years, is to us just as
mysterious as leaving them so for a million years.   "Even so,
so, Father, so it seemeth good in thy sight."   Jesus, as revealed to us in our English Bible is as stern a reality as
any we know.

          Have been reading a short biography, pity it was
not an autobiography, of Sir Walter Scott.   Felt at the conclusion, "How have the mighty fallen, and the weapons of war
perished", but Scott's works remain.   Sir Walter Scott stand-

eth or falleth to another than me. He is above any crit-
icism of mine, as he would be entirely unaffected by it.
I always remember however in reading his works, that in
them it is Sir Walter that speaks, not the characters he
depicts in $$$$. his effusions.

.Was recently requested to ad-
dress a meeting in a mission district. Did so, from the
words, "To us a child is born, to us a son is given." The
sons of Napoleon i, and Napoleon iii, "Vanities of vanities."
And yet what a future may lie before the occupant of a cra-
dle! What a future for one and all, in the light of Eternity. What possibilities for those who seek pardon through
him who suffered, though Divine, was, is, and is to come. Man
may not become God, but God has become man, and so revealed
himself in a way not otherwise possible for the object in
view. So at least we understand the revelation, "God suffering". Fearful things seem to be involved in that fact.

To-day I went in search of a boy, James Mair, supposed to
have gone to Donton on Saturday during half holiday. "John
Street" was my only guide, and somewhat uncertain whether
that was correct, having got it from a school boy. Grandmother said she did not know her daughter's address. Her
daughter was my boy's mother. Another woman, a neighbour,
said the grandmother knew quite well. I went, hoping to
get information through factors. Found the street, not
very populous, but containing three or four blocks of houses.
Inquired at some residents, found some people of the name,
but not those I wanted. Tried another block and was informed concerning some others "coming", but who had not come.
Returned to the end of the street, John Street, where I re-

newed my inquiries. "O, yes, James Kean" the name I was after, "he is coming to reside next door." "He is at present in Flying Street, where he has kept a small shop during ten years past. Fooling for me, out again, must go and
have some dinner, and then try House Factors. Tried one
but failed. Went to dinner, obtaining but a poor one; but
perhaps as good as could be expected for the money, sixpence.
I paid the money, leaving the most of my dinner behind me.
To visit my next factor meant a diversion of a mile or
more, so I would inquire near by, and make further inquiries
in my street, as I had now come to regard it. Could obtain
no satisfactory information, so I started again in a somewhat despondent mood, not sure where to go. It was now one
o'clock and workers were thronging to their dinners. Went
along John Street again, as at first, but intending to break
new ground, when suddenly a boy came running out of an entry,
raised his head, evidently saw me, knew me, wheeled round, and
returned to the full as quickly as he came. He had changed his clothes, but I knew my boy, or had no doubt it was him,
and after some further searching, found him and brought him
back to school. Now, was all this merely chance, or something more? Different people will probably give different
answer. For myself I may say, that prayer at such times
of annoyance and worry with me is customary, but I avoid dog-
matism in the matter. There are many remarkable occurrences and coincidences when answer to prayer, as a factor in
the case, is not thought of, or suggested. But when one
prays for guidance, it may be in a moment of irritation, and
weakness, and seems to receive answer, no matter though to
other eyes the occasion may appear trifling, by all rules of
consistency and true sincerity, he is bound to regard it as

guidance in answer to his prayers; be he right, or be he wrong in so thinking. Those who pray only in dire extremity, and in praying receive deliverance, should never give the cold shoulder to prayer in fair weather. A wise man in fair weather, will not laugh at his former self in the storm.

In Chambers' Journal I read as follows. A young newly married couple were standing among the rocks by the sea side. The lady dropped a valuable diamond ring. She saw it fall into a crack, or space, between two large stones that were firmly fixed in the ground. Expecting to find the ring without much trouble, they searched, as can be imagined, but the ring they could not find. After a long and anxious search they had to go without it; trying to find the ring appeared to be useless. In a year or more thereafter they revisited the same spot, when the lady addressing her husband said, "You remember dear, it was into that hole my ring dropped when we were here last." and suiting the action to the word, she pushed the point of her umbrella into the opening. Withdrawing the umbrella, one may judge of her surprise and joy on finding the lost ring on the point of it. Now in this case we have no reason to suppose that prayer had anything to do with the recovery of the ring. But supposing that the lady much annoyed and vexed, had prayed that she might recover the ring; could she have come to any other conclusion, but that she had recovered it in answer to her prayer, in the singular manner related?

Many ignorant and uncivilised people have sought for rain, and by virtue of supposed charms and fetishes, as they thought, the rain has come.   We may smile at their simplicity, but can hardly find fault with their logic, as we endeavour to point out to them their utterly wrong headedness.   Bad money implies good money; so ignorance in prayer, and superstition in expecting answers, may indicate that prayer is an instilled function of the soul, and suits the reasonable expectations of an intelligent mind.

For a number of years past one of my vocations has been to teach boys to swim.   We had the daily use of a pond, about forty feet square and sloping in depth from two and a half feet at one end to four at the other.   My plan was to put a boy into the shallower part, tell him to lie down full length in the water, his back being uppermost, his hands stretched out in front of his head, his legs straight behind him, his face well down in the water, his eyes open, his mouth shut, holding his breath while under the water, and so lie still.   Should he sink to the bottom, though I knew he could not, he was told to lie still there, or rise up, as he felt inclined.   That was lesson one, and if properly learned, any further teaching was seldom required.   However, the second lesson, when required, was, draw in hands and arms in the manner of swimming, at the same time drawing up the legs.   Then throwing out hands and feet together, feet well apart, but hands close together repeat the process and the boy could swim.   Further, at first the boy was to aim at swimming with his head under water, so long as he could hold his breath.   It was wonderful, by this method, how soon a boy could learn to swim; that was when he had faith in his teacher, and implicitly acted as he told him.   Thereafter improvement was obtained by

frequent, but not prolonged practice. It was a standing
joke among our boys, that a certain mother continually
warned her dear boy, on no account to enter the water till
he had first learned to swim: and with some boys, to get
them into the water on any terms was the great difficulty.
In such cases the boy had to be stripped, and not infrequently thrown into the water, in spite of all his entreaties to have pity, and so on. With some boys any other
plan would have been useless. When a boy was thus thrown
into the water there was generally a tremendous hubbub and
outcry; and pitying boys around the victim would hurry to
assist him, and take him to the bank. The teacher inter-
fering would cry, "Leave the boy alone, shake him off, and
let him find his way himself." Almost invariably, doing
so answered the purpose. When the boy discovered that he
was not drowned, and that he could stand with his head
clear of the water, which was not very cold, he would laugh
and splash, and henceforth there was no more trouble with
him. Only on one occasion, in our experience, was a boy so
frightened at the first go off that without assistance he
would have been drowned.

Now the analogy of all this with
the prayers of a Christian can be easily seen. A man's
fears, ignorance, timidity, or anxiety may cause him to pray
when in reality there is not much occasion, and his prayers
requiring no special answer. And again, a direct assent-
ing to a man or boy's request, might not, by any means, be
the best thing for him. Still, nothing can be lost by
prayer; nor is the Hearer by any means indifferent to the
request.

I have known more than one man, Christian men as I

I have regarded them, who have split on a common rock, a
desire to be looked up to, to be considered as occupying
an elevated platform among their fellows: not by a simple
and faithful performance of duties lying to their hands
and devolving on them, but by ample, or seeming ample possessions: as if after all, a man's life does consist in
the abundance of things which he possesses.   These men,
Christian men, as they aim at appearing, and in many ways
acting as such, I am unwilling to look upon as hypocrites,
but if so designated by those who suffer at their hands,
no complaints can well be made.   An elder borrows a
large sum of money from a lady, which he is never able to,
or does not, repay.   Another Elder invests his own savings in a business which does not pay, and is entrusted
with money which he applies to his own use, hoping to be
able to repay in course; he dies in the middle of his in-
debtedness, and leaves no money to repay any body.   Another Elder in business difficulties, borrows money which I
presume no one knowing the real state of the Elder's af-
fairs, would have lent him, and which he could not be expected to repay, be the consequences to the lenders what
they might.   Becoming caution in such cases, is as great
a snare as lending; it generally means simply giving away.
I never lend to any man more than I am willing to make
him a present of, nor become surety for a larger sum than
I am willing to lose.   Now, these Free Church Elders, highly respected for a time, and trusted, all aimed honestly e-
nough at being at least like Christian men, and could not in
law be regarded as criminals in their doings.   But such
ways do not belong to Christianity; and these men cannot
complain if branded as hypocritical scoundlers.   I knew

these men intimately, and regard their doings as mistakes, as blunders, founded on desires to be grand, to possess, to appear in positions which their legitimate incomes did not entitle them to.   Perhaps the deference and consideration paid to wealth on all hands, and as much in our Churches as anywhere else, has much to do with the fallacy, that the highest types of Christianity are conjoined with riches. This is not said in irony, but as simple truth.   And yet while the world is what it is, and men continue to be what they are, things cannot well be otherwise.

I knew, and do know, Miss Blair, an educated, elderly spinster lady.   She was well provided for, in virtue of what she inherited from her deceased relatives.   Whether she was quite contented is doubtful.   An intimate friend, dying, left Miss Blair a considerable sum of money.   This legacy somehow turned Miss Blair's head.   She set about building a house, and laying out grounds in a grand and expensive style; and in the midst of the worry and responsibilities connected therewith had to be removed to a lunatic asylum, from which there is no hope of her return.

Similarly, a gentleman of our acquaintance on receipt of a bequest, lost his head, got himself into endless trouble, and I believe, shortened his days, all through such another newly sprung ambition.   Is there not danger in coming suddenly into possession of much money; not less to be guarded against than in having too little?

If a man has the desire to live hereafter in a pure and perfect state, with the capacity to enjoy such an outlook, and can love, or desires to love God though unseen,

can gaze into space, and try in a measure to comprehend
the Eternities; do these facts not indicate that the longings of the soul have their foundations in reality? In
this thought we are probably anticipated by other thinkers,
as sooner or later we find to be the case with many if not
with all our thoughts. Thus it is cheering to find that
other minds in other ages, have thought on similar lines,
and that faculties possessed by man indicate probable truth
when free from prejudice there is the desire to find it.

How utterly beyond my powers to conceive in any satisfactory way, of God, the fountain of life and being. But is it
necessary that I should have such powers? Perhaps the
highest wisdom existing in the creature is that which sees
the futility of trying to search out God, but aims at living to God, in so far as God has revealed himself to us, and
rejoicing in the faculties that God has given us to apprehend and love him. Wealth is not the highest evidence of
God's favour. A far more to be prized gift is the capacity with the inclination to love God, to enjoy God's works
and ways, and to have real pleasure in instructing and otherwise serving our fellow men, especially such as inquire
Godwards.

viii

26th. May 18-- 8,45, a,m, .As I was seeing our boys into breakfast, I received a letter from our Inspector, "Sorry to give
so little notice &c."but the long and the short of it was
that I might expect him in ten or fifteen minutes. Janit-

or at breakfast, Work Master from home, Schoolmaster residing several miles away, and not expected in less time than
an hour and three quarters, so I am in a pickle.   Had it
been another Inspector who was a reasonable man, and having been at one time a Superintendent himself, he would
have spoken reasonably in such circumstances; but as for
"Fiery" I shall not write what I think of him, beyond that
he has a bad temper, an overbearing manner, and sometimes inclined to mischief.   If, in certain moods, "Fiery" could not
find a grievance, he was bound to make one.   We cannot be
said to love one another, but why pursue the matter?   He
gave a bad report, causing me pain and annoyance.   Why
should we deserve a bad report to-day any more than during
ten years past, in which time we have invariably received
good ones from both "Fiery" and his Chief, can only be guessed.   Some one has said, that what is must be right; so on
this line for the present I stop.

R. Cromer, auctioneer, I
knew him well, has gone over to the majority.   No, he has
not gone over to them, although gone over from us, as they
have gone.   C. was a good man, had all the temptations of
an auctioneer, but none, or few, of an auctioneer's faults.
He was one of the very few men, but this in confidence, whom
I regarded as a better man than myself.   But why should I
say so?   Things are in a bad way if there are not thousands in the world of better men than I.   Ours is but a
small circle, and by no means very select.   Really good
men seem to be suspicious of the writer; and as for good women who have loved him, he can only mention his Mother, his
Sister, and his Wife.   Possibly, he has not loved others
any better than they have loved ▓▓▓▓ him.   But then, to be

loved truly by one, singled out and loved, is far and away
better than to be loved merely in the lump, in the mass,
in the crowd, one of a multitude, although that in itself
may not in any way be a bad thing. When we think of the
advantages and blessings enjoyed by people under British
rule in these times, to the Christian it is in reality
election; and special gratitude to the Almighty becomes
those who enjoy these privileges. And special blessings
received by individuals will, or at least, should, produce
corresponding thankfulness and gratitude, in a way that ordinary mercies, given to all promiscuously, could hardly be
expected to do. Election we receive as a truth, we are
shut up to it by facts, not by mere fancies. Is there no
election in being born a Scotchman, of Christian parents,
with good health, pleasant surroundings, and every inducement to make one's "election sure" for time and for Eternity?
not by presumption, trying to pry into the secret counsels
of God, were that to serve any good purpose, but seeking to
act as if all depended on one's right doing, while praying
as if nothing depended but on God's good pleasure and one's
active faith in the Christ.

Another acquaintance, not an in-
timate, my hair cutter for well nigh thirty years, is, I am
told, dying. Regarding the man's religion, the facts indicate negations. A Christian's life should be something
more than negatives. Positively doing right is better than
merely doing no wrong. However, with one exception the
commandments are given in the negative form, "Thou shalt not,"
so better not to dogmatise. One thing, my hair dresser
seems to have been sagacious in worldly matters, and prosperous in business. That, however, is not enough for a man's

true welfare.

Have just returned from a conference of the
London Reformatory and Refuge Union, on this tri-annual
occasion, held in Glasgow. The company was a "mixty, max-
ty, motely squad", (quoting Burns) but with somewhat modified meaning. In the meeting there were good men and
women, not a few, we cannot doubt. But of religious profes-
sions, there were Evangelicals, Roman Catholics, Unitarians,
High Church, Low Church, and judging from papers read, men
of no Church. One subject discussed was the employment
of our children during leisure hours. "Inter alia" there
were recommended as permissive, or to be encouraged, novel
reading, card playing, dancing, and secularising the Sabbath.
Decided dissent was made to these proposals by some present. But what coherence can there be among men of such
varied theological and religious opinions? What we regard
as the most important factor in forming, or reforming the
character in youth is religious education. But that subject, in our conference, seemed to be studiously avoided by
the leaders; no doubt for good, or bad, reasons, that no una-
nimity could be obtained in the heterogeneous gathering.
This may be noted as a significant sign of our times, that
occupations and amusements that not long since were regarded by religious as dangerous, if not altogether sinful, as
improper spending of time, and so not to be encouraged, are
now recommended as means of reformation, with very little
expressed dissent, at a meeting of Directors and workers
aiming at reclaiming the fallen, and preserving the pure.

When starting to join in a day's outing given to the members of Conference, I observed four of our Superintendents

all smoking and entering a whiskey shop together; while
the aroma of other workers, some of them, gave clear enough
evidence, that whatever good precepts they impart to their
children, their own example in the matters of whiskey and
tobacco, cannot count for much in the right way. There
was common sense in that old copy book heading, "Example is
better than precept". Men, women, and children spend their
lives, to a large extent, merely copying. Are there any
who do not copy? And yet what a multitude of well meaning people there are who seem to regard example in their
own actions as of little or no account. Among the careless and Godless that needs not to be wondered at; but why
aiming to be upright people, and successful workers, should
not see the force of practicing all precepts in their own
persons first, is surely strange, having regard to ordinary
intelligence and common sense.

Some of our teachers and min-
isters think and say, that religion should not often be instilled into children, in case they come to dislike the subject, and so turn from it. To say so is not Bible teaching. It says, teach your children in your house, and by
the way, when rising up and when sitting down, going out and
coming in. And in secular education, more especially in
so called accomplishments, children are by no means spared
whatever their likings may be. Dailly drillings in arithmetic, dead languages, living ditto, and piano playing, all
much against the grain, or causing disgust, it may be to the
youngsters, are taught without stint; and why make religion,
God service, an exception? "Turn out your toes, Annie
dear," says the fond mother; again in a little, "Remember
your toes, Annie." Six or eight times in a short walk, the

erring young one is reminded of these turned in toes, that
after all seem to be pretty straight to any one apart
from the anxious mother. Not mothers alone; I was recently walking down a country road with a gentleman friend,
his daughters trotting along in front on their way to
school. I saw nothing wrong, but the father had a sharp
eye. "Turn out your toes, Mary." and quite right; no doubt
it was "a word in season", and how good it was.

                                                Spurgeon,
Muller, Quarrier, and Barnard are all workers among the
young. Judging from my own and certain of my friends'
experiences, I presume they, the workers, have more or less
difficulty in obtaining the right sort of assistants, like
minded with themselves. As for us, we can manage only to
obtain average men and women, too often below average, having
regard to character and abilities. Now, some prominent
men, as those indicated, profess to get funds in answer to
prayer, which enable them to go on without halt or hinder-
ance for many years. The sincerity and truthfulness of
we cannot for a moment doubt. But then, are their prayers equally efficatious in procuring for them the best assistants? We believe in prayer, and pray continually yet
often do not get exactly what we pray for; as it was with
Paul and some others. Moreover, is there not a temptation present with some of us, to expose to the public, only
the light side of our work? We are inclined to say little concerning the dark side, of our work, perhaps altogether hide certain things when we think it expedient to do
so. Another temptation is, to prefer for admission into
school or institution, nice good looking children, it may
be the children of needy but respectable parents, in pre-

.ference to the low, the repulsive or the vile.   I have
.sometimes, I do not say often, advised poor but respect-
.able mothers to cling to their children; nor break the
.tie which is God made: in my opinion a thing more to be
.feared than even a struggle for bread,   However wellwe
.workers may do, or try to do, for children under our care,
.she is but a sorry mother who would not, or could not, with
.a little timely assistance, do far better for her child
.than we can possibly do in our barrack institutions.

.Another
.departure, T.O.P. a man, agentleman so called, whom we have
.known for many years, took final leave of all, ten days ago.
.Poor, very poor, Tom---rumour has it that in his youth he
.sought pleasure to excess, and found it with the drawbacks
.of prolonged illness and impaired constitution.   He was
.introduced to us as reformed and respectable, one of the
.Managers of a charitable institution.   Tom dressed well,
.had gentlemanly manners when not crossed, and had a great
.dislike to being in any way bothered, or troubled about
.anything.   On one occasion I was rather sharply rebuked
.by him for talking about death in his presence.   When C.M.
.a mutual acquaintance died, after a short illness, the event
.affected Mr. P. very much, deprived him of comfort, and even
.of sleep for a time.   When first known to us, Mr. P. was not
.rich, but by and by he had bequeathed to him many thousand
.pounds, it was said.   His age at that time might be between
.forty and fifty.   He married but had no family.   When
.thenCity Bank failed, with which Tom had some small connec-
.tion, #### the poor man fairly collapsed, losing vigour of ####
.life and power of limbs, sank away till latterly he had to
.be tended and treated as an infant; which mentally and in

other ways he had become.   To this man what was life?
On the one hand, what desiring after the fancied good
things of life; on the other hand, what miserable, soul dis-
appointing results.   The City Bank failure gave Tom such
a fright, that subsequently when it was said that he had
lost every penny that he possessed by a different disaster, he was too far gone to be much affected by it.   For
the last few years of his life Tom had no bother; a striking realisation of his paramount desire.   I must endeavour to find out where he lies buried and visit his grave,
at present to me unknown.

In writing, or attempting to write,
an autobiography, I fear there are repetitions, not intended but difficult to delete, and more numerous than they
should be.   Portions have been written at intervals of
years, and resuming when what had been written had been forgotten, a saying over and over again the same things must
be borne by indulgent, if not sympathetic readers.

In speak-
ing to children I have doubtless repeated my words and
thoughts over and over again.   Be it so, I have as a rule
received attention from them; I think they have felt interested, and benefited in an average way, in what has been presented to them from time to time.   Preaching to children,
setting before them truth, with a view to their everlasting
salvation, a duty incumbent on parents and all guardians of
the young, is often regarded as difficult, and to those who
have no personal interest in the matter, to speak, or instruct effectively, may be considered as impossible.   "Very
difficult to speak to children", said a gentleman to me; he
had come to address them them on a Sabbath forenoon.   I

assented and George went on. "Now boys, I am going to speak to you about great men; can any of you give me the name of a great man?" "President Lincoln" said one boy. "The apostle Paul" said another. "O yes" said our preacher, "President Lincoln, the apostle Paul, and all them fellows". George got through, but evidently it was difficult.

Another to our boys spoke thus. "When a boy tells a lie, that lie remains. When a boy takes to himself what does not belong to him, in other words when a boy steals, his stealing makes him a thief, and so far a thief he remains. When a boy in anger strikes his companion, that blow remains, at least in the memory of the victim, and rightly so, it may be for ever. The consequences of evil doing in many cases, if not in all, remain, they cannot be got rid of. Law, among men, knows nothing of forgiveness. Law regards the crime and the criminal as evils to be got rid of. The reformation of the criminal is not the prerogative of the law. With the law the first consideration is that crimes are evils that cannot, and must not be tolerated in a community. The law cannot pardon crime. There must be something wrong, or weak, in a law which threatens punishment it cannot, or dares not, inflict. A parent may pass by, or be blind to a fault in a child, and because he is dealing with an infant not quite responsible; but were a boy to persist in setting fire to premises, even were said boy a fool, the law must effectively deal with him, either by corporal punishment, or by depriving him of liberty. In Heaven, or in any perfect condition of existence, there can be no liars, no thieves, nor evil doing of any kind. The doers of wrong cannot be permitted to reside there. In this world they may be tolerated, but only for a time; the law of God cannot assent to their continuance, nor regard them with indifference.

Our Queen may pardon; but in reality her pardon is a fiction resorted to in cases of uncertainty or wrongous conviction: that is conviction in error, or in pity for half witted criminals. God alone can pardon, and even he pardons only in virtue of what the Christ, our Redeemer has done. Do you, boys, wish to be pardoned? Probably not, and certainly not, if you think that you have never done anything requiring pardon. In any case you do not wish to suffer the pains and penalties of wrong doing. What are you to do, or are you to do anything? First then, remember that it is not an easy thing to be a Christian, a boy seeking salvation and eternal life. Few things worth having can be obtained without exertion, and it may be much self denial. In other directions we see great and continued exertion with corresponding self denial, if in these cases it can be called self denial, to be a good batsman, a good bowler, goal keeper, dancer, or singer. No doubt, pleasure may accompany these exertions; but what of research in the Polar Seas, in the deserts and swamps of Africa, or in Cannibal Islands. What about our Army and Navy? men leaving ease and comfort, and even laying down their lives at the call of duty. Even the pains, and penalties connected with many School boys' lives, at lessons and discipline, remind us that life is not intended to be all play and indolent ease. Boys who would be Christians must be brave. We do not mean the bravery of mere daring and foolhardiness; but the

bravery of not being afraid of being laughed at when going
to Church or prayer meeting, for praying on one's knees before lying down to sleep at night, or after rising in the
morning, refusing to enter a beer shop, refusing to desecrate
the Sabbath, or refusing to frequent questionable places of
amusement. Not easy certainly, to expose one's self to
laughter and jeering, it may be on all sides, when it can be
so easily avoided. But remember, God will take nothing
less than the best you can give, when you enlist in his service. "My son give me thy heart", more a man or boy cannot
give, less our God will not accept.

Another thing to be remembered is, that God fearing and God serving must be for ever.
Effort for a time and then drop off will not do. Think
well over the matter, it must be effort while life lasts;
mere fun, amusement, or even happiness must not be the chief
end of a Christian's life. The ultimate reward to a
Christian is eternal life; something worth striving after,
depend upon it. A healthy baby is a happy baby. A healthy boy is naturally a happy boy. A healthy man is a happy
man, barring very unfavourable circumstances. It is health
that gives happiness. Only to a very limited extent do
circumstances, apart from positive pain or sorrow, affect
the happiness of a healthy soul. Eternal life means eternal health, eternal happiness. Eternal death involves the
opposite. Jesus, the Christ has spoken of the latter in
words of fearful import, that cannot be misunderstood. Lay
these words to heart; time is short; to some of us it will
turn out very short, at the longest can only be short. Determine to do right; believing that God for Christ's sake
will assist you. Pray that God by his Holy Spirit may

teach you. Be not discouraged by partial failure. Strive
earnestly, and while you live. True happiness will ultimately accompany earnest endeavour. But happy or not
happy fight on, relax not; even a hundred years of effort
and struggle on earth will be but a short apprenticeship
for that life in Eternity which lies before us, one and all.
In striving, faith reveals itself. Without faith in God,
that he will pardon past wrong doing for Christ's sake, neither man nor boy will aim at a life of doing right. He
will merely seek to live so that life will be pleasant, or
at least not uneasy. Most men and boys in passing through
life have one darling pursuit which, though not right, they
cling to, while quite willing to relinquish bad habits which
they are more or less indifferent to. But Christianity
insists that that which we love most, if sinful, must be given
up. And generally speaking, if one makes up his mind to
part from that which he loves most, because it is sinful, other faults will be turned from without much self denial and
with no regret. By a course of right doing, and open profession of Christianity, a man or boy comes very soon to
love God, and will seek to walk so as not to displease him.
By loving God we positively please him: at least without
loving God we cannot please him. The best way, the only
true way, to shew love to God is by keeping his commandments.
Never boast of your Christianity; live it as far as you can,
and leave it to others to judge by the life you live. On
the other hand never be ashamed of your faith. Do not
hide your colours, though not called upon to shake them in
the face of every one you meet. In conclusion, a lazy do
nothing faith in Jesus Christ will save neither man nor boy,
pity if it did. God will pardon for Christ's sake, but not

if you do not desire salvation, nor in spite of yourself.
That which is not worth effort to obtain, is not worth
trouble to accept.' But to the earnest, the desirous, the
willing, the anxious, I say, pray often and alone, that God
by the Holy Spirit may teach you. Shew that you are in
earnest by right living and acting. If you fail, try a-
gain, not once, but while you live; and trust that God for
Christ's sake will do all that he has promised; and you
will do well."

Not all en one occasion, nor quite verbatim
were the foregoing remarks addressed to a school of boys
under sixteen years of age. The boys listened attentive-
ly, and evidently understanding, for half an hour at a time.
Longer addresses were deemed inadvisable.

It is well to re-
frain from sin, even when our motives in doing so are entirely selfish, and due to fear. Indulgence in sin ever
tends to make a greater sinner. Refraining from sin tends
to righteousness and to the love of it.

.ix

Have been reading of late,"Plutarch's Lives." Here we find
depicted abilities of no mean order; marked intelligence,
with ambition, superstition, and cleverness, but what a lack
of vital goodness. Specious veneers, aping the truth, with
what cold hearted wickedness do these ancient heroes, so
called, appear to us. Can the authors of such evils as
are in these stories recorded, the originators of pain and
sufferings on the heads and hearts of many of their fellow

creatures, comparatively innocent, themselves escape all ill
consequences in the world to come, as many of them have escaped in this?   Can Neros, Ilvas and Napoleons play the
parts of devils incarnate in this world, escaping any punishment worth the name, ultimately "Scott free?" get off?
One's soul revolts at the thought.   No, such cannot be,
God will bring them into judgment.   May they, then, in any
way be converted and pardoned, the tyrants and their victims alike, one and all?   Conversion and pardon in this
world are gospel truths; but the very brilliancy and glory
of gospel truth in time make sin and impenitence in Eternity al the more fearfully dark, hopeless, and despairing.
A fearful subject, but the Ruler of all will do right. " A
man cannot be more just than his maker".   As we have said
elsewhere, the existence of sin is our great difficulty, not
the final disposal of the sinner.   The existence, or the
toleration of sin, that is sinful sin, is a fact we cannot
understand.   Possibly it may lie in the imperfection of
all created intelligences: intelligent and responsible, but
falling short of inherent perfection.   Further, were sin
non-existent, we could not expect to find a very high, or at
least so high, a standard of virtue as when sin is known to
exist, and is a possible thing among the created.   Truth
will be more admired and valued where lying prevails.
Where dishonesty is rampant, probity will be enhanced in value.   These virtues, truth, honesty, and such like, it would
be difficult to appraise in the absence of their opposites.
Again, vice is somehow natural, certainly easier to man than
uniform right doing.   Virtue has to be learned; vice is at
hand, ready made, almost.   Certain of this we may be, that
God's purposes, somehow, are served by the presence of sin

in ways that they could not be were sin entirely absent.
Man suffers from sin, and the innocent and comparatively innocent and sinless suffer from its commision.   Whether
this is so in any proper sense with God, apart from the sufferings of Jesus the Christ, we cannot say, nor dare presume
to guess.

        A most difficult subject to us is, the large num-
ber of men who are, so far as we can fairly judge, not good
enough for Heaven, nor quite bad enough for Hell, as we incline, and are prone, to think.   It may to some extent sim-
plify our difficulty, which in reality has no occasion to
be a difficulty, it being a matter that will be wrought out
our assistance, if we divide all men into two classes, those
who aim at doing better, and so in a hopeful way becoming
better, and those who carelessly are ever becoming worse.
These two classes do exist, but the fact does not quite dispose of the difficulty: so good as to be fit for Heaven, so
bad as to deserve Hell.   And yet, it is a fair inference,
who heads to JohnO'Groats will to John O'Groats; and who
heads to Land's End will to Land's End, both in due course.
Does Christianity solve the difficulty?   It does, so far,
but the subject is a grave one, and causes trembling: think
well of it, only two ways.

                But returning to daily work and
daily experiences---Dan Sharp was a rather troublesome boy.
Sharp by name and Sharp by nature.   In the Superintendent
's absence, and while in charge of an under official, in the
dormitories there was a considerable disturbance.   Dancing
over beds and disorder being prevalent, in the midst of the
row Dan was heard to shout, "Hurray for Home Rule in the Industrial School."where the young rascal was then and there

located.   Mr.Gladstone was agitating for Home Rule at the
time, for Ireland, and the Superintendent was a supporter of
his; but Home Rule as exemplified on this occasion was sadly lacking in good taste.

                            Early one morning four of our boys
left school, much to our annoyance, and went no one of us
knew where.   Next morning, another boy, an English boy, not
long in school disappeared.   After the latter I started by
train, hoping to overtake him on the tramp, possibly catch
sight of him from the railway, come out at a distant station,
and returning meet my boy on the highway.   So it turned
out; with his jacket reversed I saw him, and in due course
returning, saw him again.   But he saw me, and running down a
side was lost to view.   I went into a small plantation
searching, but in vain.   Vexed and annoyed I returned to
the main road, and had not gone many paces when who should
I meet but the four boys who had gone off the preceding day.
Forthwith I took the four to school; my Englishman I never
saw again.

         Captain D.Mc.Kay and Mr.Arch.MC.Nab were both Di-
rectors in our School, at that time dubbed "Ragged School",
which in reality it was; they were partners in business.
Captain Mc.Kay was hard and old fashioned to a degree. In
the early years of the "Ragged School" the children, as a
rule, had no clothing beyond what they obtained in their respective homes.   Shoes and stockings for the most part
they had none.   However, for appearance sake it was considered advisable to supply shoes and stockings at the beginning of winter.   After the matter had on one occasion
been amicably settled, Captain Mc.Kay turning round to his
partner in business remarked in the hearing of all present,

"You and I, Archie, had tae gae tae school bare fittit."
Archie became rather red about the lugs, and yet, Why?

Have I ever said, or uttered words that have caused me subsequent unavailing regrets?   When herding, and then about
thirteen years of age, provoked by the persistent trespass-
ing of a hungry cow into soft muddy ground, I waded after
her, not removing my shoes and stockings, and sinking deep
wept with vexation, cursing the cow in bad language.   I
remember well, and wish I had not cursed, but the words remain.   On a later occasion, thoughtlessly, but without excuse, I uttered words the full significance of which I
might not know.   Another then present, may have forgotten
the words: I have not, nor likely ever will.   I wish the
words had been left unsaid, but the wish is a vain one.
In Aberdeen at the Barracks gate, I heard a young woman utter words so blasphemous that I shall never dare to repeat
them; I wish that I had never heard them.   They fell on
my ears without invitation, would I could forget them, but
they remain with me, a legacy from the evil one.   That was
sixty years ago.

Last Sabbath we were requested to address
a meeting in a Mission Hall.   Text, "Abba Father".   Among
other remarks it was said, that to love requires two.   One
sided love, as to endurance, is limited.   It is not enough
that God loves us; we must learn to love God; otherwise,
God's love to us cannot be enduring.   To say so may be
startling, but it is true and scriptural as we conceive. In
like manner it may be said anent forgiveness, two parties
are requisite, the forgiver, and the forgiven.   Forgiveness
must be asked, or begged for before it can rightly be grant-

ed.   Further, it was said, that men in earnest are not easily driven from their purpose.   A good man though he fall
will rise again.   We have seen a man in a race stumble
and fall, evidently with intention; not expecting to win he
pretended an accidental fall to hide defeat.   Are not men
sometimes quite willing to be led, or fall into temptation?
Do not men search for excuse to sin? seem anxious for excuse so that they may cease fighting against desire?   Sin
loved, and presumptious sins are not consistent with "Abba
Father".   But unknown sins of omission, forgetfulness, wear-
iness and moral frailty, God is just and faithful to forgive;
when forgiveness is prayed for with true penitence, earnest
desire, and "full purpose after new obedience", in Christ's
name and for his sake.

In the case of a man who has been try-
ing these forty years to serve God without sin, but ever with
sin, "Abba Father" comes in hopefully, and stands between him
and despair.   In reality, the earnest man has been loving
God, in a way, but too often failing in the best way to shew
it.   Such a one comes again and again, yes, daily, praying
for pardon and aiming at amendment.   Calmly looking ahead
and judging by past experience, he has little hope of much,
or even any betterness, during the few days or years that
will finish his course on earth, but "Abba Father" by the
Holy Spirit in Jesus Christ seems to cover all.   If some
with incredulity smile, what then?   Can any man living
shew us a more excellent way?   We know not any.   So nail-
ing our colours to the mast, we fight on, win or lose; our
course is all our wisdom, to do so our only choice, we can
conceive of no better.

When I sit listening to the

Reverend B.C., or not listening, he in the pulpit, I in the pew, in spite of exertion to prevent, I feel drowsy, even fall asleep, discovering it with a start.   But why sleep? Somehow the Rev.B.C.cannot, or$$ at least does not keep me awake.   Another man, in another place, will not permit his hearers to fall asleep, or even seem drowsy, why? This we know, the latter uses no written paper, he speaks as believing what he says, and appears anxious that his hearers should also believe, and do as he himself does; that is so far as the speaker succeeds in doing right.

Some suggested alterations in our School premises have been under consideration by our Directors.   One suggested alteration meant, that certain spaces belonging to the Girls' Department should be added to the Boys.   Consideration was given, but decision deferred.   Same day, Boys dinner hour, Matron dividing dinner, I am requested to speak privately.   She did speak, but with what a volley of bad temper, and why? "That you should speak to the Committee about such a thing without first consulting me."   I listened quietly, perhaps provokingly so, asked if she had any more dumpling to give us, and so ended the interview: when to be resumed I know not. Infection seems to have spread to the Schoolmistress, but I take no notice of it.

The foregoing by the way, but another subject lies on our mind, to wit, the absence of hurry with God.   In God's works no hurry, no fuss, no retracing of steps, no halting, no hesitancy, but a quiet irresistible going forward.   We do not mean uniformity of motion; which at times is comparatively slow, often inconceivably swift are motions and operations around us: but never in a hur-

ry, or making up for lost time.   But as for men they often
cannot get along quick enough; or they lag, fall asleep, or
die over their work.   How utterly different with the Auth-
or of all things; calm, quiet, ceaseless, effective.#### never
ending work.   One gets into a flutter, trying to say what
he cannot.   I stop, but what an overbearing thought; infinite work, perfect work, no mistakes, no over-driving, no stopp###
age, Orion, Sirius, Pleiades.   Those who have gone know somewhat unknown to us who remain groping.

At a meeting of Kirk
Session last night.   Church has a Mission Station near by
with rather limited operations.   There is a short meeting
on Tuesdays at seven in the evenings, and a similar meeting
at the same hour on Sabbath evenings.   An earlier meeting
was suggested to be held on Sabbath, either forenoon or afternoon, but strong opposition was manifested, evident enough
though slowly confessed, and why?   Because, it was said, that
certain people might leave the regular congregational services, and worship at the Mission Station.   It seems that
at the Mission services there are more Church members than
"lapsed masses", hence the fear, perhaps rightly grounded.
But O, alas, what about converting the world, if such poor little jealousies divert us from the Church's proper work.
The fact seems to be, that many of our churches free and
bound, calling themselves Christian, are in a rather sorry
condition.   Would it not be well to aim at higher life
standards, stricter discipline, and letting the World ascend
to our standard, while the Church resolutely declines to
come down to theirs?   And this, even if sustentation funds
should go down, and less ornate congregational buildings be
erected, with an eye to keeping clear of debt.   Bazaars and

lotteries for the maintenance or propagation of Christianity, we regard as little short of an abomination; while the promotion of dancing, and amateur theatricals in connection with certain Church gatherings known to us, are altogether out of place, and foreign to the mission of Christ's Church on earth. The "lapsed masses" as most others who have eyes and ears, dislike humbug. They may like enjoyment, whiskey, and theatres, with athletic sports and gambling; at the same time admiring a Luther, a Knox, or a Chalmers, but milk and water nobodies have but a slippery influence over them. Thoroughly good, or ditto bad, they may admire by turns, but the lukewarm they have no taste for. Has this lukewarmness in ministers, elders, and leading members, anything to do with the scant success in even retaining many of those connected with our churches, and practically no success in reclaiming those who have lapsed away from them?

Our Ministers nowadays differ in our hearing from the majority of Ministers fifty years ago. In those days sermons were much more of a doctrinal and practical character than they are now. While defining and explaining doctrines our old ministers spoke much more to the feelings, or to the hearts, of their hearers than they do now, in these latter days. They urged, warned, directed, and instructed in a manner which has now become almost obsolete. In these days preachers may speak to the head, or to the intellect, but seldom in any way to alarm, to make afraid, or bring tears to

the eyes.   They seldom preach on the work of the Holy
Spirit, or of its necessity in a man's obtaining salvation.
Everlasting punishment is seldom alluded to, or a day of
Judgment hinted at.   Our present preachers may condemn
sins of certain sorts, but they are mostly sins that their
hearers are not addicted to.   If their hearers, or some
of them, are given over to certain sins, no notice is taken
of these sins in the pulpit: and in other ways there is
evidently more a desire to please than to edify.   In former days, it may have been that, ministers aimed at preaching like the apostle Paul.   Many modern ministers appear
to preach because they have to preach, but without much aiming at anything beyond filling up the time, and pleasing as
far as they may or can.   There are exceptions, but they
are exceptions.   Evangelicalism appears more prevalent a-
mong elders and private members than among our ministers,
and in certain directions there is indicated a higher morality among the laity than among the clergy.   If in these
asseverations I am in the main correct, the facts are to be
deplored, and remedies are desirable.

Are our Scotch methods
of making ministers the best that can be devised?   Are
the most suitable men, or rather say boys, attracted to, or
placed in the profession?   It is a profession, and all over, a good one for men of fair qualifications.   It is to
be feared that not a few enter it, or are entered for it,
merely as a profession which is respectable, easy, and tolerably certain of success.   Once a minister, always a minister, and provided for during life, in a tolerable way; with
not a few prizes for really able men.   Is it not parents

more than youths themselves, that have most to do in decid-
ing to make their sons ministers? and when their course
is once started it is not regarded as creditable to halt
or turn back.   Students go forward, their principal aim
being at the end of their studies, to secure a congregation where a good stipend may be looked for with moderately easy work.   Our present system of finding and training cannot be the best.   A young man spends eight years
of his youth in acquiring College lore, Greek and Hebrew,
or a smattering of them with the rest, and at the end of
his course is no fitter, perhaps not so fit, to undertake
the duties in a congregation than not a few men who know
no language but their own.   Education and training may be
necessary, but in finding the right men much less time and
expense might well suffice to secure efficient ministers,
quite suitable for many of our congregations.   If a young
man in his twenties has shewn himself capable and active
in Church work, able to secure for himself a hearing when
opportunity is given him to speak, giving evidence of
Christian character, and well approved in the congregation
of which he is a member, why should not two years training
suffice to fit him to perform a minister's work in any
congregation giving him a call?

In our hearing, a minister,
who had stood high in College attainments, an elderly man
in charge of a town congregation, was lecturing seriatim
in Samuel and Kings.   He, the minister, had just read Solomon's injunction to Shimei anent remaining in Jerusalem,
and leaving the city at his peril; when he, the minister,
added these words, "Whether Shimei did remain in Jerusalem,

or

or what became of him, I really do not know." Nevertheless, the minister by the following Sabbath found out; perhaps by reading a little more of the narrative, concerning which he was trying, or pretending to instruct others. Again and again this Reverend gentleman has expatiated concerning "Aunty Okis", bringing the smile to the faces of certain young hearers, too young to make allowance for a minister, who I believe means well. Speaking of Felix's words to Paul, "Go thy way, Paul &c.", this minister said, by way of comment "There is good reason to believe, that Felix in this world never met Paul again."!! Describing rocks about the dead sea, he said, "There were a great many rocks, the whole of which might be taken for Lot's wife, or as she used to be:" one of the elders gave a "snicker". In our hearing this clergyman said, "The poor widow had only two mites, she gave one of them, which was half her living." however, on further reading he gave the correct version, but without alluding to his previous error. Recently, in lecturing on Adam and Eve, he speculated as to whether any of Adam's flesh was adhering to the rib removed from Adam's side to form Eve. He assured the congregation that the operation had been very neatly performed, and that the wound healed up immediately after. Re. leprosy, "incurable disease, but hungry lepers, very curious and venturesome; even in our days doctors are found so venturesome and clever, that they will remove a man's eye from the socket, clean it, and return it to its place without injury." Not merely in scientific knowledge are some ministers deficient, but in Biblical knowledge as well, and shew culpable carelessness in their preparation for the pulpit. We have heard of Isaac and Ish-

mael represented as two boys quarrelling, Isaac being at the
time an infant, incapable of quarrelling with any one. Sug$$$$$$
gesting that Paul's "thorn in the flesh" might be sore eyes,
the minister requested his young hearers to search and find
out all the passages in the New Testament where Paul speaks
of his eyes." In another connection, from the pulpit such
an utterance as this on behalf of temperance, is by no means
up to the mark; "It is an awful thing in a man, to sell his
soul for the love of drink. Were a man to cut off all his
limbs, one after another, and sell them for a sweetie, he would
not be such a fool as the man who loses his soul for drink?"

We have no sympathy with writers in novels, or otherwise, when
they try to cast ridicule on ministers by portraying them
in false colours, or putting words in their mouths that were
never uttered, the mere product of the writers animus, or de-
sire to depict smart and clever things, no matter at whose
expense But of all men our ministers should be careful as
to their utterances, whether in the pulpit or elsewhere.
The specimens we have given are probably exceptional, but
why should he that uttered them be a minister at all? The
minister alluded to was a highly esteemed one in a working
class congregation. At College, we have been informed, he
stood high, at least in some of his classes; and judging by
the praise and laudation bestowed upon him after his death,
by the leading men of his Presbytery, he must have stood
high in their estimation. But we do not complain of this
minister alone. A D.D., much esteemed for his wisdom, and
admired for his learning, in alluding from the pulpit to
John 5th, chap 4th, verse said in our hearing, that "There is

no reason to doubt the reality of this miracle any more than the reality of any other miracle recorded in the gospels." and this although our Revisers have dropped the passage out of the text. This eminent man either did not know, or was too indifferent to find out the truth anent the matter.   ?

Here are a few gems from the sermons of a young minister in his first charge, fresh from College and Theological Hall, with A.M. annexed to his name. "Do not lose respect for yourselves, by any means." "Men outside our Churches are not bad hearted, but dilatory." "It is not the love of sin that leads men into sin, but the distant coldness on the part of people, calling themselves Christians, in our Churches, that drives men away from Christianity." Do not regret sins that are past." "God's punishments are not penal, but corrective." Possibly grey hairs are inclined to be critical somewhat, and puzzled when their young pastor deprecates their coming to Sabbath services "merely as a duty", and shews a torrent of virtuous indigation when such little matters are pointed out to our fledgling. A Free Church deputational minister

recently addressing office bearers anent Church services, urged rather forcibly, that a minister to preach good sermons must have good listeners. It may be so from the minister's point of view; but should not a minister in preaching, try so to preach that his audience may feel interested, or shew themselves good listeners in virtue of what is said to them and the manner of its delivery? Try to be as earnest in preaching the truth as the actor is in propagating fiction. In the absence of

earnestness, we think, lies not a little of the apparent failure of the pulpit in these days.   Sleeping and trying to
keep awake in Church may be partly owing to weariedness, a-
rising from daily toil or continued occupation.   When so
is the case, a man seats himself in his pew to worship God
in a public manner.   The minister conducts the service,
but in such a dead and alive style, too often it is, there
being nothing either in matter or manner beyond what has
been given over and over again, till even the truth becomes
insipid: not the truth, but the manner in which it is presented.   The best of food may be spoiled in the cooking,
and offensive serving may cause nausea.   And so, in our
experience, it not seldom happens in so called preaching of
gospel truth.   Under such circumstances do not over readily blame a poor man for looking drowsy, or even falling a-
sleep.   In these cases the minister should see the fault
as lying entirely with himself.   On the public platform
a speaker is expected to interest his hearers, and keep
them fully alive to what he is saying, or try-ing to say.
Otherwise he cannot complain if his hearers nod, sleep, or
leave the hall, hoot him down, or laugh at him; in any case
they have no scruples in doing so.   Ministers in the pulpit should bear such considerations in mind.   An audience
in Church may suffer long and be kind, listening, $or trying
to listen, to dull platitudes delivered "ex officio" with no
effort at any effect, except to kill the time set apart for
the sermon; yet complaining of empty pews and listless
hearers, in such cases will not mend matters.

Some months ago
at a meeting of the Free Synod of Glasgow and Ayr, on the

report on Religion and Morals being read, an elder took occasion to speak of the excessive laudation of the poet
Burns, and in somewhat strong terms condemning the praise,
more especially by ministers and elders of the Church.
The remarks were not kindly listened to, and no indicated
support was given to the elder's opinions. That evening,
and next day, all the daily newspapers reported the elder's
remarks, some going the length of inserting articles for
and against his audacity in insulting the National idol.
But strangely, so far as we could find out, not one of the
Church magazines, or religious periodicals took any notice
of the matter. A straw may shew how the wind blows.

xi

On the thirteenth of December, after having had before, five
boys laid up with measles, a case of scarletina occurred,
which was sent for treatment to our local Infirmary. On
the eighteenth another case of scarletina, and one on the
twenty-third were both sent to the hospital. On the twen-
ty-seventh, early in the morning, I was told that Willie
Scott, eight years of age, had been ill during the night.
I went to see him, found him insensible, feet cold, and altogether in a very bad way. Our nurse, poor woman, was almost driven out of her wits, being much afraid of fever.
Fear seemed to drive her from the sick, rather than lead
her to attend to their wants. We at once sent for the
doctor who came without delay. He pronounced the illness
to be acute meningitis, a hopeless case, "The boy might be

removed to the Infirmary, but only to die."and die poor little Willie did, some twelve hours after removal. I felt it
much. Willie was a rather dull and peculiar boy, but not
deficient in intelligence, and was a very fair scholar; easily annoyed, but not given to romping. Meningitis, (infla-
mation of the internal covering of the brain) has, I think,
occasioned more deaths in our school, during my experience,
than all other causes together. Recovery from meningitis
is said to be very rare, almost hopeless, as I have found it,
and not infrequently very rapid in its action. Willie
had a brother, James, who died even more suddenly in school
from the same affection. In all these cases of meningitis
coming under our care, the parents, one or both, have been
known to us as drunkards. Whether parental drunkenness
in these numerous cases, sixteen noted by us, caused the disease in these poor children, we cannot say, but the facts
point in that direction.

When sickness occurs to one or more
of our children, our invariable practice is to send for the
doctor. The practice is a good and necessary one with a
view to keeping things right with the public, and guarding
against neglect or carelessness on the part of officials.
And yet concerning Physicians (we do not mean Surgeons) we
have been surprised at how little they can do in the way of
curing disease. They can tell us when the patient is ill,
and they can tell us when the patient is getting better;
they can go farther, and tell us with an air of authority
what is wrong, by calling the trouble measles, scarletina, &c.
but beyond telling that the patient must be kept in bed,
and taking a look at them daily or oftener, in most cases

.they.seem.able to do nothing more.   In saying this,we.do
.not.wish to.draw odium.on the profession;.we merely draw
.attention to the fact.   With Surgery.however,it appears
.to.be very different;in it great.advances.have evidently
.been made in recent days.

　　　　　　　　　　　　　　　When I was in my twenty-fourth
.year,I took.part in.a district visitation connected.with
St.Peter's Free Church.Sabbath.Schools in Glasgow.   .I
.remember well putting my.head inside a house.door.when
.I.encountered a smell which caused me to shrink backward.
.That was on a Thursday night.   I was at my work in Arthur & Compy.on Friday and on.Saturday.   But on Saturday.I
felt very sleepy and done.up,and had to go early to bed.
.I.had abad night,and in the morning my.skin.was as red.as
.a soldier's.jacket.   Dr.Morton pronounced my.trouble.to
.be.scarletina and I must keep my bed.   .Quite a sharp attack,but I was out.of bed.on Wednesday,and in.the fashion
.of.those.days ,convalescent.   My landlady.found.temporary
.lodgings in Gourock for me,and at.the end of the.week I
.was there in cold.weather,but not feeling uncomfortable.
.There came on a.heavy fall.of.snow,and I took.exercise.by
.wading through it.,and up to.the.hill.top behind Gourock.
.After.a week's.absence I returned.to my Glasgow lodgings
and to my place in the wholesale warehouse in Miller.St.
.after an absence of.two.weeks from the first appearance.of
my illness.   For weeks.thereafter.I was peeling off pieces
of my.skin.from my legs and.other.parts of my body.   .I
.do.not remember any.bad after.effects.   Nor.do I know.to
.what extent I may have been the spreader of the.disease in
the place where I went as a lodger.   .My conduct in those

days was not found fault with by the Doctor or anyone else,
but were I to do so now, I fear I would be looked on as a
criminal.

Two of my acquaintances, each aged seventy-two,
died recently. Mr.A.was an amiable and quiet man; Mr.B.
was good tempered, but at times sarcastic. To use Mr.B's
own words, both were "good average going men". Will said
average be enough in the world to which we all hasten?
Very much I fear not, if I understand the Christ aright.
What then?

The Railway Strike 1890-91 has come to an end.
It has occasioned much evil; as to any good that has accru&&
ed from it we have doubts. We are surprised at the amount
of sympathy evoked on behalf of the strikers; we did not
share in it. We have little faith in strikes as a remedy
for evils which are to a large extent occasioned by the
workers themselves. For instance, there is Sunday labour;
I am told that many of the men are eager to obtain work on
Sundays, when receiving Sunday pay; but to the public they
talk as if such work were forced upon them without adequate
remuneration. No doubt, workmen have a right to strike
when by so doing they expect benefit, but further we cannot
go. Workmen have no right, directly or indirectly, to interfere in the way of other men being prevented to do the work
refused, making their own bargain as to wages. The laws of
the land may permit pickets to dog, worry, and threaten me if
I do not act as certain strikers command me; but equitable
laws will endeavour to protect me from all molestation. Our
Lord said, "Beware of covetousness, for a man's life consist-
eth not in the abundance of things which he possesseth." To-

day, popular opinion says, "Our Lord was altogether wrong."
Covetousness lies at the bottom of all these strikes and
socialistic tendencies.   Better men are more needed than
better wages.   Given, in our Country, and in these days, to
a young man health and strength with average intelligence,
and whether his life is to be prosperous and happy, or wretched and debased, depends more on his own individual character than on any adverse circumstances we know of, apart
from himself.

I was giving to a number of our boys new jack-
ets in place of old ones considerably out at elbows. $Cas-
ting my eyes on James Munro, a boy of medium size, I saw him
earnestly set on examining the left elbow of his jacket.
Altogether, his jacket was in fairly good condition; in too
good condition for him to expect, or request a new one.   To
qualify for a better chance, he seized the sleeve of his
jacket with his teeth, trying in that manner to tear a hole
in it, but without success.   I called him out, and gave him
an admonition by three strokes with the tawse on the bare
breech by way of emphasising my advice.   Could I, or should
I have done otherwise?

Our Inspectors have often urged us
to adopt a "good system of marks", attaching a money value
to each good mark given to a boy.   Then put said money into a Savings Bank, or in some way to a boy's credit, so that
on leaving school he might have the money to assist him in
starting on his own account.   Such a system was suggested
with a view to minimising corporal punishments, if not to get
rid of them entirely.   Now, to aim at doing so is laudable.
I understand similar methods exist in the Army, Navy, and

Prisons. Hitherto, however, we have not seen our way to
adopt, or recommend such a system among our Industrial
School children. Children should be taught to conduct
themselves properly as a primary duty, failing in which
they expose themselves to penalties; and that virtue, due
to God and our fellow men, is its own reward. To attach
a money reward to mere ordinary good behaviour, tends to
lower and eradicate the idea or conviction, that virtue
is incumbent on one and all, and should be our rule in
life, even though rewards may be wanting and penalties to
be feared: as in the World's history has often been the
case. Let us inculcate higher ideas of good conduct
then that it is a mere commodity worth a sum of money,
but not otherwise to be looked for. We cannot speak $$
from experience to a large extent; but evidently such
a reward system, while rewarding the good, would not un-
likely reward also the bad, though not so intended. I
have known marks in a Reformatory work so, that workmas-
ters could make nothing of the boys without granting to
each their full quota of good marks, though not in any
way deserving them. Otherwise to get satisfactory work
or conduct, out of the boys was hopeless. Some bad boys
are adepts at keeping out of scrapes themselves, while in-
citing simple boys to become involved. But we much
doubt whether in any case, good marks would make good boys
any better; while with the bad, we fear, these marks would
be inoperative, except in the way of raising envy and bad
feeling against their better companions. We cannot
make the thief, who steals twenty shillings, honest by a re-
ward of half a crown; neither does the fear of inability

to pay debts count much with the fraudulent bankrupt.   A
boy who is down, and unaccustomed to rewards, will not be
much influenced by promised rewards, which he has no hope
of ever obtaining, or if obtained, almost immediately for-
feited, for what he will regard as "no fault at all" or a
very little one.   Ill doers never get fair play; at least
they generally say so.   When the promise of reward thus
goes for nothing, there remains for the master, instead of
reward, only positive punishment of some sort.   Deprivation of food we regard as a bad form of punishment, and a
poor deterrent.   Deprivation of privileges, liberty for example, within definite and reasonable limits, we think a very good method.   But it must be remembered, that perpetual
confinement becomes rather hopeless in the way of getting
debts paid, or securing improved conduct from a bankrupt
boy.   Lastly, we have corporal punishment, $$$ which, all over,
we regard as the best for children not over fourteen.   But
the power of inflicting corporal punishment should be only
intrusted to thoroughly reliable men and women, and even
such require to be on their guard against their own unreli-
able tempers at times of provocation or resistance.   Pun-
ishments of all sorts should be accompanied with appeals
to the culprit's better nature, and with due allowance for
circumstances and possible mistakes on the part of the pun-
isher.   Money may, and does, buy labour fairly enough; it is
questionable whether money ever does, or can, buy good con-
duct.   We know that desire for gain and thirst for money
are very often incentives to bad conduct.   Certainly where
money is in question, a bad boy will do his best to seem
good, while being really good may form a secondary consider-

ation.   Mere rewards cannot make people good; the absence
of them should not make people bad.

.At a congregational
meeting held the other evening, a speaker urged upon his
hearers the duty of more liberal giving on behalf of missions to the heathen World.   Many of our local missions
are by no means successes.   Among the heathen, wherever
the Gospel is faithfully preached, some, though it may be
only some, receive it, and live by faith in it.   At Home
all have the opportunity of hearing, but only a small number pay any attention to the Gospel.   On the other hand,
in the most unpromising fields in Africa, Uganda for instance, where zealous missionaries have gone to labour, many have professed Christianity and shewn themselves to
be true followers of our crucified Saviour.   Had Paul
and the early Christians confined their labours to Jerusalem, waiting for the conversion of all its citizens before preaching to the outside world, where, or how, would
we, the inhabitants of these islands, have been to-day?
Our aim as Christians, and as a Church, should be, to send
the Gospel to all nations, peoples, and tongues.   Difficulties did not keep Paul from ever aiming at the "regions
beyond", Asia Minor, Greece, Rome and Spain: and farther we
cannot doubt, had life and strength been prolonged to the
enthusiastic Apostle.   While many among Mahomedans, Hindoos,
and Buddhists may, and probably will, refuse to listen; equally sure may we be, that some inquiring, humble souls among
them, will listen and believe when the truth is presented to
them.   Under God, what an eternal debt of gratitude to that
missionary, or missionaries, who first brought the good news

to our kith and kin in ages gone by, do we not owe?

vost A.--- The last time I saw him was in the Railway Station about five in the afternoon, Tuesday 28th.April 1891.
"Looks like Mr.A.,but he seems very ill. But if ill, how
comes he to be here?" He speaks to Mr. B.,I shall look again
again from the carriage window. It is he, but why not in
bed? Only a few days ago I saw him, apparently quite well.
On Thursday, two days thereafter, I heard of Mr.A.'s death.
A good man, we think, hard head, soft heart, when got at. A
thoughtful man, not easily cheated by another; but capable
of being cheated by himself. Determined in having his
own way; in the main, we think, the right way. It has been
mentioned in our hearing, the grave offence which he took
when not long since, a younger man offered to carry his top
coat for him on a somewhat steep ascent. "Did the young
man think that Mr.A.was not able to carry it for himself?"
he in effect said, with a face blushing crimson. Yet, such
men as Mr.A.tend to make their country rich. Some ten
days before his death, and on the eve of going to London on
business, he called on Mr.C.,who was then on his death bed,
to bid him Good Bye, in case he, Mr.C., might depart before
Mr.A.'s return. Mr.A. returned all right, but died two
days before Mr.C. We propose, but it lies with another to
dispose.

Attended yesterday the funeral of Sandie Blair, age
seventy-four, an intelligent, but used up labouring man.
Thoughtful in old age, but "foolish in youth", so he said.
Two months ago his wife died. He was a great admirer of
Burns the poet, and a stiff Calvinist. In conversation

anent Burns Sandie's final thrust to silence all conten-
tion on our part was, "Bit yae see, it wus tae be."; there
was no getting over this statement.   On Thursday the
14th May 1891 Sandie took a rather long walk from Brig O'
Weir to Quarrier's Homes.   On again reaching his own
house, Sandie had a shock, and within an hour or two died.
Attending Sandie's funeral was a friend, a Free Mason, too
much free, as we thought.   During some conversation with
this friend of Sandie's, the remark was made, that to die
as Sandie died was in reality desirable on the part of a
man fully and quite ready to go.   An indifferent remark
was made by Sandie's friend.   Not long after, whether
ready or not we cannot say, this friend tumbled down a
stair, and so ended his earthly sojourn.

An Episode---"O,
Mr.M., I have just heard that my adopted son J.Y. is dead."
The speaker was our female night attendant among our boys,
an elderly woman.   "Have been told by various parties,
but can get no certain particulars.   I have an insurance
on his life.   He was a seaman and much given to intemper-
ance.   Must have fallen into the water &c."   Again some
days thereafter, O, Mr.M., J.Y.'s body has been cast ashore
at Gourock, his features unknowable, but I have seen his
clothes, know them perfectly, but the body I did not see".
Another interval of several days, "O, Mr.M., on presenting
the Registrar's certificate anent J.Y.'s death, they paid
the insurance, sixteen pounds and some shillings."   Yet
again, not many days after, "O, Mr.M., last night my adopted
son, J.Y., came to my door, about midnight, drunk.   So after
all he is not dead, what am I to do?"   Now, what can, or ¢¢¢¢$¢¢¢¢¢

what should, Mr.M.do or say about this whole business?
Just hold on a bit, until he see. Eh, pu-gh, J.Y.is not
dead. The Insurance Office has found out as much. "Return the money, or so much of it, and that will do." The
Procurator Fiscal who registered the death, supposed or
affirmed, must regard the man as dead, until, well, until he
is found to be alive. So meantime rests the queer business.

On Wednesday H.M.Inspector inspected our School. He
had given us two days notice. Found us all ready, and
was well pleased. We cannot, however, make out, so good
this year, so bad last. Too bad last year, too good this.
But H.M.Inspectors, like some other people, can be managed.

5th June 1891, this day I am fifty-seven years of age. "An
old man"says one. "Young man"says another. "Prime of
life"says ninety. "Done"says twenty-five. "Of little
consequence what is said,"say I. To-day I am as ready
to die as I can ever hope to be. Happy to remain, but not
unduly alarmed at the thought of soon going. Extreme
old age has no attractions for me, but a grumbling spirit
is far more to be deplored. Many things I have said and
done in the past, that I regret, but trust for forgiveness
through the one Mediator between God and man, shut up to
that my only known resource. Positively, in my faith, I
think I shall not be confounded. Let me not be ashamed
of my hope: everlasting life granted by Almighty God for
the Christ's sake. So be it, I know no better way. All
the same, let me struggle after that holiness, without which
I cannot see, or enjoy, God.

J.W., husband of my wife's aunt, has gone over. Sold whiskey in Paisley. Drank whiskey there and in other places.
And yet, not too much, it may be said, for he lived till
past ninety. And yet, perhaps a little too much, when one
thinks of the agonies occasioned by senile gangrene, which
was the immediate cause of J.W.'s death. It was said of
an old Jewish king, that "he departed without being desired."
Sometimes, were the truth told, such departures are desired.

Prince of Wales, Knights, and ladies playing cards. The
last time I played was with my fellow herd laddie for amusement: we had no money, so we could not seriously cheat.
Pitch and toss for bawbees, three thimbles for "tanners",
and cards for bigger sums; what's the difference? In our
mind all are connected, or associated with select society.
To cheat at pitch and toss, at the thimble trick or cards,
well, we suppose Satan himself, draws the line somewhere;
but we would rather go by a line drawn by some one else, in
whom we could put more confidence. But hold, hush, enough
anent a prospective king.

Elsewhere I have alluded to menin-
gitis in speaking of sickness and ailments among our boys,
the rapidity with which it may develope, the seeming futility in trying to arrest or cure, and its almost invariably
ending in death. I remember one case of a stout healthy
looking boy, fourteen years of age, or thereby. I was called
out of bed early in the morning to see this boy. He had
been found lying in the water closet by a companion, who a-
roused an assistant in his room close by. The boy was insensible. We laid him in bed, and I went for the Doctor,

rather less than a mile away. The Doctor came and told
us what to do; mustard to back of neck, castor oil, and reé
moval to Infirmary as soon as possible. All these instructions were attended to; but John, a quiet well behaved boy,
died the same day. Concerning his mother I know nothing;
his father was, or had been a confirmed drunkard; so I was
informed. On the other hand in attending to ailments a-
mong our children, anxiety has at times led us to go for
our Doctor in the middle of the night, who on coming and examining our patient, found little or nothing wrong, beyond,
may be, a disordered stomach, or other slight ailment. A
boy at night might complain of illness, when a simple remedy applied seemed to put all right, or tending that way.
And generally, I may say, that a doctor's midnight visit,
while so far putting one's mind at rest, made little or no
difference in respect to an ailment which in any case would
take its time, and run its course. Our rules said, "In
cases of sickness, call the Doctor immediately." and this was
attended to so far that a message was sent without delay:
but it might not be possible to find our Doctor without considerable time elapsing. In case of an accident requiring
urgent attention, the patient was taken to the Infirmary .
On another occasion, I was aroused out of bed to see a boy
who could not very well say what was wrong with him, beyond
a sore head and general sickness. He was a brother to
Willie Scott, who as already mentioned, died of meningitis
six months previously. The boy seemed inclined to vomit.
He rose from his bed and, without assistance, walked to a
night stool across the dormitory, vomited a little, and returned to bed. I spoke a few encouraging words to him,

told him to try and sleep, and hoped he would be better by
morning.   The night attendant, who acted as nurse, was instructed to look to the boy now and again, but if he slept,
she was not to disturb him.   The boy slept; but on being
examined some time after was found to be dead, presumedly
of meningitis.   To a Superintendent such an occurrence is
very sore.   Blame, if with any one, lies with him.   An error of judgment is very apt to be regarded as a criminal
act.   It was not supposed that a Doctor's visit would have
averted death; but the Doctor should have been sent for, and
he was not till too late.

Collection for Foreign Missions
next Sabbath.   On looking over our Free Church accounts
we find, that about £225,000 are given to our Home Ministers
by way of stipends, annually.   Then, for Foreign Missions,
Female Education in India, and Missions to the Jews, roundly
not much more than a tenth of that sum, £25,000, are given.
Our Lord's last injunction was, "Go and disciple all nations"
and Paul says, that "they that preach the gospel, should live
by the gospel."   But relatively, does not the Free Church,
if not doing too much for the ministers to say one million
at home, do far too little for the thousand millions abroad?
It is reported of the Moravian Brethren, that they have more
missionaries abroad than ministers at home; and we presume
more money is spent on the former than on the latter. which
Church manifests most obedience to our Lord's last injunction?   It was said at a Church meeting not long since, "To
sustain ministers at home we give money abundantly, but not
our prayers, at least in public.   We receive as much as possible from man, and still ask for more.   On the other hand,

"Thy kingdom come" is our daily prayer, but how little comparatively we give to hasten its coming." We, or our ministers, seem ashamed to pray for the former, and are too lukewarm to urge giving for the latter. Our prayers ought to run abreast with our money; and our money ought to go in line with our prayers. But how stands the matter in these days? Except from an occasional missionary on furlough, I do not remember a warm hearted sermon from the pulpit, on behalf of the heathen world during these forty years.

Among Christian men, active and willing workers in our Churches, our ministers of to-day do not seem to stand so high in their estimation as the ministers of a past generation. Whatever the reason may be, our pastors nowadays are not the leaders of thought they have been in the past. Poets and novel writers lead the majority of men in these days. They seem to lead our ministers, judging by the quotations they repeat in the pulpit, and their readiness to worship at the shrine of a popular poet or novel writer. However much to be regretted, our experience justifies us in saying so. To regain this lost position, simple gospel truth, in simple language, will have most power with the mass of mankind; when earnestly urged by earnest men, free from sacerdotalism and academical conceit.

xii

At the Boys breakfast table the other morning. "Where's Brown?" "Not well; he's in the dormitory." After breakfast I went and found Brown lying on his bed, uncovered.

He had been vomiting, and was evidently ill. He was taken to the sick room, where hot water bottles were applied to his feet and stomach, but with slight apparent result. The Doctor was sent for, but he was not at home. He was sent for to the Infirmary, but he was not there. Finally, he was sent for at the shop of call, but still could not be found. Slowly, the boy seemed to recover somewhat. He asked for water, and then vomited. I gave him twelve drops of chlorodyne. Three or four hours thereafter the Doctor arrived, prescribed for the boy, and next day he was practically better. But here lies the puzzle: the night attendant did not know that the boy had been ill, and the janitor was quite sure, that he saw the boy in the play ground in the morning, to all appearance quite well. The boy, himself, says, he did not leave his bed during the night, except once to go to the closet. His companions, who were in bed around him, say, some one thing, some another. How difficult at times to find out the truth in such matters. In any case, I got a sore fright; but perhaps that is all in a Superintendent's bargain. These frights and worries, we fancy, disagree with comfortable digestion. Be it so, it seems to be the lot of most men in their surroundings, to meet with their share of experiences that make afraid. What bearing have they on that future to which we all hasten?

Have been reading Don Quixote. Tried it years ago, but got tired of it and laid it aside. But frequent allusions to Sancho Panza in current literature, have induced me to try Don again. The book is often prosy, but now and again good things turn up. We condemn novel reading, as rather a waste of time, and too often pernicious in tendencies; but yet find it needful in a manner, to read what the multitude reads; and we find more or less pleasure in doing so. But some of our so called best novelists, such as Dickens and Thackery, are by no means to our liking. To sample, we have read a few of these writers' novels, but are by no means tempted to invest in the stock. Scott in his novels, depicts historical scenes; and to read his works is a pleasant way of learning history. As to their historical accuracy, that is another matter. But still, the reading of Scott fixes on one's memory events that otherwise are prone to be forgotten: events that are substanially true, though the setting be imaginary. Whether the Pilgrim's Progress can rightly designated a novel, we think not. We regard it more as a parable, wherein the truths taught could not be taught in a better manner, nor perhaps not so well in any other manner. Almost without exception, novels appear to us as overdrawn; even when to some extent true, they are often false to real life; and written more with a view to make money than for any higher purpose. In saying this, we include the many stories in Church and religious magazines. Simple and unadorned truth, even when common place and unexciting, as in a daily newspaper, we can read, if not much enjoy, but many of the imaginary yarns presented to the public, partake more of caricature than photographs of current life.

      J.J.G. has gone; his going accelerated by a fall, or the fall accelerated by his going. J.M. has also gone. The first, eighty-one, the second seventy-two. Such deaths are perhaps the most solemn of all. "Soul, thou

hast much goods laid up for many years". "This night thy
soul is required of thee". Some one has said, "Only that
man who crossed America in an ox wagon, knows how broad it
is." Similarly, we may say, Only the man who lives a hundred years, realises how short men's lives on earth are.
We try to look beyond, or look beyond, or in a way, try to realise what lies beyond.

We hear now and again of Agnosticism.
There is truth in the idea, "One thing I know, that I do not
know." Also it is true, "One thing I know, that I do know."
And what is this latter? That man is a monstrosity, if regarded as without a spiritual, moral, and responsible nature.
Deficiency of the moral element tends, at times, to turn
earth into a hell; a suffiency would go far in turning
earth into a heaven. Having regard to one aspect among
men, how much, and how often does the female sex suffer at
the hands of the male. Among the lower animals the female
is protected by provisions and instincts Among men these
provisions are awanting. In man, moral principles should
fill the void. But in a large number of cases, if not in
the majority, it does not. Man has surely fallen. Whether man as constituted, is capable of standing, is a question
more easily asked than answered.

On Thursday, when returning
from a walk and nearing the school gate, I saw our shoemaker,
brushmaker, and others, carrying some one out. Found it to
be, Bobby Gray. He had been swinging on the play ground
swing with another boy, and when some sixteen or eighteen
feet from the ground, lost his hold and fell right down on
his face. His nose was split open after the manner of an

opened mussel.   That was the worst, bad enough; the boy is
now progressing favourably in the Infirmary.   The previous day, William Stewart had an epileptic fit, so bad that
he had to be removed to the Infirmary.   On Sunday last another boy had a convulsive fit, not very bad, yet enough to
trouble us on starting for Church.   We had two deaths recently, and have another boy seemingly dying.   Sometimes
when it rains, it pours.   "It wus tae be"; old Sandie would
have said.

Yesterday, as I sat at table, having finished my
dinner, a common house fly found its way into a dish of
milk which was standing on the table.   The fly was promptly thrown out, and lay struggling with its back on the table.   Presently another fly, call him number two, an acquaintance seemingly, flew over to the half drowned one, set to
and licked him carefully all over, head, body, and wings.
Number two fly then left number one, and flew to an adjac-
ent window opposite, ten feet, or thereby away.   Number one
managed to roll over from back to belly, but was still unable either to fly or walk.   He rolled over on his back
again, and I could see his two front legs doubled up, stick-
ing together, and for the time being useless.   Then, fly
number two, presumed to be, returned on wing to its prostrate
companion, put its trunk into the loop of one of the doubled
up legs, straightened it out, the other front leg somehow
getting right at the same time, and thereupon departed on
wing.   Number one then gave himself a shake or two and
mounted into the air.   Number two must have come from Sam-
aria.

My religion, I must confess, is very selfish.   I am ve-

ry anxious to obtain, and pleased at the prospect of obtaining, everlasting life. I am anxious to do right; and anxious, it may be, to please God; and anxious that certain
loved ones may obtain everlasting life. Then, in a certain
sickly fashion, I am anxious that all men may obtain everlasting life, but ever returning to first principles, "O, that
I may obtain that everlasting boon, come what may to the per-
ishing millions." Can such a state of mind be justified?
Is it reasonable? Is it in any way right? Well, to desire
the good for one's self, and at the same time to be indifferent to the fate of others, is wrong, must be wrong, utterly
wrong, and akin to the evil one. If this is our sin, our
own words condemn us. No doubt, to be indifferent as to
one's own salvation implies, clearly enough, indifference as
to the salvation of others. He who, himself, has no over-
powering desire for everlasting life, cannot be very anxious
about a gift for others, which he, himself, cares not for, nor
desires. We do not seek, nor expect, endless life for the
lower animals; nor regard that as a loss to them for which
they are neither intended nor fitted. The Alpine climber
has an ambition and a joy on the summit of Mont Blanc. He
achieves in perfect innocence that with which he never expects his grandmother to be a partaker. So far both are
contented, and all is well. The Geologist, the Botanist,
the Explorer, may each in his place, work, achieve, and enjoy,
with few or no companions to go hand in hand with them; and
although self is ever present the egoist may never appear.
But does the Christian, or should he, run on parallel lines?
Is it lawful to be careless regarding those upon whom everlasting life would be practically thrown away? Is it

right to be careless concerning those who seem to have no
desire above the brutal, in whom intellectual or spiritual
aspirations after love to God, or love to God's truth, seem
to have no place, in whom those higher faculties that differ men from brutes, look as if dying a natural death?
An intelligent working man to whom I was speaking recently,
asked me the question, "Would not everlasting life be very
monotonous?"   To that man it probably would be, and possibly
worse than monotonous.   The man was a daring blasphemer,
talking of God as he might of a little respected companion.
Can I, or should I, be equally anxious about such a man, as
about those in whom the "smoking flax" is not quenched, nor
the "bruised reed" altogether broken?   Is it not more natural to sympathise with those who do not lend a deaf ear,
or defiant mind, but who listen with humility, if not with
very ardent desire?   And still more clearly, may we not be
desirous regarding those who have never had an opportunity
of hearing in the midst of dark heathenism?

What does our
Lord, Jesus the Christ, imply when he uses the words, "Where
the worm dieth not, and the fire is not quenched", and "everlasting punishment"?   We fear to answer.   The ordinary
meaning attached to these words, but often with little
thought, is so terrible, so fearful, that we instinctively
start and shudder in calm reflection, at the thing suggested.
Even supposing hyperbolical language, to some extent, it does
little or nothing to alter the meaning.   Further, shudder-
ing at truth does not in the least affect its truthfulness.
Perhaps there is no greater blunder among men of the nineteenth Century, or of all Centuries, than the latent thought,

that loving or hating a supposition somehow affects its
truthfulness. There is a difference between trying to
find truth, and trying to make it. And yet, very strangely, we are prone to become angry with the man who believes
things that we, ourselves, deny. How useless to aim at
making truth; true wisdom lies in trying to find it. In
many ways concerning many things, we must wait for more
light. Let us so wait patiently, when it only indicates
folly to do otherwise. There are, or have been men in
the world for whom Hell seems not inappropriate, though we
may shrink from assigning it to any. Yet, "more tolerable
in the day of Judgment" evidently implies a difference, or
differences, so we pause. The lot of the presumptious sinner, the unconverted, the unpardoned, will after death be
such, we cannot doubt, as should fully incite us to do all
we can for their salvation, and while we live. It was not
on a needless errand that the Christ came to earth to suffer and die, we may be well assured. Let us then seek the
conversion of the wicked, the enlightenment of the ignorant,
the instruction of the foolish, ever remembering, that "The
Judge of all the earth will do right." The wicked have
had, and do have, awful power in their hands for evil; let the
would be righteous try and shew that they also have power
for good. But then, how easy to do evil; how difficult for
even the best of men invariably to do right. Still we are
under law; and must either be judged by it, or pardoned in
virtue of a Daysman..

It is a fair question, Can any created
being certainly be assured of not falling into sin, if temptation assails him? Further, if the created, and consequent-

ly, ### finite being, be in no way ever tempted to do wrong,
is their stability in doing right much to be relied on?
Is virtue much to be accounted of, if it cannot survive
temptation?   Where no temptation to vice exists, if such
a condition there be, can virtue attain a perfect state,
that is perfect by comparison?   Many like questions we
have proposed to ourselves, and continue proposing, but almost invariably find, sooner or later, that others before
us have asked similar questions, and have got similar answers, or no answer at all.

            Duke of Clarence, Cardinal Mann-
ing, and C. H. Spurgeon have been sent for and have gone.
The Queen can make another Clarence, the Pope another Cardinal, but when shall we obtain another C. H. Spurgeon?
What a mass of bona fide work has been achieved by Spurgeon during his life of fifty-eight years?   Spurgeon's
departure we can only regard as a loss to his Church to
Christendom and to our age.   To Spurgeon, we expect no
successor.

        How easily can good men accommadate their con-
sciences to evil doings when companions of good repute,
join hands with them.   A large number of our Free Church
congregations supplement their ministers stipends while
aid receiving from the Sustentation Fund.   To us the
practice seems downright dishonesty.   It cannot so appear
to many of the ministers implicated, men of Christian character and above suspicion.   Are God's laws elastic?   Is
a thing right merely because I do not consider it wrong?
Is a thing wrong, merely because I do not consider it right?
Must we bear the consequences of error in such matters? In

money matters we are conscious of trying to escape taxa-
tion, and that apart from the justice or injustice of the
tax.   To pay nineteen pounds nineteen shillings instead
of twenty pounds to escape house rent tax, is an example
of what we mean.   In doing so, what might an enemy, or
even a friend say of our conduct?   Do we pray to have
known and practiced sins pardoned?   Very risky proceeding, is it not?   Rather pray to be delivered from them,
and quit them now, and for ever.   And yet, and yet, how fond
of compromise.   How prone to give doubtful practices the
benefit of the doubt, and go on doing as hitherto.   They
will be saved whom God saves, but"let us run so that we may
obtain."

        Yesterday a young man, thirty-two years of age, mar-
ried recently, was buried in our local cemetery.   He was a
healthy and robust young man, but in looking at a foot ball
match got chilled,   The chill ended in pneumonia and death.
Coming down a rather steep street two weeks ago, snow lying
on the ground, to avoid slipping and falling I left the middle of the street and stepped on the newly cleaned pavement.
Scarcely had I done so when slipping somehow, down I came
very heavily on the last bone of my vertebrae, said bone being all but smashed in the operation.   Nothing very serious resulted beyond considerable pain, some faintishness, and
some gratitude that I had not fallen on the back of my head.
Are such occurrences, or accidents, avoidable?   In the one
case death results; possibly with more prudence would not.
In our case why, or how, the fall, or what good purpose was
served by this very innocent tumble?   One cannot very well
see; it was the very thing that was being prudently avoided.

141

There seems danger sometimes, in too much caution and circumspection. However, since then, a good many years ago as I rewrite, I have not fallen on a slippery pavement, and am extra careful on that particular street where I had my nasty fall.

A Teacher applies over and over for situations advertised, with no apparent result, till one morning comes a note "Meet Board on Monday at 6,15,p,m,you are on short leet." Next morning comes another note, from another quarter, "Meet School Board at 2,30, on Tuesday, you are on short leet of two." Same evening come a third note, from a third quarter, "Meet School Board on Friday at 2,30,." Till now, no attention has been given to many applications, from any quarter; but now apparently more than enough as it turned out, one having to be accepted, two declined. But how much humming and ha'ing, weighing of supposed advantages, counselling, soliciting guidance, &c. before coming to a decision. How many things there are in the world that one cannot see clearly through. But seeing so much, and so far, goes to mould character and habit of resolution. Surely in the world to come, there will be found real and solid reasons for definite and reliable character, and real and solid work for such characters to perform. Not the popular view this, we opine, but very often, truth and popularity are not found in company. Again, what bearing will dullness, stupidity, wooden headedness, or doubtful intelligence, have upon the being and existence of such in the world to come? Without trying to answer, we cannot doubt, that experience in this world has, or will have, a most important bearing on our future life.

xiii

In Glasgow the other day I was standing at a bookseller's window in Dunlop Street. Directly I began thinking about an old friend, Mr. Kay, whom I had not seen for a long time, I think not for years. "Is not this person like Mr. Kay? No, but---" Then stepping on a yard or two, and turning into the shop, I found Mr. Kay standing before me. It was a meeting quite unexpected by either, and yet in a way thought of by one of the two, a minute or two before. Mr. Kay had not been thinking of me at the time, but such premonitions have so often happened in my experience, that this strengthens a previously formed idea, that there is an unseen influence, as between minds or souls of men, that somehow makes itself felt, although the manner of its operation is, or may be, unknown. It suggests itself as an involuntary influence in operation, but not always active, or equally potent. It is somewhat like a "glint" from the spirit world. When a good man or woman, whose character and general conduct may be quite unknown, enters a company, and before either speech or actions indicate character or attainments, has not the very presence of that person a beneficent effect on all present? Or the incomer may be of bad character; but certain it is, that as we glance at the new arrival we form an opinion of him, good or bad, even when neither speech nor action has in any way indicated the manner of the man. That company tends to influence and form character none will deny. But it may be questioned, whether an unseen, occult force from one's person goes to affect the spiritual or mental condition of another. If it exists, and we think it does, it is no

doubt more or less reciprocal, though not equally so. In
any case, I should aim so to frame, not merely my external
conduct, but also my inmost thoughts, as if both reacted on
my fellowmen. Especially, children seem to be open to
these influences; they form likes and dislikes to different people, without reasons being apparent to others, or dis-
tinctly known to the children themselves.

We have had a
good deal to do with temper, passion, or rage. Is bad temper criminal or excusable? We read of our Lord looking
round in anger, but not in a passion as we understand the
words. In the course of our observations we have seen
individuals with what are usually termed bad tempers; but
we have also noticed that such people could quite restrain
their tempers, when they had sufficient inducement to do so.
They might become pale, livid, or even tremble under temptation to break out, but still could, and did, keep silent or
civil, when it was clearly their felt interest to do so.
Ebullitions of violent temper we regard as luxuries, that
certain people indulge in, when they can do so at no great
cost, or at a cost which they are willing to pay for the
pleasure. Certain folks feel that they cannot afford to
be passionately angry at any time, or give expression to
that which would imply passionate anger. Others may regard calmness and equanimity under all circumstances, as a
greater luxury than the exercise of blind passion under
any. They may regard control of the spirit as a duty
they owe to God, and essential to the true course of a
Christian man, as that spirit of Christ "without which we
can be none of his." Practice may, and we think can, go far

to make a naturally bad temper a good one; but in any case we cannot excuse bad actions on the plea of having a bad temper: far safer to regard bad temper as a crime, a sin to be guarded against. We have had under our care boys with very bad tempers, clearly in some instances inherited, vixen mother, vixen child; but never in our experience of over thirty years, and dealing with hundreds of boys from six to sixteen years of age, have we met one who could not quite control his temper in our presence, a leather tawse being near by. "O come" it may be said, "the tawse merely made a pretence of calm temper." Of course that may be so; but all the same, the power to control was clearly there, tawse or no tawse. Passion is often nothing more or less than a crime. When a man in a passion says or does a wrong thing, his passion can be no valid excuse, though likely enough it may be an aggravation. Let me then avoid passion, that luxury of proud and silly minds. It is well to remember that a passionate word, or thrust unmerited, to a friend can never be forgotten, nor fairly forgiven; it knocks a hole in the friendly vessel, which neither putty nor solder can ever cover from sight, or put out of memory.

In climbing a hill, (in Scotland we seldom lay claim to mountains) after more or less ascending, with vigorous puffing and blowing, we have enjoyed now and then a halt, a look back, and in a general way make estimate as to how we have been, and are getting on and up in our journey. In like we have pleasure in trying to glance over our past days and years, and if possible make estimate in a general way. One may do so fairly enough after spending forty or more years in shouldering his way through the World's motley crowd. And calmly speaking, we cannot congratulate ourselves on much wisdom, cleverness, or superior intelligence evinced hitherto in our goings thus far. Other people's opinions need not count for much; often when they praise we know better, and should honestly confess, that praise given is frequently not merited. We may sometimes have been wrongly blamed; but on the whole it has signified little. When residing in Limerick, so regarded we the native blessing and the native curse, both given with equal unction, and both equally harmless, so long as "hands off" was the rule. In childhood our arms were thin, not by any means brawny; our health did not seem robust, head was big, the only big thing about us, and a poor hard working father sadly mourned over a son who gave such meagre promise of being able to make his way through the world by the sweat of his brow. In the matter of muscle the "loon", himself had some doubts anent strength, and so took fancy to being a merchant, that meaning a draper's assistant, or grocer's or both combined. He thought that comparatively easy work and fair pay would be more to his mind than digging drains, or even making shoes. In due time the laddie became a draper. He stuck to it for nine years; but drapery, as pointed out, did not prove a success. In the way of giving the young rustic a good brushing up, however, these years were by no means lost to him. But looking back, we fancy the drapery did a good deal more for us than we did for it. Then, re-, our Reformatory and Industrial School career, we cannot but confess that somehow our achievements have come far short of our expectations. Successful so far that we have been well provided for; but as

to the amount of real good we have done, we cannot easily
appraise it.   If generally more concerned about our wages than our work, presumedly it is a fault that poor humanity is prone to.

A little over three years ago I attended
the funeral of James Brown's wife, seventy-six years of age,
James, the survivor, being then seventy-two.   A careful, fru-
gal, and hard working pair they had been in their day.   Having no children, they gathered some three or four thousand
pounds by making and selling "sweeties" in the kingdom of
Fife.   When in their forties, they retired, and thereafter
spent their time in cultivating a garden and fattening pigs.
James remained in his house for two years after Mary's death,
then for reasons known to himself, married again.   A few
weeks ago, while on a journey, he was suddenly taken ill with
cramp in the stomach, and in ten days thereafter died.   I
attended his funeral, and heard his wills, for there were two
of them, read.   Things have got wofully mixed.   The wills,
intended for the first wife, are now knocked topsy turvey by
the second wife claiming one half of the estate movable, and
life rent of heritable tierce, the Trustees nominate being
all dead.   There remains a host of brothers and sisters, or
their children on both sides, whose claims on the departed's
belongings have all to be adjusted: a real kettle in Kettle.
James intended to make a new will, and for that purpose made
two journeys to the County town; but his man of business
happened to be absent on both occasions, so before James
could settle matters, the last messenger settled him.   "What
thy hand findeth to do, do it quickly" very quickly
if you earnestly wish to have it done.   Hard worker, did I
say of James?   Yes, rather, often working at night, and driv-

ing his van by day.   Mary made money by making and selling pies.   On one occasion James was extra busy, and extra tired.   He had been at work, night and day, from Monday morning till Saturday night; during which time no
proper rest had been alloted to him.   On Saturday evening, in view of the coming Sabbath, James stooped down to
untie his laces, fell off his chair, went to sleep, there
and then, and did not awake till the fire had burnt a hole
in his bonnet, and set about roasting his head.   But
James was working for himself then, and considerably over
nine hours a day.   Mary, we presume, would be busy selling
pies.

In a large drapery warehouse in Limerick half a century ago, in the forties it must have been, evangelical or
revival work on the part of a few young men, protestant
and religious, was conducted in this fashion.   The particulars we had from a partner in the work.   Fixing on a
warehouse hand, careless and Godless, without any external
action, the party of evangelisers took to praying for the
wandering and erring one; and keeping to the practice, generally ended in success, at least for a time, if not always
permanently.   In these days we hear much of prayer for
money to maintain charitable institutions, and apparently ####
with success.   I believe in prayer, pray daily, and cannot
doubt as to its being often answered; and I would strongly
advise every earnest soul to pray to God, for good things
in the name of Christ.   But we cannot blink the fact, that
other influences may be at work, that may lead one to regard prayer as answered, when in reality it is not, at least
in any special way.   (Conscious of repetition here in our

remarks, the importance of the subject urges us to go on.)
May it not be that ######## when a mind, or a number of
minds, are earnestly interested in an individual, that said
individual may become influenced, without exactly knowing
how? We are only searching for truth, not professing to
have found it. Still, we incline to believe, that when a
man prays earnestly on behalf of another, he may, and probably does, influence that other one, apart from influence
from a higher source. It will not be questioned, that
when an earnest and good man prays audibly, his hearers
may be, and often are, affected thereby as by an orator.
Nor is it new doctrine to say, that an earnest silent soul
may influence another, apart from spoken or written words.
The exhibitions of magnetism, though of little practical
account as hitherto exhibited, may not be altogether unworthy of credence. We do not insinuate that answers to
prayer are merely apparent; but that answers to prayer
are sometimes only apparent, we cannot doubt. Let one
pray however earnestly, he should avoid jumping to conclus-
-ions that his prayers are answered, or otherwise, till time
reveals. On the other hand he must not forget, that when
he prays, and his requests seem to be granted, consistently,
though cautiously, he should regard his prayer as answered.
One, we know, has in his time made many mistakes in thinking
prayer answered in certain ways, when subsequent experience
shewed that in his surmisings he was wrong. It must however be added, that this one's prayer seemingly unanswered
at the time expected, and in the manner looked for, were in
reality answered, as afterward appeared, and more fully than
were even asked for, or expected. But reverting to that

supposed real, though hidden, influence that one human soul
has upon another, if not on all others, within a given circle, an influence imparted without speech, sight, or hearing,
though accelerated by them, if real, as we incline to think
it is, what a duty is laid upon us, not merely to act rightly, but to think with purity of heart and soul, and as in
the sight of God; remembering that our very thoughts may
have an eternal influence not merely on ourselves, but on
souls innumerable around us. Has the growth of public
opinion in a community anything to do with such an influence? It may be remarked, that even the wicked often
like to have a reputed holy man residing in their vicinity.
Superstition this may be, to some extent, but there may be
something more in it. What if a something in David, apart
from his harp, helped to mollify and quiet the perturba-
tions of the heart of Saul. Whether our surmisings are
correct or not, our duty is clear, to act as if they were.

Recently, several boys spoke to me concerning a wish, desire,
or resolve they had, they said, to serve God, to become new
boys. Many more, they said, had expressed themselves in a
similar manner, and our encouragement was evidently sought
for. We listened, but with mixed feelings. Glad to
think that any words of ours should so incline our boys to
good, yet remembering that in another place certain boys
who set about building a Church, suggested to the Devil the
erection of a chapel. We did not however, throw any cold
water on the movement; but reminded our young friends, that
the reality of their good intentions, their conversion,
could only be manifested by good behaviour in time to come.

Meantime they should be watchful, and pray to God to teach
them, with humble but hopeful spirits.   The evil one must
have been listening; for since said movement we have had
more bad conduct in School than for a long time previous.
The Fair holidays upset some, we have had several cases of
absconding, and the other night we were called out of bed
to deal with an attempt at fire raising on the part of
some boys; for no special reason beyond this, that if the
School premises were burned, the boys could no longer be
detained in them.

It was in August 1859, at the time of the
Revivals in the North of Ireland and elsewhere, that a movement began among the boys in Duke Street Reformatory, Glasgow,   For a few days there was much excitement, about one
half of the boys, two hundred, being more or less affected.
They conducted prayer meetings by themselves in preference,
and much earnestness was manifested during their continuance.   A number of the boys of the worst character were
seemingly changed for the better, and the reality of the
change we could not doubt.   Subsequent inquiries on our
part, after leaving the Reformatory, did not confirm our
first impressions.   Some twenty or thirty boys, of whose
conversion we felt most certain, al fell away into their previous bad ways.   We believe in revivals of religion, but
what we saw in Duke Street gave a rude shock to our implic-
it faith in them: that is, only time can shew their reality.
In such movements, all excitement and late hours in conduct-
ing meetings should be avoided.   Professing convertsshould
ever be reminded, that alone in their closets is the most ap-
propriate time and place for seeking a change of heart, and
that time alone can give satisfactory evidence of true con-

version.   After this so called revival in Duke Street
things got into a very bad condition; much worse, we believe, than at any previous period of the School's existence.   Reaction from spurious conversion tends, we cannot
doubt, to "the latter state being worse than the first".

As New Year's rejoicing times have drawn near in the past,
we have on occasion said, "Wish we could fall asleep, children and all, for say two weeks, till New Year's hub-bub be
past and gone."   Cowardly, if not worse, perhaps, but note
what follows.   Thankful, that at Christmas in very cold
weather, our children were in very good health.   On 31st.
of December, one of our biggest boys took ill of meningitis,
became insensible, and died on New Year's day: the Doctor
and attendants able to do nothing to prevent; only to look
on.   On the third of January another boy was seized early
in the morning with purging and vomiting, followed by a condition of collapse.   The boy was seen by the Doctor and
prescribed for.   The boy was quite sensible but cold, could
not be kept warm, and so continued for two days.   On the
third day he was removed to the Infirmary, but on arriving
there was found to be dead.   Since then, two weeks ago, we
have had several cases of pneumonia; two have recovered, but
another was removed to the Infirmary yesterday.   We feel
these events very sore, but are powerless to prevent such.
This however, may be noted, that we have never twice passed
through precisely similar circumstances or experiences.
Whether that may be regarded as consolatory is questionable,
but God's will be done.
                    My friend, Mr. Duff, is strongly op-

-posed to Mr. Gladstone and Home Rule for Ireland. His "earnest to God is that it may be averted." Strange, I am not afraid of it much; I would like Home Rule for Scotland. Consistently, I do not see why I should refuse it to Ireland. Might we not give it a trial? Perhaps Ireland thereupon would become more loyal! Mr. D. says, "They, the Irish, are not fit to rule themselves." "Perhaps, it is so, but how can they ever become fit without practice?" "They would persecute the protestants in Ulster and elsewhere in Ireland." "Let us take order that they do not; and stand by ready to interfere, if they, the Roman Catholics attempt it." "But", says our friend, "they do not need it." "But they think they need it, and that is as bad in the way of securing loyalty as if they did not need it." But my friend, by and by, on a later occasion proceeds, "First put down violence, let the Irish be law abiding, and so shew themselves worthy, then we shall consider the matter." Again, when Ireland is comparatively quiet, my consistent friend will have it, "They, the Irish, are now quiet and contented, and evidently do not want Home Rule." In all this, exaggeration is not aimed at, the logic is pretty well understood. In my boyish days I remember my Mother's voice, "They who get porridge and milk require nothing else; and further "Unless you finish your porridge and milk, you get nothing else." In other words, the good boy required nothing else; the bad boy deserved nothing else. A woman's logic perhaps, but the boy saw through his dear Mother; and possibly Irishmen see through the English dealings with them these eight hundred years gone by. Should not a Christian nation treat another, a weaker nation, even if a pagan and very wicked nation, as one

Christian man ought to treat another? "Do unto others as ye would that others would do unto you." The good, or the bad character of the others, does not much, if at all affect the matter. I cannot say that I make Home Rule a special subject to pray about. I have my doubts about granting it, without such safeguards that I fear would be regarded as not granting it at all. It cannot be said with certainty be said how it would turn out; a benefit to the British Empire, a benefit to Ireland, or a benefit in any way. But in some form it should be granted: perhaps in the form of Home Rule all round, as with the United States and our British Colonies. We owe the money; as to how our creditor may expend it, that hardly justifies us in refusing to pay. We need not be much afraid: surely England and Scotland with their over thirty millions, could hold their own against Ireland's three millions of Roman Catholics, assuming that the remainder in Ireland are Protestants, and ever on the side of the larger Island. Have we become poltroons? or a lot of selfish intriguers? After all, we shall be surprised if the G.O.M. manages to carry his measure?

The British have nothing to boast of anent their motives in going to war with other nations. But clearly enough, by these wars things have been done, and good achieved, as if somehow Great Britian has been an instrument in the hands of the Highest, to turn up and polish the rough stones of the world. Our Country may have often aimed badly, but she has shot wonderfully; and if at times a poacher, she has brought up a large family in a tolerable way, and done much in clearing the world of vermin. We cannot always credit her with good intentions, but on the

whole, cannot but see in her actions abundant good results.
Our war with America, when she fought for her independence,
was a blunder on our part; and the Crimean war was a crime; $$$
but ultimately good has resulted from many of our British
wars, even when unjustly waged.   When such a war as the
Boers' causes consternation and alarm among all classes in
our community, it is a pleasing thought to the Christian to
know that God is over all, ever present, and will irrespect-
ive of ultimatums and determination on either, or both sides,
order all, or see that all, work out his plans in Africa, from
Cairo to the Cape.   This has been our assurance allthrough,
even in the dark hours of Colenso, Magerfontein, and Spion
Kop.   However deplorable war is, or has been, very clearly
it has been God's agent, or overruled by Him, for good, that
seemingly in other ways was unattainable.

xiv

Surprise visit by H.M.Inspector to-day.   We met and parted
on good terms.   As mentioned elsewhere, one of our boys died
on New Year's day, and another some days after.   "Bad begin-
ning" says Mr. S. "must not let any more die."   We passed
through the Sick Room; two boys ailing, hoped they would both
be better soon; but a few days thereafter one died, and the
other suffering from consumption, does not look like getting
better.   O, these terrible averages.   A long time of good
health, and no deaths among our children makes us fear what
may be coming.   We have been told of an Institution contain-
ing nearly four hundred children, without a death among them

during nearly four years. Otherwise however, we were informed, that in that house, weakly and dying children were
got rid of somehow, so that they might die elsewhere; and
we believe it was, and is so. The public are prone to be
jealous of Institutions, and at times unreasonably so, and
hence the public must be managed, or gulled: we think that
is the correct word. It is by no means difficult to gull.

Have been visiting the Granite City, and made some calls at
a venture. One, to see a married lady whom I had not seen
for a long time. I saw, and spoke to, her husband; his wife
had died five years ago. Made another call on an old
shopmate, J.A. "J.A." was over the warehouse door, and I was
requested to wait for my friend, who would be with me "immediately". In a little time we found out, that "J.A." meant
the firm, that was all. He who made the business, giving
his name to the firm, died eighteen months ago. After
much early struggling, and years of toil and worry, he achieved prosperity, and died aged fifty-eight, the last of his
family, I understand. Of his property, he left the whole,
or the largest part of it, to his workmen and other employees. J.A. was not married. O, vanity, when our hopes ex-
tend not beyond earth and its good things, but we gladly
cherish the hope, that it was not so with J.A. He was the
last of eight, myself excepted, who were all busy in Black's
Buildings in the fifties. Next on the leet, be ready.

Four

Australian Banks have failed within the past year, two of
them recently. I had lent them three hundred pounds.
When I told my wife she said, "O, Johnnie". Sorry I am, but

not much cast down, if no more be taken from us.   Bad enough
to lose the money, without breaking our hearts about it. How
things will turn out, meantime we do not know.   Let us try
and be thankful for past and present good things.   If He,
the giver, sees fit to take away, what right have we to complain?   Perhaps we were too greedy for high interest; not
wise enough in our generation.   Perhaps, perhaps, --but
that will do, remember Job.   Thank God for health and fair
strength, good situation and fair salary.   In any case our $
days are numbered, and if we have to die in harness, to do so
has been the lot of many a good horse.   To unduly love money, or mispend it, has not been our prominent sin.   In any
case submit, and wait without much grumbling, or the shadow
of anything indicating unthankfulness.

                                        To do a good action,
without the remotest expectation of reward, either in this
world or in the world to come, beyond the satisfaction of
having done it, the good action unknown to any except God
and one's self, is perhaps the purest form of goodness that
exists.   It is a form of goodness existing in most mothers,
although mankind are, as a rule, not good.   And yet, to obey
God, to obey promptly and without question, is the highest,
perhaps the only real goodness that by man or angel can be
reached. Our School playground

                                Our School playground is better
lighted now than formerly in the evenings.   On last Sabbath
evening, between six and seven o'clock I observed a group of
boys in a far off corner, and being suspicious, I set about
finding out.   Three boys 58, 112, and 180, not the best of our
boys, along with five or six well behaved boys, and younger

than the first three I might examine. The younger boys I
examined separately, found that the first three wanted a match
and threatened blows because they did not receive one. I took
the first three into the Schoolroom to further examine. "
Felt a smell of smoking, and by asking for a match sought to
find out whether the other boys were smoking".so said one.
And now follows one lie, two lies, lies all round, until "130"
acknowledged that "53" had a pipe &c. "Well now, "53"where
is the pipe and tobacco?" "Have none, threw them over the
wall last night." And only when nine rather smart strokes
were given him on the bare hips, was I informed, that the pipe
and tobacco were in the keeping of certain boys into whose
hands they were slipped when on their way into the Schoolroom. "113"got six strokes for his unabashed lying in the
matter. Then addressing the entire school of boys, then present, I said, "Your companions "53"and "112" have told lies
concerning the pipe and tobacco, and have so far got their reward, but as yet I have got neither pipe nor tobacco; can any
boy tell me where either or both are?" No reply. Again
the question is put, but no reply. A third time the question
is put, but with the same, or no result. Then taking off my
coat, as if meaning business, up jumps a boy, ⚇ "Here's the tobacco." "And now, my boy, what about the pipe?" "Oyes" says
the boy"I was holding up my hand, but you took no notice."
"Just so my boy, I was doing my best to find the truth without
flogging; but I have found my doing so of no use; do you remember Achan?" · He confessed, but not till otherwise found
out. The use of tobacco forbidden is bad; but lies and refusing to tell the truth is much worse: take your reward, a
whipping.

By chance the other day I met an old friend and received a
very cordial greeting.   At one time this friend was said to
have put "my eye out"when he got married to,well,to an acquaintance of mine,without my being consulted.   I must confess to having been somewhat stunned,and chagrined at the
time.   On another occasion I remember being advised to pray
for a wife,by one who loftily gave me to understand,that it
be useless to pray for her in any case; and so we parted,I
at least,feeling very uncomfortable.   But now,my male friend
and I had a talk,inquirings,and relatings,a good many,and I
arrived at certain conclusions.   To be jilted,to be declined,to be despised,or even to be laughed at in one's early
days,may turn out not a bad course of training in life,when
looked at from first to last.   More pertinently,if a young
man prays for a wife,(and if he wants a wife,he is a fool if
he does not pray for guidance in the matter.) he should not
say,that "he does not care",while in reality he does care
very much; nor on the other hand break his heart if things
go not as he may at the time wish.   If a man submissively
prays for somewhat,let him do so patiently and hopefully,
and he may find out in the long run that guidance turns out
much better than he could foresee,or even hope for.   The
advice of one who has had some experience,is"if crossed in
love,or disappointed in hopes,do not forthwith regard life
as not worth living,but calmly and quietly wait.   Seek
counsel and guidance from the infallible quarter,and trust
for the best.   It is well when either man or woman,calmly
and without grumbling,can assent to a "No" when and where
their fondest hopes and expectations are involved.   In
any case ,one sided love is but a poor affair.

Ten days ago I followed to the grave the remains of a young
man thirty-three years of age, a married man.   I felt, and
do feel sad concerning him.   A free mason he was; yes too
free.   He was an admirer of Burns, the poet; and very like
him in what was least to be admired in Burns' character.
What a multitude does Burns cover under his free and easy
wings.   My friend, or rather my acquaintance say, moving about
on Monday as usual, died on the following Friday evening.
"Very resigned" it was said.   Yes, there is a resignation be-
gotten of utter inability to ward off delay.   The motto of
such a man is "enjoyment", cost what it may in detracting
from the happiness of one and all having claims upon them.
No more; poor Robert has gone to a higher court.

                                                      On Monday
evening last two boys "32" and "19" were brought before me
charged with having engaged in a regular stand up fight in
their dormitory about six o'clock in the morning; and thus
it occurred.   "19" in distributing the morning pieces of
bread, gave an unsatisfactory one to "32" who in anger threw
it back to "19".   Words followed, and then blows, of which "19"
bore traces on his face.   "32" is a big lad, and had he re-
sisted, I, alone, could not have managed him.   Quietly he lay
down at command, and received six strokes on the thighs.   As
a rule, "32" is a well behaved boy, and I was sorry to flog him,
but I felt that I could not well overlook his fault.   Some
hours thereafter, "137" seemingly a sympathiser with "32" handed me two small sheets of paper written over with pencil. One
sheet was a love letter to aforesaid "19", one of our biggest
boys, from one of our school girls.   The other sheet was headed "this is a bar".   These sheets had been slipped through

a door slit, designedly for "19", but "137" had picked them
up. This latter boy said that he had not read them, and I
was pleased to think so. In the letter was not much to be
found fault with beyond certain expressions that could bear
a double meaning; and that all correspondence by writing letters between boys and girls was forbidden, and as far as pos-
ible prevented. But the other sheet, "this is a bar" was simply a retailing of such obscenity that transcription here is
out of the question. I know of no way of bringing such a
girl to her senses, or of humbling her in her shameless conduct, than by giving her a sound flogging. Of course flogging of a girl should be done by the Matron, or in her presence. But in these days public opinion would be shocked at
such a course; and so, we fear, a girl will be lost whom a
timely castigation might save. A modern idea is that punishment is intended merely for the reformation of the criminal,
as if hanging a man would reform him. A chief end of punishment, if not the chief, is to deter others. My experience is
that a deserved punishment is seldom resented, by even big boys,
and girls are largely made up of similar materials. It was
subsequently found out, that some twelve girls had got out of
bed about midnight, adjourned to the sick room, and turning two
sick girls out of the room to bed elsewhere, forthwith set to
writing the letters alluded to. I cannot say that any one
of our officials were to blame in connection with those proceedings; but perhaps such doings give reason for the entire
separation of boys and girls in such schools, that is detention in separate premises. And in girls schools one can
hardly doubt, that rigid and continuous confinement in an Institution does much to aggravate those tendencies to prurien-

cy that might be greatly modified if there were given to
them more outdoor amusements, or occupations of an attractive kind, to occupy the minds of the girls, and to which
they could continuously look forward to, as near at hand.

Serjeant Moore, pensioner, with his wife, has been in our service these nine months. About New Year's day, the Serjeant
came to me rather abruptly, demanding rather than requesting,
four days leave of absence. "Out of the question." I replied; having regard to the season, that imposed extra work
which had to be attended to by some one. Thereupon the
Serjeant got into a violent passion; "he had no fixed ag-
reement", would leave to-day, and so on. By and by, he cooled down on being promised one day, a week hence. One month
later, our annual meeting day, he gave another exhibition of
passion and violent language. "Insulted by your son, willgo
to the Sheriff &c." then rushing away to his own room, he
told his wife to "clear out "at once, then he away down stairs
pitching the school keys against the schoolroom door, and a-
way no one then knew where. As quickly as I could, I set about arranging to get on without the man, his wife, a very decent woman, included. After making the best arrangements I
could under the circumstances, I started for our Secretary's
office, to acquaint him as to what had taken place. On
reaching the office I found our Serjeant there, who having
thought over the matter, was ready to beg pardon, which he did,
and returned to his work. Had the man been a boy under my
charge, I would have certainly given him a flogging.

                                                A Christian
ought to be able to control his bad or passionate temper.

If he cannot, or rather will not, for I hold he could if he
would, so much the worse for his reputation and character.
Of late I have been disappointed in some Christians, by the
manner in which they have spoken to me, found fault with me,
charging me with a lack of conscientiousness, and positively
saying concerning me what was not true.   But then, I have
also regretted my own somewhat hot and passionate manner in
resenting these imputations, and intend to improve, should
occasion again occur, that is if I can manage it.   When re-
viled, we must not revile in return, nor cherish revenge in
saying, much less in doing.   Perhaps silence is at times
the Christians' duty, and calmness of spirit, under no matter
how much provocation.   Neither is it wise to feign contempt when wronged.   This one thing however I have learned
in recent experiences, and in a way not learned before, that
one should not try to put wrong right, unless he is quite
prepared to suffer for it.   Specially beware of in any way
touching a man's pocket, if not to put somewhat into it, or
your reputation is gone in that quarter.   Possibly at the
suggestion of dear friends your name goes under; these
brethren being so good, that they do not wish to be made any
better.

        As an old man now, at times I fear, that holiness of
heart and conversation, after which I have been professing
to strive these many years, is by me unobtainable, beyond my
efforts, my ability or willingness.   I fear that old saints,
so called, are sometimes downright wicked, without clearly
seeing it, or being in any fit condition to excuse it.   Rather discouraging, even when remembering a vicariously suffering Saviour.   For our faith in vicarious suffering does

not carry us beyond the necessity of that holiness without which salvation is impossible, and which with varying success every Christian struggles after. I feel as if I must end my Christian life pretty much as I began it, asking forgiveness for Christ's sake and hoping to receive it: but with less, rather than more, of that joyous assurance which makes the young Christian ready to die, that he may enjoy. Nowadays, I feel a little, or more than a little, submissive to live on earth, and obtain all that can be got out of it, my anticipations of Heaven being modified by my being--well,--useful on earth?

XV

Is drunkenness an effect, or a cause? To a large extent, both; we cannot safely ignore either. We dare not say, that only the previously bad become drunkards; nor go to the other extreme, and say that character has nothing to do with it. That souls are ruined by it, we cannot doubt. It is their darling sin. That to become a drunkard is highly criminal, we dare not but affirm. We regard that man as a sinner, or a fool, who is not a total abstainer from intoxicants, as a means of enjoyment, or ordinary factor in health giving or conserving. Among Reformatory and Industrial School Superintendents we have taken notes, and among these officials: who of all men and women should be above suspicion. A fellow worker, a woman, six or eight years in the work, was discharged for drunkenness, took refuge in a silly marriage, and died an early death. Not long since a

wretched looking woman came to me as a beggar; she had been
known to me as the Superintendent of a large Institution,
in a leading city, but drink proved her ruin.   Mr. T. of B.
Industrial School, a Superintendent for years in the work,
was discharged for drunkenness; and yet shortly before his
dismissal, two of our most respected Superintendents of
large $$$$$$$$$$ schools, spent in this man's company, a
large part of a night, smoking and drinking, all as a matter
of course and to shew good fellowship.   Mr. C. of D. Indus-
trial School, a Superintendent of experience in the work, was
discharged on account of drunkenness, and no wonder, remember-
ing the condition of intoxication in which we have publicly
seen him.   Mr. E. of F. Reformatory, is evidently hurrying on
to discharge, if something worse does not happen to him be-
fore.   Two young men of our acquaintance, competent teach-
ers, engaged in Reformatory work, both about thirty years of
age, have recently gone to their graves, their deaths, if not
directly caused, yet clearly accelerated by intoxicating
drink.   And yet in the face of such well known facts, I see
otherwise respectable workers ever tippling and guzzling, as
if no good can be achieved, or pleasure enjoyed, without the
never ending imbibing of intoxicants.   But how often do
reputedly wise men conduct themselves as poor fools.

                                                I seldom
play at draughts; never did, never could to any great purpose.
I rather despised the game as trifling and a waste of time.
Paid sixpence to see the "Herd laddie" play for a money
prize with another professional.   Curiosity prompted, but
our admiration for the game was not enhanced.   Still, I
might play a game, now and then with a boy, and generally win.

But "Charlie" had been for a long time a patient in our
local Infirmary, and had there learned to play the "brod"
ageinst some good players, elderly men. Charlie I found
to be too many for me. Playing with him, the game became
more and more interesting to me; but for all that, I was
often beaten in most provoking manner. "Be blowed" I was
stupidly often. In laying traps for Charlie, the "maister"
himself, was trapped. In a word, the boy was almost always
wide awake, but the master asleep. It was more than Ø I
had bargained for, and more than I liked to endure. At
times I won, and was then inclined to break off with flying
colours. Venturing again, I would be beaten in three or
four games running. I never lost my temper, but felt annoyed. In dogged earnestness last Friday evening I sat
two hours after the boys, Charlie excepted, were in bed, and
managed to beat him twice, and draw once. The question
now is, shall I face him again, or rest on my laurels, and
give up the game? To really enjoy any game, one must lay
his mind to it, spend considerable time at it, and attain
some proficiency in playing: for in continuous losing of
games there is not much, if any, enjoyment. But then the obvious drawback comes to be, the spending of time, not as an
occasional relaxation, but as a continuous pursuit. Experts
at Chess, Draughts, and the like, seem to expend their leisure
time doing little else than studying their favourite games;
nor care for any pursuit outside of them. It is not without reason, that earnest men taboo these games as a waste of
time, that could, and should, be more profitably spent. And
yet, for myself, I am unable to walk abroad continually, no
matter on what errand. To read without interval, time would

become drudgery; music after much practice becomes monotonous; and I do not care to sleep, except at nights.   Eating I find pleasant for half, or rather a quarter, of an
hour three times a day; but to smoke, or drink intoxicants,
to me would be a punishment.   Changing from one pursuit
to another, not too long at any, I get along very pleasantly,
and might find amusement in chess or draughts, but frankly
I am afraid; so avoid them, and feel happy without them.
Unceasing devotion to scientific pursuits, may be necessary
and laudable; but the tendency to excess in many out of
door games, such as football, bowling, and boating, would lead
one to think, that their votaries regard their favourite
game as the chief end of man.   It is this manifested tendency, ever present, that makes one look askance at games otherwise innocent, and in moderation worthy of approval.   Dancing may be put on the same platform; to young people it is
delightful and healthful, when moderately indulged in.   But,
what is moderation?   Two hours at most, in the twenty-four,
and that only occasionally, not oftener than once a week, and
by day in the open air.   Under such conditions, dancing
needs not be objected to; but dancing is generally pursued
in a different fashion.   To dance in moderation may be easy
enough; but it is far more agreeable in most cases to dance
too much.   And some find it better, to dance not at all,
than resist the continual and urgent solicitations of those
who do.   Cards and games of chance, we regard with something akin to contempt, and so never engage in them.   Gambling is a disease, and generally associated with crime.

It has
been said in our hearing, by one who had ample opportunity

to judge, that women are less conscientious than men.   Men
are bad, if women are worse, then may we say, alas, poor women.
Our experience anent Institution Matrons has led us at
times to think, that there is some apparent truth in the
statement.   But our thoughts lie in this direction; that
women are more impulsive than men, more actuated by their
feelings than men are.   A man thinks, where often a woman
only feels.   Where a woman loves, there she may be trusted;
but if love be absent, a woman should invariably seek counsel from a man.   Men should listen to women, that is, hear
what they have got to say, in every case, a man to his wife.
Man is prone to be deficient in affection, woman in correct
judgment.   To be conscientious in an Institution, where being found out is reduced to a minimum, requires a high type
of character; and we know that failure on the part of both
men and women in such places, is not so rare as to deserve
no attention.   Appropriating for one's own use that which
rightly belonged to the inmates has in our experience, been
a failing common to both sexes: but from giving particulars
it may be better to refrain.   In these cases Directors are
not always blameless.   They are prone to refrain from inquiry and investigation when these are rightly called for;
and at times are more given to hushing up% than to laying
bare, for fear of the "horrid public" as represented in the
dailies; and we can sympathise with them.   Certain newspapers seem more anxious to procure news, than to make known
truth, and exaggeration is their element.

　　　　　　　　　　　　　　　　X. & Y. Z. were bro-
thers, and as Colonial Traders became very rich.   X.'s eld-
est son, John, was born with a silver spoon in his mouth, and

in course of time came into possession of the greater part of the firm's property.   John attended to business in a way, but in a very small way; he also attended to his pleasure in a much more extensive way.   He also did a little in the way of taking the chair at philantrophic meetings, but shewed a very poor figure at them.   If John did not perspire himself, he made the cold sweat break out on his hearers, who posed as his supporters,   At the same time John had a laudable ambition; having money, why not have a seat in Parliament?   If he, himself, was not an orator, he might get others to orate for him, as ultimately it turned out.   John got his seat, at a cost of four thousand pounds it was said, sat in it a while, making only a so so member. By and by he became alarmed at somewhat, resigned M.P. and returned to private life.   John is now a comparatively poor man, bad times having ov/ertaken him.   He is in poor health, and quite possibly, or probably, one of these days may arrive at the end of his tether. John is only one of a considerable number known to us in the past, over whom may be written, "All is vanity":   To hear, or read, of like cases is instructive; but to have known, and to have been more or less intimate with these men, brings truth home with sledge hammer force to the soul.

Peter Gray has been Superintendent of Dryhill Reformatory during many years. A few months ago I met him on a holiday drive.   I sat next to Mrs. Gray as we rattled through one of our beautiful Highland glens.   Mrs. Gray spoke as an ardent admirer of poet Burns, "poor fellow".   We differed on some things that concerned the poet and his lasses; but by and by we

wended our wordy way into the subject of true religion and
communion with God, when in a manner squeezed out of the
soul by troubles, well nigh past endurance. I enjoyed the
conversation much, and at parting, the lady hoped, we would
both remember the subject of our talk. We each returned
to our work; the Grays to Dryhill, and I to Grumbleton. Ten
days thereafter, at Dryhill, the sudden death of an inmate
bent on mischief, which returned on his own head, caused commotion, inquiry, and trouble, ending in the resignation of Mr.
Gray, and much else not desirable. Observe, what has doubtless been noticed by others, earnest thought and cogitation
on possibilities, scanned as they are on the eve of their
being put to the test in life's grim experience, but the re-
alities unknown to the subject of them, at the time. And
again, strange how lightly we are prone to regard the pains
and tears of others, while most seriously taking to heart
the reverses and sorrows that overtake ourselves.

Miss Grand
was a farmer's daughter, and as such had to work, and without
stint. Nothing wrong in that, except possibly in the
young woman's own estimation. By and by she became an assistant in a public Institution; afterwards got married and
had a house of her own. But circumstances sent her back
to Institution work. She seemed to satisfy her employers
for a number of years, but ultimately was requested to resign. The lady is quite indifferent, resignation of no consequence to her, but nevertheless how difficult to get Madam
to resign. Altogether too humbling, after these years aiming at a lady's ways and manners; when among strangers, we
mean. When at home, disguise was impossible, and by fellow

workers the woman was not loved.   To have to return to
menial work, so called, and lay the lady aside is to most a
crushing blow.   .But why regard honest manual labour as
in any way a disgrace?   Of course we remember the disgrace
of the prodigal son in having to tend swine for a subsistence; but why regard undeserved poverty as a crime, or even
make excuse for it?   Yet to do so, by not a few people, is
the rule.   Or what is the same thing, they are ashamed to
acknowledge their humble origin.   Then, many men and women
alike, though otherwise intelligent, go utterly down, at the
thought of going down.   They die through fear of dying; or
through fear of wanting the necessaries of life.   Then a-
mong al classes, how often does the possession of a full
purse mean purse proud?   If one has not a full purse, or
cannot persuade his neighbour that it is full, he hangs his
head as if guilty of a crime, of a sin unpardonable.   No
doubt there are men and women above such foolish weakness,
but among acquaintances we do not feel equal to pointing
them out.   There is one, we know, who is not exactly ashamed
of his poverty in the past, nor of the poverty of his parents;
all the same, he likes his acquaintances to understand that
he is not poor now; and he therefor carries his head more
bravely in public now than when he was poor.   Ministers
and Teachers are as bad in this respect as any others, we at
times think, worse.   When poverty is no result of crime on
the poor's part, why should those who are poor act, and in a
manner plead guilty, as if it were a crime?   Humble origin
can never be a crime; but men are weak, and often shew themselves, poor fools.

Having ascended a little higher the hill

of life; or, rather being fairly over the top and stepping
down the opposite declivity, but still having in sight our
path of ascent, we muse and note, that two things, from time
to time, have been matters of regret, the first that times
move so slowly, the second, that time flies so fast.   Then,
the question, Has our life been a success? presses itself
on our notice, though now too late to avail much.   Regarding what we have done, we cannot boast much, or perhaps at
all.   Concerning what God in his good providence for us,
our life has been a great success.   At school the boy was
too lazy to become a clever scholar.   He was too deficient in energy, and too dreamy, to make a good herd laddie.
He was too discontented, and perhaps over scrupulous to be
a smart draper or commercial man.   And although a so
called reformer of the young these thirty-five years past,
he has felt much more depressed by his failures than elat-
ed by his successes.   Yet he is by no means without hope,
that in a future state of being, or even in this world according to some estimates, his life may be finally entered
as a success.   And we must ever remember, that with the
Creator, such a thing as failure cannot be admitted, or even
thought of.   If negatively, one may be permitted to boast
of not doing certain evil things, then might he sum up a very respectable list in that direction; or even in attending
to incumbent duties in a perfunctory way, his case might not
look bad.   But taken all over, this one's life and doings
may be regarded as somewhat ordinary.   Yet he was born a
Scotchman, and of Christian parents.   These last seven words
mean a great deal.   Few of earth's great ones can say as
much as they imply.

Our annual Fair has come and gone.   I was at the Fair,
and spent twopence there.   On Thursday, while observing
several men, whom I regarded as swindlers, pretending to
drop shillings into purses, and offering to sell them for
a shilling each, I met Dr. D.D. of the Free Church also stepping along and looking through the Fair.   I spoke to the
Reverend man, and referred to the Fair as a malignant growth
&c.   Much to my surprise, the Doctor seemed to regard the
whole show, not with mere equanimity, but with approval. "All
enjoying themselves, might be much worse employed." so said
the Doctor.   In reference to our swindling neighbours
whom I pointed out, "O" said the Doctor, "people who want to
get a shilling for nothing, are worse than those men who pretend to give it to them."   I have always regarded the Fair
as a nuisance; very little in it on this occasion, beyond
swings, merry go rounds, and gambling in small ways for cocoa
nuts, cigars, and coppers.   So unqualified praise from a
Free Church minister of first class reputation, surprised me
not a little.   But minds differ; perhaps the Doctor is
broad, and possibly I am narrow.   I saw a poor woman, seemed
very poor, grasping a purse, containing as she supposed, a
shilling, or several, and paying for it, honestly enough, her
own shilling.   "Go away now" said the vendor, an able bodied
young man, "and don't look into the purse till you get home,
in case the people laugh at you."   She did however look in
and found a halfpenny and a bit rounded tin, large enough to
tingle and make believe.   To that woman I might have given
advice, but to the young man the tread mill, could I have had
my way, and notwithstanding the worthy Doctor's opinion.
Does the Doctor get only his deserts, when he in search of

higher. than current interest, loses his money in a bankrupt concern?   But of course that is different; for the Doctor cannot be worse than the bankrupt, nor by any means so bad.

The foregoing parenthetically,   To resume, what has been given to the writer?   Good health, on the whole very good, and it has been taken good care of.   Intelligence somewhat above the average, that is if looking to the future implies it.   One may be too wise in his generation; not rightly assigning to the present and to the future in due measure. In family relations , some keen cutting sorrows have fallen to our lot, by the early removal of much loved ones.   But then, to die early is not always an evil to those removed, let us fondly hope; and more especially when we have good reason to believe that "gathered" means "safe".   As for the rest, happy in one's family, contented and grateful for what has been given to us in possession, what more on earth can a son of man ask, or wish for?   Our early days were spent in dire poverty, but now we have abundance and to spare.   All has been with small ability, or very ardent seeking after on the receiver's part, so far at least as mere material goods have been concerned.   No doubt, prayer has been resorted to, but often from felt weakness and fear, rather than from strong faith, or earnest endeavour.   To young men beginning life, an old man who must soon end it, may be allowed from experience to say, "Seek God in prayer, by trust through Jesus the Christ, alone in your closet, even when against your inclinations, and much more may come out of it than you at first wot of.

                    And now, out of harness, how

how does the old man feel? Leisure is, and may be enjoyed,
but pleasant work is pleasanter than no work to the
healthy soul. One is apt to tire in the continued pursuit
of any one thing, and the changes available for an old man
are limited. Yet one of the most unreasonable things a
man or woman can do, is to complain of growing old. It is
a complaint that one did not die young. Unless one is
tired of life, let him be thankful that life to him is prolonged. Long life to a good man is an advantage; he will
continue to gain experience, and grow so much the better by
it. With a bad man the reverse is true; the longer he
lives, the greater a transgressor he becomes. Perhaps the
saddest feature in an old man's life is his loneliness; his
companions of early days one after another are removed from
earth, and for ever; so far as our senses go to bind the ties
of friendship. Happy is that man who can spend the evening of his days with the cheering hope, that partings now
are not for ever.

Concerning an Industrial School that needs
not special designation, I have been creditably informed,
that religious instruction, as such, is forbidden by the Directors, and why? Because in said school, there are under
detention, children of Protestants, Roman Catholics, and so
on; and the teaching of religion, except in very vague terms,
might cause ill feeling among both parents and children.
Surely religion among said Directors, is a religion not
worth dying for.

A few words anent Directors generally in
public Institutions set apart for the young. To begin,
they do not seem to perceive the amount of drudgery they

may indirectly impose upon children, say in an Industrial
School, by their (the Directors) fondness for seeing every
thing clean, some one has said painfully clean, tidy and
spotless in every way.   It may be very good so far, but
how does this praise of absolute cleanliness too often
work?   Why, in children being kept scrubbing late and early, at dinner hours, play hours, and extra hours; and not seldom, in children being kept out in the cold for fear of dir-
tying the premises inside.   Directors seldom make any effective inquiries as to how children are fed, that the food
be properly cooked, nicely served, and divided so that each
child gets sufficient quantity, and time given, so that the
eater be not forced to gulp his food, or leave a portion not
eaten.   No doubt Directors should have confidence in their
Superintendents; and the Superintendent may have confidence
in his assistants.   And possibly all this good natured confidence may not be unmerited, but one known Superintendent
has found his wisdom a good deal overtaxed, to secure that
such little matters were fairly attended to.   We have never found a Director request that a child be stripped of its
clothing, with a view to seeing that its body was clean, and
its underclothing in good condition, sufficient to keep its
body warm.   Even Inspectors, we have found very cursory in
these matters.   In the matter of feeding it is difficult
to judge correctly.   A farmer has two calves; he gives one
its stated drink of milk two or three times a day, and grass
"ad lib", and in time it may turn out a fairly sized ox; but
allow the other calf to suck its mother as it and she feel
inclined, and at the end of six months this second calf will
weigh from forty to fifty per cent heavier than the first.

There can be no doubt, that properly fed children grow much bigger, and turn out, both physically and mentally, much superior to children insufficiently fed, or otherwise not properly taken care of. Neither Directors, Doctors, nor Inspectors can be fully equal to seeing to all this. Only an intelligent, conscientious, and experienced Superintendent can fully recognise his responsibilities in the situation he fills. But a Superintendent may take things very easy, and yet not stand any worse in the eyes of discerning Directors, or discriminating Inspectors. If a Superintendent seeks merely to please and gain popularity, then he, or she, must aim at having everything seen by the eyes, in tip top order, the outer clothing of the children included: especially on fete days and in Church on Sundays. Further, he should endeavour to get a few of the children to recite cleverly, comic pieces are the best, perform a little in the way of amateur theatricals, sing a song or two nicely, perform at musical drill, play the bagpipes, or dance Ghillie Callum, and the reputation of that Superintendent or Teacher will at once be securely established: even supposing that these same children cannot write a letter to a friend in any other manner than in the stereotyped fashion, "writ thes $$$$1 fue lines hopping your the same", do a simple count without $$$$ blunders, or sweep a staircase without sending all the dust from top to bottom in one cloud. In saying all this, we do not try to insinuate that such practices exist in all schools, nor are followed by all Teachers; but the pictures are not merely fancied ones. Have just been to see an old

acquaintance, a companion of my twenties. Poor fellow, how

changed.   He has had a shock of paralysis; "getting better" his wife says, but to me his condition does not seem very hopeful.   "Good by, my boy, let us pray for one another" I said as my friend's eyes became watery, "you and I must go back to first principles, Jesus Christ and him crucified, is it not so?"   "O yes", said my friend, and with a fervent hand shaking again we said, "Good by."   My friend has been a reader of German and many other writings.   I remember him saying in my hearing, "O, how I wish I knew nothing more than I did in the days of my youth, concerning my faith in the Bible and what it teaches, that my faith to-day were as clear and strong as it was then."   How naturally, when all else fails, can some of us frail ones turn to him, the Saviour of sinning men, God manifest in the flesh.

Why is it that I, as a Christian, have been so often, as I have been, ashamed of my colours?   Why have I been afraid to speak as a Christian when I should not have been silent?   Is this shame excusable?   Am I ashamed of my country, or of my political opinions?   No.   Then examine somewhat and analyse.   If I happen to be in the company of refined English speaking people, am I ashamed of my uncouth Scottish accent?   I may have been in times past, but not now.   But why **ever** ashamed?   "Dinna ken", perhaps afraid of being laughed at, or wished to be thought more highly of , by speaking, or trying to speak, fine or pure English.   If so, I might save myself the trouble, unless very clever, which I am not, in trying I would utterly fail, and very likely make matters worse than by going on in my natural way.   Old folk know all this, young folk have to learn.   In society, so called, with evening dresses and

jewelry being the rule, do I in my plain attire, devoid of
gold or silver ornament, feel quite at my ease, or move a-
bout without wincing, amid a splendour and decoration entirely beyond my purse and station? In spite of myself,
my better self, do I not feel like a fish out of water,
wishing that I were at home, and why? Is it fear of being despised, thought little of, or avoided? Or again, may
one be inclined to indifference affected to meretricious
surroundings, which is not felt, and be proud of his humility? Further, in conversation with certain friends, or
with those whose good opinions I wish for, they express
themselves strongly on political, social, or religious subjects, where I utterly disagree with them, but sit dumb, afraid to offend, does not moral, if not criminal cowardice,
lie at the bottom of silence or fear to differ? Now, coming, to vital Christianity, a profession, or confession, of
faith in the Christ of God, my Saviour, my hope in time and
for Eternity, that I have been ashamed of my said faith, if
not of my general practice, I would not dare to deny. I
bend my knees, morning and evening, daily, when I rise from
bed, and before retiring to rest, and occasionally at other
times. I may be careful to close doors and lock them, but
if these arrangements have been overlooked, and a neighbour
abruptly enters and finds me on my knees, how confused and
startled I am, if not ashamed: as if caught stealing, or com-
mitting a mean action, and yet, why? To some extent the con-
fusion may be natural, and not blameworthy. Startled con-
fusion may be seen when a bird is frightened out of its
nest, away from its eggs or young. Our Lord seems to sympathise somewhat with the feeling when he says, "Shut the

door of your closet, and pray in secret",. Young lovers/
&and innocent hearts, when a stranger, or rather one who is*
/prefer to talk by themselves, and may, and do, blush with pure%
.*not a stranger, suddenly and unexpectedly, causes interruption in their mutual tattle. Indeed we might rightly regard the young couple as not exactly what they ought to be,
if they did not blush. But to be ashamed of one another,
would be an entirely different matter, a thing not to be tolerated on one side or the other. A true lover can never
be ashamed of the object of his attachment. Applying all
this to loving God, serving our Creator as far as we can, or
on the other hand being ashamed, what is my duty, how should
I act? A wise and true Christian will not noisly parade
his profession of religion before men, or be eager to shout,
"I am a Christian, you are not." But neither will he hide
his light under a bushel, nor fail to rebuke when and where
rebuke is called for. For a Christian this duty is, perhaps, the most difficult of all duties. When one recognises
his own shortcomings, he may be loathe to rebuke his brother,
not feeling inclined to expose his flank, even to a feeble
enemy. Then, a fault may be a comparatively trifling one,
or so regarded by my neighbour, if not by me, and to clear his
&&& mental and moral vision, while aiming at my standard, may
not be an easy matter, though a necessary one, if my rebuke is
to effect any good. To whistle "Maggie Lauder" on my way
to Church on Sabbath, or on that day at all, I may regard as a
sin; but I might not be able to convince in reality a far
better man, that said whistling would be a sin if done by him.
When a man or brother says, or does, wrong, evidently knowing
it to be wrong, I ought to rebuke him; but in such a way as

he may best receive it, the rebuke, or most likely be well
affected by it. Speak to him when alone, except circumstances demand instant and unhesitating blame. Ashamed
to speak, too often I fear, keeps me dumb. The Christian
should quietly and patiently reason with a man; not in a
dogged argumentative and angry way, but in a way that may,
if possible, disarm opposition, if it fail to convince.
But after all, he confesses the Christ best, who quietly
lives Christianity in honesty, truthfulness, and good will
to his fellowmen, while publically and regularly attending
his stated place of worship, and so far as he can inducing
others who act differently, to do as he, the Christian does.
There are however various ways in being ashamed. A young
man was invited to tea on a Sabbath afternoon, and declined
because it was Sabbath, without giving that as the true reason. Was acting so, being ashamed? Had certain other
people invited this young man to tea, he would have gone,
had they been of his own way of thinking anent Sabbath observance. To tell a man that I will not drink tea with
him, because he is not so good a man as I am, puts us both
in a rather tight place, does it not? This same timid
Christian has been invited to have somewhat to eat and
drink by a few friends in whose company he chanced to be,
and quietly followed till he saw the leader heading into
licensed premises, when contriving to be last on the file,
he slipped away without ever saying why. Was that being
ashamed? Very like it, I fear. This man has not on all
occasions been ashamed; and when so excited as to be angry,
has talked loud enough in defence of his faith and practice. So far, so good; but on all occasions, in amiable

mood or otherwise, to show his colours without boasting or
brag, without bounce or railing, but constantly and consistently, has not been exactly his fort. Then the worst of
the matter seems to be, that to be ashamed in this connection is a sin for which there is no forgiveness while it it
exists. One might offer many excuses for being ashamed,
but seeing that our Lord suggests none it is better to refrain. Ashamed of him, ashamed of us. Does being ashamed
of my position in life, my country, my poverty, my religion,
when no blameworthiness is present, serve any good purpose?
If my poverty or my mean estate, is the result of my own im-
providence, intemperate$$$$$$$$$$$ habits, or lazy life, I
ought certainly to be ashamed, and do what I can to mend mat-
ters. In such cases, shame augurs well for amendment; but
shame when no fault lies at one's door, is moral weakness, if
nothing worse, and will certainly result in pride if riches
follow. Despise no man on account of his poverty; defer
to no man on account of his riches; and avoid causing unnec-
essary offence to either. It is a difficult thing to con-
ceal one's origin, "our speech bewrayeth us." and trying to
conceal, may end in being laughed at. To appear quietly in
one's true colours may ensure some measure of respect, at
least not undeserved scorn. Pretence is hardly worth the
pains; it is a weapon which is prone to injure the user. A
pretentious man is incapable of true friendship; such a
man can find no friend good enough for him; and those who
might be friendly with him, can have no confidence in him.
A man who in his own estimation has no faults, is altogether
too superior for ordinary friendships. If I pretend to be
rich, I expose myself to envy; expensive clothing and dis-

plays of jewelry may cause envy and latent hatred, certainly never love or esteem. The poor man is never envied for his poverty. Concerning religion it is somewhat different; it must be looked at in another way. A truly religious man cannot be a hypocrite; but there may be those who bear him ill will for not being one. Those who themselves are insincere, do not like those who honestly appear in their true colours. They are hypocrites who wish to be regarded as not irreligious themselves, but their standard being a low one, they cannot take kindly to those who walk in a higher plane than themselves, and are inclined to be intolerant of any religion, or professor of religion, that appears to throw them into the shade. Their religion comes to be merely pretension, hypocrisy, or shame in another form. Thus consistent Christians have had very often fire and sword as their portion in the world's history; and ashamed of Christ has often meant no more than afraid of Christ's enemies. Fear may have not a little to do with a Christian's shame, not exactly ashamed, but afraid. Then, is fear a sin? In battle cowardice is treated as a crime; and "the fear of man bringeth a snare". Men have been shot by their commanders for cowardice in the presence of the enemy. Rather hard lines for timid people, but faced they must be. Cowardice, as popularly understood, is a crime, and fear of men's opinions is the constant companion of little souls. "Fear not him who can only kill the body." "I forewarn you whom ye shall fear". "I say unto you, fear Him." So, to fear may be a sin; and not to fear, may be a crime.

My friend alluded to on page 176 has gone.

when I saw him for the last time, as it has turned out, two months ago, neither he, himself, nor his relations seemed to expect his early death. Removed to the country, he appeared to progress fairly well, but on Thursday he was seized with a sharp pain in his head, for which there was found no remedy. On the following Monday he became insensible and continued till the Tuesday forenoon when he died. In recent years I met him seldom, corresponded not often, had not much intimacy beyond remembering our intercourse in earlier years, before marriage. But now that my old friend has gone, I feel as if I had lost a second self. My friend was ambitious in his own way; (who is not ambitious in some way?) aim at being a literate in some form. Poetry and certain other subjects occupied his thoughts a good deal. Question, if much he did in those lines will long survive him. How much we would like to speak after death in an articulate way, to abide, somehow to live, to be remembered, to be thought well of, to fill a corner that could not be so well filled by any one else. A right and laudable ambition, doubtless, but do we always pursue the right, or the best way to attain the desired end?

In our experience, a boy, a friend, or an acquaintance has at times called to our remembrance a something said by us many years before, a something forgotten by one's self, but remembered by our hearer. The words may have been for good or for evil, yet remembered, let it be hoped for good. What a far reaching effect may result from these remembered words. The speaker may never have written a book, not even a letter to a newspaper; on no occasion have addressed an audience in public; and yet by such a one a few words fitly spoken may

have certain beneficial results to people; at the time un-
born.   What opportunities for good lay with the nurse of
our queen Victoria!   How much may the British nations and
the world at large, owe to that woman's words to our then
future Queen!   The converse should also be noticed.   Evil words uttered, too often become crystalised in the minds
of hearers, to their sorrow it may be, to their trial, some-
♦♦♦♦♦♦♦♦♦ times to their ruin.   To be able to speak wisely and well, without fear on the one hand or pride on the
other, on fit occasion and in proper place, may in the annals
of Eternity count for much more than the writing of a book,
which possibly few will read: the book itself being regarded as not worth reading.   Are not such considerations encouraging to the quiet, earnest, and pessimistic soul, as well
as a little ballasting to the ambitious literate.   Yes, ambition often misdirected, and often directed to catch gewgaws.
To that man who starts, and continues in life aiming at fair
dealing with all men, worshipping as becometh a Christian,
shirking no duty in the pursuit of pleasure, while rejoicing ♦♦
in the lawful enjoyments given to him, and not straining after any other, there lies a noble ambition and capacity to enjoy everlasting life: which he is fitted to possess.

One morn-
ing in 1896 a young woman in an Industrial School(Boys and
Girls) came rather excitedly to the Superintendent, then a-
bout to conduct worship with the boys, bringing a girl with
her, and said that the girl had been trying to set fire to
the premises.   "The fire is now extinguished,"so said Miss
Seam, and worship was proceeded with.   Shortly thereafter,
the Superintendent went to the Girls' Department paraffin

had been sprinkled upon the dormitory floor and set fire
to. The Matron, who properly had charge of the girls' Department, was absent from the school. The girl, about
fourteen years of age, in the Superintendent's opinion
should be flogged. Some people who have never had charge
of an Industrial school for girls, think that under no circumstances should girls be corporally punished. In any
case the Superintendent had no expressed authority to punish girls by flogging; and so he requested first one, and
then another of the female staff to flog the girl. But
no, they declined; so the Superintendent was in a fix. A-
mong the girls might arise a spirit of rebellion, or general fire raising, and all this alongside the boys, some of
whom were fit enough for mischief. To hand the girl over to the Police was not desirable; so the Superintendent
must quickly decide as to his course of action. He did
decide; taking the girl into a side room, with the tawse
he gave her six strokes on the bare body, admonished her
and sent her to her seat, among the grave faces of her companions, and trusting that the whole affair was ended.
Not so, however, a second message intimated that the school
was on fire, policeman making inquiries, and so on. The
Girls' upper dormitory was full of smoke, and the Fire Brig-
ade was sent for. It subsequently appeared, that an intelligent assistant after extinguishing the first attempt
to fire the premises, a trifling affair, went away to her
breakfast, leaving the delinquents to kindle as they
pleased. The Police were on the premises now, and five
girls were removed to the Police Office. Precognitions
by the Procurator Fiscal, trial by the Sheriff, and an of-

ficial inquiry by the Home Office ended in instructions
that Boys and Girls be henceforth accommodated in entirely separate premises.   But the one great thing that had
to be considered and dealt with, above all others, was that
a girl had been flogged by the Superintendent, and done as
had been done.   No doubt, the girl had tried to set fire
to the premises, but then she was a girl, and should not
have been punished in such a manner.   The Superintendent
was an old man, old fashioned in his ways, and thought then,
as he still thinks, that he did the best thing under the
circumstances, as then known to him.   The Home Secretary
censured him, but did nothing worse, and the following night
the Superintendent slept, as sound as usual.   There may be
times when a man is so placed, that action, prompt action, is
imperative; but queer rules, and queer public opinions, make
risky any action worthy of the name, or suited to the circumstances.   In such cases a man may run considerable
risk, no matter how he acts, or does not act.   To stand and
merely look on, would be somewhat akin to cowardice, might
even verge on criminality.   In like cases might it not be
well on the part of authorities to take circumstances into
consideration, and be blind at times to infractions of
rules and regulations, when the culprit is placed in difficult and exceptional positions?   In about a year thereafter, the girls being removed, and numerous changes in general arrangements contemplated, the Superintendent resigned,
entirely of his own accord, after thirty-six years service
in the same school.   He received no pension, it was not in
the bargain.   However, the Superintendent had made hay
while the sun shone; and on the whole his Directors had

been. kind. to. him.

xvi

I have. just. read. a volume which. aims. at. proving. the. extreme,
. or measureless length. of. time since. man. began. his. life on
. earth.   One. should not. resist truth, but is. at. liberty to
. question. surmisings.   Men may. have existed much longer in
. the world. than orthodox Christianity. has been in. the habit
. of believing.   Granting. that he has, it. does not much, if at
. all. affect. our faith in Christianity.   Concerning. the. ques-
. tion. however, some. relative questions. arise.   If. ancient
Egypt and Chaldea attained. such high civilisation in. such
remote. ages as. the writer. avers, and. there. seems to. be no
. doubt. about it, from whence did. they. obtain it?   How came
. they to. lose it, why have they lost it, and. themselves be-
sides?   Evolution, is the answer. to the first question. But
. why Evolution. should. not go on, and continue to go on, in
these ancient nations, after having gone. so far, $$ is not ex-
plained.   If Evolution did so much for. these two ancient
and now lost. nations, how comes it. that there. are millions
at present in. the world, for whom evolution has done. nothing,
or next to nothing?   If Evolution has done everything for
the British. and other European nationalities, how comes it
. that it has done practically nothing for Central Africans
. and Cannibal Islanders?   We do not deny evolutionary facts
when such come under our notice; but evolution. apart from
a directing intelligence, we cannot comprehend.   I am shewn
a handful of flint arrow heads, and am not prepared to. say,

that they are not correctly described. But when it is
averred that the chipping of these rough and badly shaped
flints, clearly indicate them to be the work of intelligent men, which we do not deny, we take notes. Now, is it
not strange to learn, to know, that the scienists who can
see so much in flint arrow heads, can in man himself, see
nothing more than the product of an unthinking, nonintelli-
gen###### ###### ###########. evolution, ## ###### nor assign
man's origin to any higher source? When these inferences
are drawn from arrow heads, and totally inconsistent inferences from the existence of men on earth, we can only conclude, that in some heads, as compared with ours, very different methods of thought exist, and logical argument as between
us, impossible. We are open to all certified facts, but in
accepting inferences must be cautious. Our author speaks
very disparagingly of the Hebrews and their civilisation, or
rather their want of it, before the times of the Kings and
the Prophets, contrasting the prophetical writings with the
condition of things as related in Joshua, Judges, and Samuel.
Granting much that he says in this connection, how does he
account for the great difference and contrast between two
such systems of ethics, and general religious opinions? By
evolution? If so, how can such rapidity shew itself in a
few hundred years in Palestine, while in many other countries millions of years, according to evolutionists, have
done little or nothing in raising nations above the lowest
intelligenceand moral levels? Persistency of type in the
various races of mankind, is in one part of the book strongly insisted on. In the oldest Chaldean tablets, it is a-
verred, that strongly marked faces of negros are portrayed

alongside of white Europeans, Circassians, yellow Chinese and copper coloured men; and at a date certainly thousands of years prior to the date of Adam and Eve as usually received. All this is urged to shew that mankind as now existing, could not have originated in a single pair. It is asserted that the various races of men now living, must have had at least four distinct origins; black, white, yellow, and copper coloured. Of course, these surmisings, are only surmisings. But now, the curious thing is, that the author goes on to argue that all these various races have in virtue of evolution descended from an ape! How easily we can believe that which for some reason, we wish to be true. And how difficult to believe that which for some reason, we wish to be false. Our wishes and general moral character have evidently much to do with our religious faith; while the converse is also true, that our religious faith has much to do with our character and wishes.

Evolution with Divine intelligence at the back of it, cannot be fairly objected to; orthodox Christianity has invariably argued in favour of it, though possibly under another name. It believes that all existing races of men have descended from a primal pair; and that all existing languages have their roots in Adam's. Much more concise definition of what is meant by evolution than has as yet reached our eyes or ears, require to be given, before we can arrive at any reliable conclusion concerning it. Nothing has as yet been advanced, scientiffically or otherwise, to shake our faith in the answer given in the shorter catechism to the question, "What is God?" nor do we think, ever

will.   So far and so long, as I regard myself as a created intelligence, and while a qualified assent to evolu-
ion, within definite limits, when verified, I cannot ever
regard Jesus the Christ as in any proper sense a product
of evolution.   When a caterpillar concludes its various
stages of existence by becoming a butterfly, with strict
propriety the process may be called evolution; and so
the evolution of many insects and parasites is clearly
recognised by all attentive onlookers.   But how can evolution in these forms of life be recognised as a non-intelligent force, or power, evolving life and adaptability to
innumerable organisms whose subsistence depends on the
lives of others?   The supposition is barely conceivable,
when we remember, that separately, at the beginning, middle,
and later periods of life, at one time as a parasite on the
skin, then in the mouth, in the stomach, in the muscles, these
living creatures exist; in each case the beginning of life
being adjusted to an utterly dissimilar middle or ending.
It may be that evolutionists, so called, are coming to see
this, and perforce acknowledging that conjoined intelligence and power must lie beyond all these evolvings, hitherto regarded by them, as the results of agencies somewhat
akin to utilitarianism or "survival of the fittest", but
now to be received as an intelligence, or a something akin
to the Biblical expression, "God, the self existent Jehovah".
We have heard of men losing their way in a mist, and after
prolonged wanderings in search of the right way, sink down
to die within a few yards of their own door: an apt resemblance to some of our modern scientific evolutionists.
Imagine certain agents, spiritual and intelligent, but limit-

ed in power, improving by alterations existing forms of
organised life; somewhat as improvements have been, and
are being made in the steam engine, the original type being never lost sight of, nor alterations made except
where requisite.   That to us would explain many of the
facts connected with supposed evolution, that are otherwise undoubtedly puzzling.

                    Have been reading sermons by
the late Professor Caird of Glasgow University.   He believes in the Divinity of Christ, but then, he seems to believe in the Divinity of all men more or less, though putting Jesus at the top of the tree.   To our eyes the Professor's creed is altogether rather misty.   If Universalism is not preached by the Professor, it looks like a possible thing with him.   Clearly, he does not believe in the
sacrificial mission and vicarious death of Christ.   The
Professor sees God's ways as different from man's ways, and
God's thoughts as different from man's thoughts, but in ways
calculated to throw our customary ideas of justice and
rectitude to the winds.   He regards repentance(without defining it)pardon, and regeneration consecutive and sure, repentance as never in vain, and pardon as a matter of course,
outside of the atonement by the Christ.   Concerning the
heathen world, and unpardoned men generally, our opinion is,
that if they are under law, they will be judged by that law;
if under no law, then will follow no judgment.   But better
to leave the unknown in God's hands, nor argue concerning
conclusions when unable to state reliable premises.   If
Christ, that is $$$$$$$, Emmanuel, came not as a vicarious
Saviour, we cannot conceive for what purpose he did come to

earth, or on what mission.   The Unitarian's sinless man
would have been enough for our exemplar.

                                   In favourable
circumstances the lower animals attain their highest development in virtue of their instincts, that answer their
requirements individually, and in reference to one another.
With man it is not so.   For man's highest development
the moral faculty necessary for this and their true happiness is almost always wanting.   Take the one instance of
men in their treatment of women, their wives, their companions, and equals by right.   Among the lower animals the
female can either protect herself from the male, or at
least is not in any way abused or maltreated by him.   Is
it so with mankind?   Not alone in the heathen world, where
women are often treated worse than brutes, but in the midst
of our highest civilisation there is painful evidence, that
wives are far from being kindly or considerately treated
by many husbands sworn to love and protect them.   The requisite morale is not there; certainly it must be the Creator's intention that it should be there; that is, that
the moral faculty as in a man's conscience, should be rightly exercised, and penalties attached to the mal-exercise
of it.   We do not require an inspired revelation to teach
us so much; we see with our eyes, and understand with our
intellect.

          I like to read reliable biographies, but I find
that biographies outside the Bible are almost invariably
one sided and profuse in applying whitewash to the cloudy
side of their subject's character.   In autobiographies,
at least as I write, I dislike the Ego, but where I's strict-

ly speaking should be the rule, it does not seem advisable to make them the exception.   Further, we cannot expect a man, even when speaking the truth about himself, to tell the whole truth, the worst concerning himself not excepted.   So, in both productions complete and accurate pictures are not obtainable; unless faults, which no man is free from, are as faithfully depicted as the good points and virtues.   Discriminating readers will judge of the stock from the sample.

Among our prominent men, such as Owen, Scott, Lyndhurst and Carlyle, while surprised at, and admiring their industry, intelligence, and wonderful achievements, we feel also surprised and pained at what may be called their negative attitude towards the vital truths of Christianity and its Divine author.   Not that we observe much directly antagonistic to our New Testament faith, but rather, what looks like a studious care to avoid saying anything that might lead readers to think that they, the men of whom we write, have, or had anything in common with simple minded, God fearing Christians.   How far biographers and editors are responsible for omissions that if inserted, would lead to different conclusions we cannot say; but we suppose that as a rule, biographers are in sympathy with the subjects of their memoirs; and that these give a fair and just picture, so far, of the minds and inner thoughts of the men spoken of.   We cannot well conceive of any good reason why, if a man is a Christian, he should systematically hide his faith as under a bushel, or be ashamed to make an open confession of it in his public life and writings.   Did Paul allude to such when he said, "Not many wise are called"?   The steam hammer of Neasmith was a

first class invention, the effect of which for the advance
of civilisation and general welfare of mankind's material
interests, can hardly be overestimated.   The researches
of Owen, however instructive and fascinating to cultivated
leisure, can never, except in a cursory way, be of much account
to the million, nor in any way essential to a useful and
happy existence.   The inventions of Watt, of Stephenson,
and of Arkwright are first class in importance, so far as
material wealth is concerned;   but these must stand on a
lower platform than the inculcation among our fellow men
of truthfulness, righteousness, and intelligent worship in
serving God, that alone exalteth a nation in the best sense.
We do not say that the pursuits of these men may not be a
serving of God so far as these works are concerned, but
when in a biography the direct $$$ worship of God as ex-
emplied in the subject/s is virtually absent as not worth
notice, we cannot but note the circumstance.   A number of
young men in our hearing, were studying and preparing for
an examination in biology, the examiner being Professor
Huxley, when the "coacher" was careful to warn his students
to state nothing but bald facts in their answers.   Any-
thing written by the examined, said he, suggesting purpose
or design by a Creator, would certainly be fatal to a pass.
Why do so many of our leading men, followed by many in more
humble positions, in speaking and in writing, "thank heaven"
"praise providence", personify nature, and sing "Lead kindly
light"?   If pressed, they may say, that in using these var-
ious terms they all the time mean "God".   But if so, why
not use the correct name plainly?   Why not with becoming
reverence use the right name without a going round about

the bush?   A Father prefers to be called "Father" rather
than "The Governor", "my old fellow", or "the Boss"; and a
really respectful and loving son will always to be careful to give that name which implies due regard, and is most
pleasing to his parent.   The habit, or practice, may be
simply a fashion, and "bettir be oot o'thi queets than oot
o'thi fashion", says the old Scotch proverb.   Or it may be
thought, that the use of sacred names and Biblical terms
lays the users open open to being charged with hypocrisy;
but still, would not a little more Christian manliness tend
to improved practice in the way of a due acknowledgment of
God at all times, and under all circumstances, braving the
risks of false or unpleasant imputations.

                        How may we account
for sacerdotalism and practice of ritualism being regarded
as a means to the attaining of a higher state of existence
in a future world?   Men do a great deal for one another
in this life.   The truth is, were each man left to himself,
without assistance by division of labour and good offices
rendered one to another, life to men would hardly be endur-
able, in some cases impossible.   Possibly this fact has
somewhat to do with men so often trying to throw all religious responsibilities on others, who for a consideration undertake to carry them.   As medicines, in small or
larger doses, and with little trouble, seem to lift diseases
from the body, so in like manner it comes to be thought,
that a dose of ceremony will cleanse a sinful heart; or at
least secure immunity from punishment now, and after death
a happy Eternity.   But salvation by Christ, does not imply
salvation easy.   Very often with Christians it has been

"through fire and water to the wealthy place."

"What does it all mean?"said an eminent scientific gentleman in Glasgow to the writer; he was alluding to the million, living, moving, dying.   The unexpected question found the addressed unprepared with a direct answer.   And what satisfactory could be given to a question, perhaps unanswerable by any man.   Christianity as set forth in our New Testament, goes a great way in giving an answer, which to many earnest men is so far satisfactory, that they feel quite contented to wait for more light.   We cannot think of a really earnest seeker after the truth, rejecting Christ as revealed in the Christians book, or books; and this apart from all questions anent inspiration, canonicity, or guaranteed authenticity.

How often in the early summer, and on the "gowan lea", has the "herd laddie" gazed on the myriads of gowans full blown, with their faces all as one turned to the sun.   Each gowan had in reality a sun to itself.   Had there been only one daisy, instead of millions, all the same that one could have had no greater share in, or benefit by, the sun's rays.   Who in thought, has not been overwhelmed at times, by the presence of a vast crowd of his fellowmen; their being fed and clothed, their cares, their separate little worlds, room enough for each and all, but above all to a Christian, their prayers, their justification or condemnation, and general condition before God.   Can God's ear be possibly open to the cries, to the requests of millions, the circumstances of no two being precisely alike, nor the wants of any one being on all fours with the re-

quirements or wishes of any other.   And yet, is there anything more wonderful in a million of men than in one?
With us numbers count for much, but with infinitude one
may be as a thousand, and a thousand as one.   In saying so,
we grope after, rather than clearly perceive; and yet returning to the gowans, how simple, no limit can be put to the
number that may open their petals to the noonday sun.   The
gowan has been made to look, and the man, if not made to pray,
has at least the capacity, and in certain circumstances the
inclination irrepressible, to pray.   Is it wise then, on the
part of those who do confessedly do not pray, to sneer at
those who do? forgetting that the very capacity to pray to
God, implies that a power too often dormant, or misunderstood,
it may be, but still existing, has been placed in the creature, man, to which we may well believe there is a corresponding ear to hear, and willingness to listen, on the part of
God, the Creator.   In other words, a key implies a lock;
wings imply flight; and feet imply motion.

                    I have a diffic-
ulty in seeing clearly much that has been said by Thom Carlyle.   The spirit of defiance depicted in one part of Sar-
tor Resartus, is on lines where I dare not follow him, even
were I so disposed, which I certainly am not.   Defiance on
the part of man with very limited powers and entirely dependent, is a very foolish, if not a positively wicked state
of mind anent that which God alone has ordained, and which
he alone can alter.   Concerning such matters, caution is
one's only safe course.   In one place Teufeldorch says,
that space and time are merely "forms of thought"; and so
disposes of his difficulties regarding them.   But a defin-

ition of the phrase, "forms of thought"is not given by our
author. The phrase either means nothing definable, or it
implies too much: that the phrase may be applied to all
known or imagined existences, and that there exists nothing
to which the words may not be applied. I cannot make out
Carlyle's creed beyond this, that he seems to believe in
the existence of God, and in work of some sort; always good
work, it is to be hoped. Like most men of "light and leading"in these days, he says next to nothing concerning Jesus,
God's revelation of himself to man, in any of his books
read by us. Jesus is either ignored, or distantly alluded
to in a patronising sort of way. There are not a few people in certain walks of life who talk of Christ as if he
were an intimate and familiar friend of theirs; and disgust at this manner may drive better educated, and more refined people, to the other extreme of virtually saying, that
they have heard of Jesus, but that he is outside the circle
of their acquaintance. But there is a reverential a respectful, and becoming way of acknowledging the Christ,
which every professing Christian should aim at, so that his
audience or readers may have no difficulty in discovering
his faith in him who is the sole hope of humanity, as delin-
eated in the gospels and Paul's epistles. However, we owe
much to the compiler of Cromwell's letters and speeches.
To one of the most puritanical of men (though possibly at
times an erring one) Carlyle has done most ample justice.
For that alone we must admire Carlyle as a lover of truth
and so far a fearless expounder of it.

In giving estimates
of certain men's characters, Charles Kingsley's for instance,

written by admiring friends, what an amount of verbosity and
diffuse laboured eulogiums, compared with Biblical descriptions and estimates of distinguished men. Of Enoch it is
said simply that "he walked with God", of Abraham that "he
was the Father of the faithful", of Moses that "he was the
meekest of men", of David that "he was the man after God's
own heart", of Barnabas that "he was a good man", and of Ha-
naniah that "he feared God above many". How delightfully
succinct and suggestive, in comparison with descriptions
that look more like flash advertisements than honest estimates of what men are in reality are or were. But of more
importance than Mr. Kingley's character are his opinions
and teachings anent the future punishment of the sinner,
and its duration, his Universalism, if we understand him a-
right. To us, the words of our Lord in the Gospels fore-
close all discussion as to the reality of punishment to
the unrepentant sinner, and its endless duration; though to
describe or deliniate beyond what is written, savours of
presumption and sinful rashness. Regarding pains and penalties in general, we may be permitted to say a little.
Among men, pains are often regarded with comparative equanimity, so long as danger to life does not seem to be involved. Toothache and sea sickness have been often laughed at; we know what they are, and regard the laughter of an
onlooker as by no means funny. Lumbago is seldom regarded
very seriously by those not affected by it, while flogging
to a villian deserving it, may be regarded with a secret satisfaction by those who know the facts of the case. On
the other hand, with what horror is hanging regarded, though
painless; because it deprives of life; and poisoning, though

it may be merely falling asleep, but not awakening.   No
doubt, to gouge out a man's eye is horrible, very, even when
death is not involved; but it is on record, that certain
criminals when undergoing unspeakable torments, have shewn
impenitence and defiance in such manner, that sympathy or
sorrow, by just and law abiding onlookers, was in a manner
out of the question.: Both Old and New Testaments recog-
the fact, that pains and penalties do not as a rule, either
soften or reform.   Then regarding Kingsley and his suggested intermediate state, would a man be more likely to repent then than now?   Might not a longer time on earth answer equally well?   When a friend dies, who in dying, any
more than in past living, gives no indication of repentance
or contrition for wrong doing during a careless and aband-
oned life, it is not surprising if surviving friends hope
or imagine that "beyond the bar" there is reserved for such
an intermediate state where a renewed opportunity for amendment will be given; shall it be said as a last chance, or
merely giving another opportunity which will, or may, be renewed until repentance and radical conversion result?   The
Romish doctrine of Purgatory hardly deserves serious attention; but the intermediate state suggested by Kingsley
calls for more notice.   He, a popular man, believing, or trying to believe in the idea, though without any proof of its
truth, will always be palatable to the many ### to whom religion in any form is a bugbear.   Many men, sinners in
their youth, have had times for amendment given to them in
middle life and in old age.   Do these opportunities produce or lead to repentance?   As a rule, it is to be feared,
not.   Almost invariably, good men have been good from their

youth: a fact much forgotten, but none the less true. Failure of capacity to enjoy sinful pleasures as life advances
does not imply repentance, nor less desire for indulgence,
could inclinations be gratified. One may regret without
repenting. Napoleon in St. Helena was Napoleon still,
though a caged eagle. Sowing "wild oats" in youth, means
a full crop in later life. Dr. Johnson stood repentant
where he considered he had committed the sin; but to repent
and obtain absolution in a future world for sins which can
have no existence there, seems not very logical in supposition, nor except for the sinner himself, does the thing appear
desirable. One opportunity in time is given; if beyond
the present time be given a second, why not also a third, a
fourth, or any greater number? Or at once say Universalism,
which Kingsley seems to have believed in, for all except
"bigots", to whom he thinks our Lord refers when speaking
of the sin against the Holy Ghost!

An autobiographer stands
at a disadvantage in one or two things. He cannot from
personal knowledge give any account of his entrance into
life, nor forecast the manner of his leaving it. However,
for practical purposes one may, after three score years
and ten, or sooner, be looked upon as a decimal repeater, and
thought of accordingly. It is questionable whether any
important change in a man's character takes place after
forty, or even thirty, ; we incline to think not. In extreme
old age dotage may supervene, but that needs not count.

How difficult to be, or at least to feel alone; that is free
from all human presence, in the way of being seen, heard, or

thought of as being in a certain place.   When in harness
I blamed the work; but out of harness I find $$$ to be a-
lone more difficult than ever.   Dear ones are so inter-
ested in my whereabouts, general condition and actions, that
at times I am tempted to sigh, and cry, "O, to be alone."
When making inquiries anent the propriety of my going to
Limerick, one question I put to my friend $$$ offering to
find me a situation there, was, if in proposed dwelling
place there was any private room where a young man could
at times be alone.   The reply was, "Walk to and fro on Limerick, Bridge, a public promenade, you gcan be as much alone
there as in your closet; no one will disturb you."but on
subsequent trial the bridge was found by no means the place
where one could feel alone in.   A much better place, to
which I occasionally resorted in summer weather was right
out by a manhole door in the roof and on to the slates in
a perfectly safe place, and free from interruption: so difficult at times to be really alone, or at least to feel a-
lone.   The fear of being seen or heard, may have a good
deal to do with the feeling of not being alone.   I think,
I could count on the fingers of one hand the number of
times I have had the assured feeling of being alone, so far
as my fellows were concerned, and acting accordingly.   How
often when one is in search of loneness, it may be in a
country walk, will another, suddenly and unexpectedly, come
on the scene, evidently on similar search, and causing to
both similar annoyance.

Wishing to hear of old friends I
make inquiries as opportunities occur.   Mrs.F. in Limerick
was an attractive Christian lady.   She was the mother of

eleven children when scarletina entered her family. First
one, and then another of her young ones were seized with
the fell disease till all the eleven had passed through it.
Mrs. F. nursed them all, and successfully; they all recovered.
But when they all had passed, or reached convalescence, Mrs.
F. herself was laid down with the disease and died. Probably a doctor will say, that the woman's strength had been
exhausted, her system down owing to previous labour and anxiety. Possibly so, but reasons are but poor comfort to a
loving husband and overwhelmed father. We live not for
time alone, but for Eternity. The lady's Mr. F. was a good
man , and a devoted husband. They were both members of
the Society of Friends in their early days, but became memb$$$
ers of the Congregational Church in Limerick, shortly after
their marriage. Mr. F. without offence, was a brewer of Por-
ter and Ale, On one occasion the business being criticised
Mrs. F. exclaimed, "But what would you do if you had to make
your living by it?" Certainly a hard question, to which no
satisfactory answer could be given. The Devonshire militia
were then in Limerick; it was the time of the Crimean War.
Mr. F. undertook the distribution of tracts among those men,
and at a time when volunteering for the general army was go-
ing on $$$$ "What a scene" said Mr. F. "what a scene of
drunkenness and all its accompaniments; my visit was useless;
I hurried away faster than I came; and the worst of it all
was, that my own porter and ale were being driven in by the
cart load to these men whom I came to benefit." His Christ-
ian brethren thought it was a good joke. Subsequently, Mr. F.
gave up the brewing of porter and ale, and as I understand,
without having made a fortune by it.

I don't think that total abstinence in those days, and even
among Christian, was regarded as in any way incumbent as a
duty.   At times of festivity, I have seen prominent Christians, at least by profession and general practice, clearly
taking more than was good for them; if not drunk, they were
certainly not sober.   Further I remember Christian men de-
fending practices that in my opinion were not right; so
prone are we to keep the law in the letter, or try to do it,
while pushing the spirit to the wall. When in a leading
Glasgow warehouse one day the head of a department rather
abruptly asked me if the price I quoted was the $"cost price"
with a view to cheating the customer I supposed. "yes" I
blurted out; but mentally saying to myself, "cost to you, but
not cost to us."   I hereby offer no excuse, I regret the
act and will regret it while I live. My companions in Limerick, the Roman Catholics, were much given to bad language,
lying, and stealing.   Scotchmen given to these practices,
acknowledged their sins but without improving their practice.
With the Irishman it was different.   In the matter of stealing, (stealing from one another was a common habit in the
premises.) it was not stealing they called it, but "making"
and they meant no harm by it.   When a lie was a lie it was
not easy to make out at times; if a lie it did not deserve
the name.   Then coming to language, "By Gor," was a favourite expression, but it seemed to be more usual to take the
d in place of the r , and become very angry if the mistake
was pointed out to them.   Much more to be guarded against
than these ordinary matters was the eating of beef on a
Friday.   There are evils in Ireland and among the Irish,
in Scotland and among the Scotch, in England and among the

English; but the cure for these evils must ever lie more
with the character of a people than with any alteration
of laws which a Government can devise.

I have known a re-
spectable old gentleman who acknowledging all the evils
connected with alcoholic drinking, said, that he drank a
glass at night, before going to bed, and thereby obtained
refreshing sleep which otherwise was denied him. That
there was some truth in what he said, or thought, we cannot
doubt; but whether this habit was an acquired one we do
not know.   In exceptionally circumstances sleep may be
unobtainable, when a glass of whiskey might ensure it, like
thirty drops of laudanum, but better wait a while than
have recourse to either. The sleep obtained by a drunk
man sleeping on the pavement is not a refreshing, nor a
good one in any way.   When a lad in Aberdeen I slept in
a bedroom adjoining that of Tom Southland, a man ten or
twelve years my senior,   He appeared to sleep very little, if any at all in a satisfactory way, judging from his
communings in the night watches; and certainly could not
be accounted for by deficiency of alcoholics which were
Tom's daily, or hourly solace.   In due course, Tom died
of delirium tremens.   All that can be said on behalf of
alcoholics is, that in drinking them, to many there is pleasure; and that like arsenic, opium, and strychnine, they may
be useful medicinally.

One thing in old age I feel much.
The friends of my youth are mostly gone, and somehow I fail
in finding new ones.   I seem to be too slow and old fashioned for the young, while the old regard me with suspicion

When young, we have pleasure in airing our prosperity to
our friends and acquaintances, or in retailing our griev-
ances to sympathetic listeners.   Now, these wise auditors
are almost all gone, or grown indifferent to our means and
ways, as possibly we are to theirs.   The young seem more
envious of what I possess, than eager to emulate in pursu-
ing to possess by honesty and industry as the more satisfactory way.   My wife is if anything rather too anxious
anent my welfare and the prolonging of my life, but I do
not think that any one else in the world would mourn much
at my departure.   In saying so I do not complain, perhaps
the cause lies in myself, it must be all right; but one cannot shut his eyes to it, or be indifferent regarding it.
I love little children, even when they cannot be expected to
much love me.   For many of my fellowmen I feel sorry, sometimes sad; so little in common anent our hopes and fears
runs in the same grooves; yet when my fellowmen die, I do not
weep for them; their departure does not much affect my happiness.   So one is paid back in his own coin.   Am I worth
loving?   Not much, I fear.   It is pleasant to be loved.   It
is pleasant to love; but to aim at winning love is an ardu-
ous undertaking.   Let us do our best to do our best, without
reference to specific reward.   Our duty is our duty, come
what may; and there is great and lasting gratification in doing what is right, even when as Paul says "though the more
we love, the less we be loved."   Then, the majority of men
love, we presume, and are loved by someone.   The reliable
steady love of one is better than the fitful love of a thousand; meantime I have my wife and am thankful.   In the
course of nature we must be separated, but only for a little.

To deserve love, though not loved, is far better than to be
loved by mistake, not deserving love.   One may be grave;
"sorrowful but rejoicing," trembling for the many, hopeful
for himself, trying to peer into the awful, unknown future,
near and certain, while exulting in the one great assurance, that the great God of all will do right, and has plea-
ure only in the best.   To me, the most fearful fact in
the world's history is, the incarnation and suffering of
the one "I AM".

Is there one who having the felt ability to
do something, with the desire to do, yet who cannot find
that something to do?   Who has a desire to orate, but cannot find listeners; a desire to teach, but cannot find
willing pupils; a desire to be busy in a useful way, but
spending the most of his time doing nothing, or too much
like nothing?   A question that has been often put to me
by acquaintances is, "How do you spend your time, now when
at the close of a busy life you have nothing special to do?"
"Well," I reply, "I am always good company to myself; to my-"
self I am a good talker and a good listener, an earnest
talker and an appreciative listener.   Then, early habits
of thinking seriously, speaking cautiously, and acting promptly, I have carried with me into quiet life.   Drinking alcoholics, smoking tobacco, or playing cards, have no attraction
for me, nor if I mistake not ever will have.   About loving
money I am not so certain.   I have always had more pleasure in saving money than in spending it.   At the same time
I am not niggardly in giving; I give away, never less than a
tenth of my income to religious and charitable purpose but
still I like to save money, and often count what I manage

to save. I have still abundance and to spare, and am seldom at a loss for something to do." I fancy any dismalness connected with a healthy old age arises mostly when the beyond appears as a dark void, and its near approach cannot be evaded or kept out of mind. To young men I may say further, that since my teens I have always been in the habit of jotting down all money spent by me, even to a half-penny worth of apples; the habit is in many ways a good one, quite apart from saving money. Only good can come to a young man in putting conscience into the spending of his money.

A matter which presses heavily on my mind is, not altogether what "my" condition may be in that future to which we hurry on; but also the condition of many of my fellow-men around. In many ways they are as good, or better than I am; they pay their debts, they are free handed in assisting the needy, in giving to promote good causes; gentlemanly in their deportment, trying to live harmoniously with all men, and in a general way faultless so far as their social conduct is concerned. Yet, with all this right conduct and action, they appear sthangers to any hopes or desires, except in a very vague way, extending to beyond their present life. They may pray, and aim at communion with God, but they generally give no evidence of doing so, rather the reverse. In their homes they have no family worship; Sabbath with them is more of a holiday than a day to be kept holy; the religious education of their children must be extremely lax, if attended to at all, and their family life in general very different from what is expected in Bible readers and Christ followers. May not the sourness of visage,

the sadness of demeanour, the repellant manners of some
Christians be laid at the door of the fault finders whose
lives go far to occasion the defects alluded to?   In any
case, gravity and thoughtfulness do not necessarily indicate self-righteousness and hypocrisy.

I am curious to know
concerning the opinions of some leading men, and have arrived at conclusions as follows.

Emerson believes in the
immortality of the soul, and enjoins, "Obey your own heart."
He lauds virtue and morality, admires intelligence, but does
not believe in the personality of the Supreme Intelligence,
does not believe in a personal God.

Robert Browning "believ-
ed in soul, and was very sure of God."   He admired Christ,
but that he had faith in our Lord, and loved him, is by no
means clear.   Jesus Christ's claim to Divinity he calls,
"an important stumble, never seriously made by another."

Mrs. Browning, as described to us, was a Christian woman; but
in her writings at times, sympathy seems to run in wrong
channels.   Am I to love the bad because bad, rather than
the good because good?   Or is wickedness entitled to love
and sympathy, while virtue receives neither?

Carlyle only in
a very misty way, if at all, professes faith in Christianity.
Whether Theist or Pantheist, to me is by no means clear.
I think the first; but if so, why not say so?   What is man's
chief end?   Carlyle is said to have admired the answer.

J. Russell Stowell, so far as may be gathered from his writings, was a Unitarian.

George Elliot in private character was outside the pale of respectability. If at one time she professed Christianity, she by and by parted with it, utterly. With her, confession of faith, of any sort does not appear. A significant remark of hers is, that big feet in a woman is a mark of vulgarity.

Matthew Arnold does not believe in the personality of God. He speaks of "Eternal, not ourselves, that makes for righteousness." Is he a Pantheist, or anything definable? In no sense is the Bible his guide: he throws it on one side. He expects no immortality for man. Is, or was, he a materialist?

Herbert Spencer believes in an "Infinite and eternal energy unknown and unknowable, from which all things proceed." but he goes no further in the direction of Bible truth, or Evangelical Christianity. He appears to be an Agnostic and extreme Evolutionist.

John Ruskin says, "Do justly*****Whatsoever he (the Christ) saith unto you, do it." John Ruskin professed to be a believing Christian; but curiously enough streniously denied being an Evangelical.

How come these so called leaders of thought to adopt such strange opinions? Or, how come men holding such opinions to be leaders of thought, and such thought? Do they refuse to believe anything and every thing which they cannot understand? Do they despise the faith of the million, because it is the faith of the million?

Would it not be better to more carefully conserve the truth
we are in possession of, than making suggestion that instead
of throwing light on matters not understood, only tend to
make darkness more dark?

Agnosticism is hardly worth serious
consideration; that is, when it is put forward as a reason
for doing nothing.   How little do we certainly know that
is, or that may be.   Yet we continually live and act as if
we knew all about all, or most things.   We provide for to-????
morrow and the day after, as if life to us were a certainty,
or the next thing to it.   In so acting, we, for the most
part act wisely.   It is the only way we can and should act.
Certainly the future lies with God; but we must act as if
the future were known to us.   In other words we do, and
must live a life of faith.   Too often however, our faith is
wrongly placed.   No matter, Agnosticism is death.   Though
many things I do not know, I follow that which I regard as
a safe, or the safest course.   Seeing that Agnosticism can
be no excuse in life for doing nothing, or for wrong doing,
in like manner it can be no valid excuse for irreligion in
any form.   To acknowledge God in Jesus Christ, and to aim
at serving him, can never be aught but a safe course for dependent man.

Recently I went in search of a New Testament
printed in extra large type.   I called on six or eight Bib
be sellers but failed to get what I wanted.   Some of these
sellers said quite civilly, that they had no copy larger in
print than those they shewed.   But other more prominent
men, of whom I would have expected better things, positively
averred, that the sort of New Testament I wanted was not
printed.

printed.   Provoked at one of these men,I reminded him,
that he should content himself by merely saying,that such
a New Testament he had not for disposal.   In Glasgow I
bought the New Testament I wanted,double pica,four lines
to an inch,and was at the trouble to shew it to these
worthies,who went so near to telling lies.   But business
is business,they wished to sell what they had.

He was an
old croftsman,I met him in Arran,sitting on the fore part
of his cart as he drove his horse along.   He was evidently not quite sober,though not exactly drunk.   I was reading a book as I stepped along.   "Is that the Bible you
te reading?"   In Scotch fashion I replied by asking,"Do
you know what the Bible says?"No drunkard can inherit the
kingdom of Heaven."   "Tis a ---- lie."said my interrogater,
and so we parted.

An old man's thoughts are apt to revert
to old time incidents,that may be of small importance
to any one but which he likes to retail to others.   In
the Industrial School one day,John Buff,a Scotchified Cock-
ney,who was Janitor at the time,came to me complaining
that a certain biggish boy,an inmate of the school,had
seized him and thrown him down stairs.   I promised to see
to it ,and in due course made inquiries.   The boy complained of said,that it was John that tried to throw him,
the boy, down stairs,and as he did not wish to go alone he
pulled John with him.   Which of the two was exactly in
fault I could not find out; but it seemed pretty clear,
that both rolled down stairs, and possibly both equally to
blame.

Allan Grant

So we shall call him, was the son of a poor labouring man.
Very poor, thoughtful, and "castle building" was Allan.
Jamie was a companion. While the two were playing one
day by a duck pond, deep enough to drown the little fellow,
Allan fell in; but a handy woman managed to pick him out,
and Allan lived on. About the same time Allan running
across the street, fell and struck his head against the stone
wall, his brow being thereby sadly cut and bruised, but not
permantly injured. But why enumerate the accidents and
dangers that many, if not all children, encounter ere reaching manhood. Even then, dangers come not to an end. When
sent to school, Allan soon managed to become a fairly good
scholar, or rather reader, and was fond of books. Park's
books for children were among the first he read; "Jack the
giant killer", "Jack and the bean stalk", and such like.
By and by Allan would read eyerything, or anything in the
shape of a book that fell into his hands. "Boston's Four
fold State" and the "Crook in the Lot", books of his Father's
were too many for him; but the "Scotch Haggis", "Wallace and
Bruce" by Blind Harry, "The Children of the Abbey", "A Legend
of Montrose", "The Children of the Mist" and so on, were eagerly read by the boy. Eventually however, in reading fiction regarded as fact, the thought occurred to Allan, "How
could a writer retail so many words and events, which according to the writer's own shewing, were only known to the speak-
ers and actors, and could only to a very partial extent be
remembered even by them?" Hitherto Allan had thought that
whatever was printed must be true, that no one would, or could,

print a lie, at least knowingly, and even yet he not infrequently meets simple folk who think that the fact of letter press should close all further discussion.   "Again"
said Allan to himself, "in these stories I find, almost always, love and murder, one or other, and often both; I'll read
no more of them." and for many years Allan avoided them.
As an old man, now beyond three score, he still dislikes
novels; and although he has read a number of Scott's with
one or two of Dickens and Thackery's, he has not changed
his mind regarding them.   With the exception of Scott's
that have a historical value, the great majority of others
do not seem worth reading, judging stock from samples.

When twelve years of age, Allan one day amusing himself
with others of his own age, assisted in revolving a thresh-
ing mill wheel by stepping from spoke to spoke as the
wheel revolved.   Suddenly he found himself jammed between
a spoke of the wheel and the wall on which the end of the
axle rested.   He got a squeeze, with a sad fright, but was
not seriously injured.   To die then, was not intended for
him.

        Allan had a brother, David, some years younger than him-
self.   Queer little fellow, David.   If he took a fancy to
a plaything, a draigon or a tap, a picture book or toy, there
was no peace in the house till David in some form, obtained
the wished for article.   When obtained, the article might
be prized for a short time only.   In this he was merely
like other children, it may be said, but with David it was
his pertinacity that was the leading feature in his manner.

With David the desire to obtain the wished for article was
akin to a passion; other children might turn their thoughts
in another direction, but not so with Allan's brother David.
 But now, for the sequel: without going into all the path-
ways of David&s life, let us jot down a few particulars. His
education in school was very meagre.   He learned to read
and write in a fair way, being of an inquiring mind and intelligent.   In addition to his ordinary work as a tradesman, when he reached manhood he set about making models of
sailing ships.   While at work for a short time in a seaport,
he spent much of his leisure about the harbours, examining
bows, sterns, masts, yards, sails and rigging, till he was able
to construct a model ship which would have done credit to an
old sea carpenter.   Having done so far, David, for a change
took to flower gardening; the summit of his ambition being
to snatch prizes from local gardeners at their annual flower
shows; and at times succeeded in doing so.   Tiring in this
pursuit, David set about collecting birds eggs; and came to
have such a collection, that an egg of almost every Scottish
bird, if not every British one, seemed to be in his possession.
He laid them carefully aside, intending to mount them properly, as soon as he might find time from his other occupations.
He has had all the time going, a good many years now, but the
eggs remain, or do not remain, as collected.   By way of vari-
ety, David bought first a concertina, and afterwards a harmonium, and managed to perform some fair work on both for a time,
but does nothing on either now.   His next hobby was coin collecting.   He came to have many coins, various and rare, new
and old, but ultimately gave them to an acquaintance who amass-
ed in that line.   In these pursuits, David certainly obtained

his own share of amusement, if not much profit.   He seems
to have done a good deal in courting the fair sex, but somehow with indifferent success.   Too cautious, he may have
been; in any case he was clearly too slow for more than one
lady who either would not, or could not, wait.   How David
came to hunt after flint arrow heads, we cannot well say, we
cannot well say; but in time he had an extensive collection,
which he eventually disposed of to the Antiquarian Museum,
Edinburgh, receiving a few pounds for his specimens, to the
mutual satisfaction of the Museum Managers and David.   Of
anything rare, curious, or seldom to be heard of, David was,
and is, always eager to be the possessor.   These curious
odds and ends go to adorn his home.   He has an entire set
of Queen Victoria's gold and silver Jubilee coins that he
keeps in a box for future disposal.   David has seriously
thought of burying the ten pound treasure, so that some
poor fellow in due course, might have the extatic pleasure
of finding them.   A few select pictures, statuary, stuffed
birds and vases with other things of more or less value,
may be noted by occasional visitors to his house, which
with an adjoining garden is his own.   Of all these pursuits and possessions, the most we can say is, that they have
yielded, and do yield, pleasure to the man and his wife, and
give trouble to no one else.   David's latest and not unpromising source of pleasure, is a small greenhouse filled
with ferns and flowering plants.   David has never had high
wages, but has always been earning wages.   He is now married, has saved money, and expects to be able to make provis-
ion for old age, should he reach it.   Now anent all this,
can anything further be said?   Why, one thing may be said,

though often said before, that one cannot eat his cake and
have it.   Had David spent his money on beer and tobacco,
theatres and singing saloons, his condition to- day would
have been a very different one.   There is an old Scotch
proverb which in effect says, that two simultaneous good
things are unattainable.   One must choose to the right,
or to the left; both ways cannot be travelled at the same
time. . Regarding David we may further say, that he has been
a traveller, at least in his native Scotland.   He has stood
on the summit of Ben Nevis, Ben Wevis, and Ben Lomond; he has
trodden the ground of Arran, Skye, and St. Kilda; he has seen
Royalty at Balmoral, at Edinburgh Volunteer Review, and in
Jubilee year at London; and lastly he has visited Ireland:
and all this on ordinary workman's pay.   Of course, self denial in other directions had to be exercised by David.   He
did not marry when barely out of his teens, which is too much
the fashion with young men in these days, without a penny beyond his daily wages; though we fear he was at times tempted
in that direction.   David has now reached the evening of
life; but he continues in good health, and comfortably provided for as a working man.   Not a bad country, ours, even for
the working man, when he patiently works, and faithfully per-
forms, relying more on his own steady endeavours than on Trades
Unions, Strikes, and expected Socialism.   David's definition
of Socialism is, "First eat your own cake and then agitate for
the half of your neighbour's".   David had never occasion to
go on strike, and in any case would have preferred to paddle
his own canoe.   Possibly his opinions and practice may have
brought him more or less of ill will and envy; but remembering the old proverb, he has not tried to hold on to the two

goods. . In the long run, hanging by his own hook has better served his purpose than the tyranny of combination.
We do not depreciate association for laudable objects in right ways.   Insurance and friendly societies for ill health and old age, we admire; but to sink one's individuality to any low level suggested by companions or circumstances, is the last thing any man should do; even to obtain high wages.   It may be good to be an associate, but certainly it is better to be a man.   The world owes infinitely more to competition than to marching in line.
Encourage your brother to hurry, and assist him so far; but to compel him to walk fast or slow, as to you may seem good, is tyranny.   Among men generally, there is an inertia which only dire necessity can overcome.   Often there is an aversion to honest labour alongside of an extravagant desire for pleasure.   Selfishness may sound harsh, and require not a few cautions; but remove it from among men, and what in the world can fill its place or perform effectively the work it does?   David was, and is, selfish; but who is not?   He has always paid his way, and was the chief support of his widowed mother during her latter days.   He can be liberal and generous on occasions; and is generally respected, though not altogether perfect.   But David's pursuits gave pleasure to himself while doing no harm to his neighbours.   Possibly, had he got a better secular education in youth, his genius might have yielded more conspicuous results in manhood.   But not lost is a good example, that shews how a man can be happy, without making others unhappy, can live and let live, contribute his share of honest and faithful work to the community, and end his days

as David hopes to do, at peace with his fellow men and not without hope in God.

ii

Allan Grant learned at times without a master, but with the aid of books. He learned to play the flute, the accordion, and the harmonium; he taught his daughters to play the piano; he learned enough of French to enable him to read in it, though not to speak or write the language. He learned to sing at sight, and mastered Algebra as far as quadratics. He did not, nor could he, spend much time at playing chess or Draughts; they became too absorbing, so Allan had to strike. Nor did Athletics ever attract him much; but he has always been fond of walking, especially in the forest, on the hill side, by the sea shore and alone. In mentioning these pursuits, we do not always admire, nor praise Allan any more than David; but we seek to point out to young men, and perhaps to young women, the amount of genuine pleasure and enjoyment that can be obtained at trifling cost; far cheaper and superior to theatre going, dancing, petty gambling and similar pursuits. Allan never did much at free hand drawing or sketching, but derived much pleasure from the little he once attempted. He had not the opportunity of regular instruction, and much to his later regret, he did not go in search of it. To all young men and women we say, learn and practice free hand drawing, even although at first it may be tiresome. At a Drawing Class recently, an enthusiastic Teacher put the question, "Now, supposing you were to draw me,

that is my body as I stand, what part would draw first?"
"Draw your neck". said an incorrigible, and so ended that
lesson.

Was Allan ever in love?   Yes, for a good many
years, we incline to think, he was never out of it.   "Bonnie lassie that Allan, you should stick up to that lassie"
so said Jock Young. Where is Jock now?   We know not;
living or dead, he is lost to our ken.| Jock was ambitious
to rise in the world, but could not very well see how.   As
a warehouse porter his wages were ten shillings per week.
One day a hundred pounds came somehow to be talked about;
says Jock, enlivened at the thought of so much money, "Had I
a hunner poun, I wudna stop in Aberdeen five minnits."
But returning to Jock's suggestion anent the bonnie lassie,
curious how it acted on the mind of the boy of sixteen.
In a moment, so to speak, Allan was over head and ears in
love with the girl in question, a girl about his own age. To
see that girl, to speak to her, or get a smile from her, was
to Allan, if we mistake not, the most exquisite enjoyment
his nature at that time was capable of.   By and by, however,
he was cured by seeing his fair one in a bad temper.   In
course of time Allan came to love another, but with less ar-
dor.   Circumstances led to the lad shifting his quarters,
both the young women got married, and well was it for Allan
that love on his part went no farther with either of the
dear ones.   But still, the pleasure yielded by being in
love was by no means to be despised.   It led to no bad results, so far as we are aware, and was delicious while it
lasted.

When Allan was about nineteen years of age his Fa-

ther died, and Allan's mother had to look to him for assistance to live.   While his Mother lived in poor condition,
and in feeble health, the young man cheerfully and willing-
ly did what he could in the way of assisting her, and a younger brother and sister.   Remembering Allan in these times,
it seems to us that for a young man to have an old Father
or Mother depending, while his assistance is cheerfully giv-
en, is one of the greatest blessings that God in his providence can bestow upon him.   If the young man cannot marry
so soon as he would like, so much the better.   Many men marry too soon.   For most men, thirty years of age is soon enough.   If a woman whom he loves jilts him, let him be thankful to get rid of a woman who under such circumstances loves
him so little, as to jilt him.   More than likely, he will
meet another who will not jilt him, but love him more and
more while they live together.   To ardent and impatient
young women we would say, never be afraid to wait for the man
who doing his duty to his aged parents, has had to delay marriage beyond young folks wishes.   He who has been kind to
his dependent parents, will be doubly kind to his wife, and
possessed of an experience and prudence that are worth waiting for.   In a comparatively long life, Allan's purest joys,
and most satisfactory doings, connect themselves with what
he gave to his widowed Mother.   In doing so, he was not expecting any return, nor wishing for any, beyond the feeling
that doing so was right, and in accordance with the eternal
fitness of things, as arranged by him who reigns over all.

Still, Allan's Mother was poor, and had often to pray, literal-
ly for daily bread.   Allan was far, hundreds of miles, away

from his Mother, and it was sadly against the poor woman's
grain, to ask from her son more than he was in the habit
of regularly sending.   One day his Mother had only one
penny remaining in her house, no more money, nor knew she
where to find more.   But Hezekiah like, Allan's Mother
laid her case before the Lord in prayer.   Next day a re$$$
lation called unexpectedly and gave her a pound.   Poor,
simple woman, she did not regard this as a mere chance; she
thought, God had sent the friend.   On another occasion ev-
en the solitary penny was wanting.   Trouble and pain send
some people to their knees, and on this occasion trouble
sent Allan's Mother to hers.   Rising from her knees she
thought that possibly some relief might be procured by go-
ing out.   Taking a somewhat prolonged walk, but without ap-
parent result, Mother was returning home heavy hearted, com-
ing up the brae, yae ken th' place, a shilling was lying on
the ground, enough for that day's wants.   We cannot doubt,
that Allan's Mother often prayed when in want-without find-
ing a shilling, or receiving a pound from an unexpected vis-
itor; but we also know, that while life was prolonged to her,
her bread was provided, and her water was made sure: Allan's
Mother did not die from want of the necessaries of life.
Our prayers are not always answered as we would like, or as
we may expect.   Often, no special answer may be required.
We often pray in fear, for protection, when there is in real-
ity no special danger.   We may pray for that which if grant-
ed, would be no blessing to us.   Sometimes our requests may
be point blank refused, for reasons good in themselves, though
unknown to us.   We may pray for things that would be given
to us without prayer.   Many good things, and probably most

good things, on earth are given to us without prayer; and
God is often profuse in his gifts to prayerless and Godless men.

Men of little profession, at times talk of "pro-
found providences" as occurring in their experiences, when
the hearer may be somewhat sceptical as to there being
any special providence in the matter.   Allan's Mother,
however, urged him to pray; and from his Bible, Allan came
to learn, that prayer is essential to the life of a Christian; as was said of the converted Paul, "Behold he prayeth".
Allan came to pray of things important, and possibly he often
prayed concerning things not very important.   Sometimes, ###
rather hurriedly, thought his prayers were answered, or being
answered, in his wished for way, when they were not.   At other times he might think his prayers were not answered, when
in reality they were.   He may at times have prayed, pretty
much as a "Commercial" solicits orders; in dubious success,
more and more in earnest to succeed.   On occasion, he may
have prayed for certain things, when he should have refrained.   At other times he may have refrained, when it would
have been better had he prayed.   Sometimes he may have
prayed wisely, at other times as a fool.   No matter, Allan
prayed, does pray, and will continue to pray to the end, we
cannot doubt.   For eight years Allan prayed for a young
woman whom he hoped to make his wife, in due course.   That
young woman did not become his wife; she would not, or could
not wait.   But Allan's petitions were more than answered
in the woman who ultimately became his wife.   Prayers were
answered, but in a different way from what was anticipated.
Anent prayer it has been said, and correctly, that God rules

the world by laws: laws inflexible and invariable.   Quite
true, but is it not also true, that by an act of will, even
regarding it as a law, a man in many cases can interfere,
if not to alter a law, to modify, divert, or avert its action.
A boy throws a ball into the air; law says the ball must
fall back to the ground.   By an act of will, at the request
of a companion, the boy with his hand can catch the ball, and
toss it again and again into the air.   So, an act of will
as distinguished from material law, may change the course, or
arrest the action of a law.   Can we suppose God as giving
a power to man which God cannot, or does not reserve to himself?   Needs one ask a question which admits of only one
answer?   Or as the Bible in another way puts it, "Does he
who made the eye not see? Does he who made the ear, not
hear?"   Or, will our Creator alone, refuse to listen to the
prayers of his creatures, however earnestly presented, or
answer urgently required?   Is man more merciful than God?
Is our fellow man more worthy of trust than our maker?   Is
it conceivable, that God has made a creature better than
God himself?   And even when prayers are in vain, as in certain cases they may be, does not the inclination, the tendency, the ability to pray, imply a hearer, an answerer of prayer?   Yet it is a difficulty, the question; one may pray to
a piece of rotten wood, to a holy stone, to a relic, and all
in vain.   Such prayers prove, that the supplicant is super-
stitious, if not foolish; may they not however, prove something more? an instinct that prayer is in a direct way pow-
erful, may be not in vain; like typical organs in the male
sex that indicate a purpose, a truth, in the being of the
race?   Bad coins imply good coins, and wrong roads imply

right ones.   True, men have spent much time in trying to
square the circle, to find the elixir of life, to transmute
base metals into gold, but all in vain.   Men make mistakes,
and may sail on utterly wrong tacks; but truth is true, and
its tracks and spoors are found in all directions.   With
care and patiencetruth in many ways can be traced and iden-
tified, though to its full extent it is probably, or we may
say certainly , unattainable by man.   By prayer much may be
gained.   By sincere prayer, nothing can be lost.   Smile
not, sneer not , if Allan continues to pray.   In praying, he
is neither a rogue nor a fool.   A man may pray that the
sun rise tomorrow, that trees bud in spring, that suitable
weather be given to ripen the crops.   All these events may
occur, probably, if not certainly, without prayer.   All the
same we like to think, that men are praying for them.   He
is a craven who never prays in fair weather, but only in the
storm.   He is a mean coward who never prays in health, but
who sends for priest or minister when on the eye of death.
"You pray for a good crop, while I do not pray" says a doubt-
er, "and by and by see who has the best crop."   An unbeliev-
ing eccentric shoemaker, known to us, put prayer to the test
in this manner, so he said.   He cut out tops for a pair of
boots, put them carefully by themselves in a corner, and as
he was in a hurry, prayed that the job might be finished before morning.   Going to find them at an early hour he was
sadly put out to see that a single stitch had not been put
in to them.   The man's story might occasion a ribald laugh,
that was all; and so may others like it.   Prayer is not answered to encourage laziness, any more than miracles are performed to gratify idle curiosity.

When Allan was a little fellow, like other such, he tumbled
occasionally., .Instead of rising and proceeding on his
way, his habit was to lie and roar, till some one lifted him.
In after years Allan.made a point of never lifting any fallen child till satisfied that the child could not rise without assistance.   We repeat, that in praying, young and ardent folk are prone to jump to conclusions; that prayer by
singular events is answered, when time may shew their surmisings to
be wrong.   Then, urgent and anxious prayers lay them open
to frequent and, not unlikely, humbling suppositions.   People who never pray, will not lay themselves open to experience disappointments.

At Cape Coast Castle resided a Christ-
ian negro; the following relation is is substantially the
negro's own.   He left his home, and as a seaman was absent
for a long time.   Home sick he returned to find a much
loved brother had left C.C.C., and had gone, no one knew
where.   Sam, as we shall call him, was a Christian man, and
so a praying one, prayed earnestly, and with a sorrowful
heart, that he might be directed so as to find his brother,
Jim.   Sam had heard of London and thought that Jim might
be there.   He started, and by partly working, partly paying
his way, reached Hamburg.   In Hamburg he had to spend, or
lose, almost all his money, and on telling his story to a
company of sailors and others in a lodging house, of his pro-
posal to go to London in search of Jim, was only laughed at;
he might as well go search for a needle in a hay stack.
Sam's remaining money was barely sufficient to pay his passage to London, but in due course next evening he landed in
the mammoth city, entered an eating house, and ate a humble

meal.   Falling into conversation with some of the inmates, Sam told his story, as having come from C.C.C., when the land- lady interrupted him with the exclamation, "Why there is a C.C.C. man next door, come and see him."   It was Sam's bro- ther, Jim.   Now, some may say, "happy chance", but we question whether an angel from heaven would be able to convince pray- ing Sam, that his prayers had not been answered.   Allan has sometimes thought, that not a little of his well being, per- haps also his well doing if any, in life, he owes to the pray- ers of a poor labouring man while on his way to daily toil, wearing his life out to keep life in: that man his Father.

How touchy young people are, for the most part, concerning re- marks, made by others, as to their personal appearance. What pain they have, Byron like, to endure over bodily defects, even when said defects are more imaginary than real. Allan's Father was a good intelligent man; but how cruelly he made his little boy suffer by remarks about his "black hair", his "big lang heed", the way in which the boy's hair grew "doon his back", his "coo lick", and so on.   To unnecessarily hurt his boy's feelings, was far from his Father's intention, but thoughtlessly he did so.   Thereby we may be taught a lesson; never to make remarks concerning the personal defects, or ev- en the personal appearance of any boy or girl, when they are in no way responsible for them.   If a boy can remedy a de- fect in his person or manner, do not hesitate to urge him thereto by such fair means as may be available, even not ex- cluding ridicule and laughter, when by them a good purpose may be achieved.   But to laugh at a boy, or to give him a nickname, so ever reminding him of a defect, for which he is not responsible, and cannot cure, is in a teacher or guardian highly blamable. even when only fun may be intended, and the want of thought the only available excuse.

Allan, a number of years ago, but then a married man, taking a customary walk on a country road, met a good looking young woman whom he noticed was wofully intoed. He had met her before this time, and frequently met her again as a stranger to him. He on this occasion spoke to the young woman pleasantly pointed out her defect, and said how, he thought, she might cure it. Meeting the maiden in subsequent walks, Allan would glance at her toes and smile; the girl would also smile, while try ing to direct aright the refractory members; and in passing, Allan would make a kind and encouraging remark. Before very long the young woman managed to guide her toes all right, was profuse in thanking a stranger for pointing out a defect, that she could, and did cure, but which no one else had been at the trouble to take any notice of, at least with a view to curing the eyesore which it was to Allan, if not to the woman herself. So there may be a right and a wrong way of noticing bodily defects in others; especially among the young. Where in such cases there is no remedy, the right and kindest way is to act and speak as if the defect did not exist; and so help the subject to forget it, if possible.

How often does a chance step, a chance meeting, a seeming bagatelle in life, turn its whole volume into a new channel? Some may regard the incidents as only a chance; others, Allan among the number, will ever in such events see the guidance of an overruling power, God's guidance. . One day in Trongate, Glasgow, Allan intended, if possible, to engage himself in a Warehouse of indifferent repute; but instead of going straight in, a something led him to take a few steps past the door. Returning to enter, he met an acquaintance who strongly advised him against offering his services in that quarter. Allan did not enter; the three or four aimless steps changed the current of his life on that occasion. At another time what might be regarded as a chance glance at an advertisement in the Glasgow Herald formed an important link in the chain of his life's experiences. We presume, such experiences are, or were, not peculiar to Allan.

As a young man out of his teens and half through his twenties, Allan had what young men enjoy with much zest, at least Allan did. He had some acquaintances among the other sex, not always younger than himself; at times they were so much older that he thought he might enjoy more or less of the pleasant ways of courtship without incurring any of its responsibilities. Rather risky these friendships may be, and probably are. While the young man is merely seeking the enjoyment of friendly intercourse for a season, the woman, though considerably his senior, may take matters more seriously, and may unpleasantly say so at a time really inconvenient. When Allan in due time arranged to get married, he received an epistle from a lady upbraiding him for his cruelty and desertion; the last thing he would have thought upon from that quarter. He could not see how anything he had done or said could have given occasion to the lady to allow such a bee to go bumming in her bonnet. Allan handed the letter to his intended who very promptly sought

out the complaining fair one, and somehow the business was
settled, or fought out, between them; satisfactorily, at
least on one side, and the wedding took place.   But we anticipate; these remarks belong to later on.

Courting with-
out serious intentions, may involve things unexpected, and
annoying, as Allan on one occasion found out.   Enjoying
the acquaintance of a lady, his senior, and regarding the
pleasure as a safe investment, things went on safely enough
till one day a mutual acquaintance informed Allan that the
lady in question was about to be married to another acquaintance whom Allan could not but regard as a less suitable
match for the lady than he himself would have been. He felt
as if he had got a sudden blow in the stomach,   No matter,
he assumed a brave face, and as early as convenient found
out the couple's new residence, went to see them, and continued friendly ever after.

Allan was getting through the twen-
ties in his life and thought that if he was to get married
at all much more delay was not desirable.   He put much
more importance on a woman's character than on her mere personal appearance, and though not indifferent to good looks
and handsome figure, yet had become pretty well proof against
the latter in absence of a satisfactory former.   He had no
idea of marriage till fully able to support a wife and possible contingencies.   He would never ask a woman to enter a
lower station with him, than what she had hitherto been accus-
tomed to.   Then curiously enough, Allan could not, or did not,
see what objection a woman fairly his equal would, or could,
have to him, if not otherwise engaged.   He was all right, and

would make the best of husbands; if that did not appear
very clear to the woman before marriage, she would find it
out in due course.   Allan did not meet with many, one of
whom he would have liked to make his wife, whatever her opinions of him might have been.   Indeed, before or after,
we do not think he ever saw or met another woman who was
so exactly what he wished and prayed for as the one he
was ultimately united to, (a common experience, it is to be
hoped.)   The light headedness of some was at variance
with his own sobriety.   The vanity and extravagance $$ ap-
parent in others were beyond his approval and his means.
The impudent eagerness of one or two to cultivate acquaint-
ance repelled him; and perhaps above all, the danger of be-
coming a victim made him cautious.   We have all, more or
less, faults in our character, but we do not care to shew
them to those whom we wish to please.   Allan so fully re-
cognised this that he actually ventured on the dangerous
experiment of saying something to his intended calculated
to make her angry; he wishing to find out how she would
look and behave when provoked, by criticism of her dress we
think it was.   The test, though bordering on the audacious,
and unfair, was a successful one.   Perhaps however, it were
well to remember, that if sufficiently astute, two can play
at such games.

When circumstances seemed favourable to Allan
for seriously looking out for a wife(for that is all the
length we have got yet.) he inquired at a matronly lady, an
acquaintance, who knew a good many young women, if she could
recommend him to one; and without much hesitation she named
two; either of whom, she thought, would suit Allan very well.

Of course this lady could not say whether the nominees
might not be otherwise engaged, though that, she thought,
might be ascertained without much difficulty.   She, Allan's
friend, would not do the work of an agent, nor did he contem-
plate her doing so.   One of the nominees he could not fancy; the other he thought, might turn out the very article
wanted.   In a somewhat cavalier manner Allan sent the chosen one a letter relating pretty much as has been stated
here.   Allan's elderly lady friend had such a high opinion
of him, that it did not seem to occur to her, that any other
woman could think less of him than she herself did, and so
gave full liberty to use her name as might be advisable.
Before any reply came to Allan he met the young lady at tea,
and it was arranged that he, happy man, should walk home with
her.   With no unnecessary delay the young man broached the
subject nearest his heart, and with a pitty-pattying held
his breath for a reply.   But O, poor Allan, the avalanche of
abuse, of all that was contemptible and mean, of all that was
presumptious, proud, and impertinent, almost made the much to
be pitied young man wonder in all the earth what had happened to the lady or what was wrong with himself.   For an
hour or more Allan tried to vindicate his conduct, and to
convince the lady that to listen favourably to him was the
right thing for her to do, but all to no purpose.   With a
sad heart he had to bid the fair one good night.   If his
intentions were right, he had gone about the business in the
wrong way.   Thinking then, and thinking still, that there
was a misunderstanding on the youyg woman's part, Allan said
to himself that he would give her three years to think over
the matter, and meantime try and possess his soul in patience.

Allan did not in a hurry propose marriage to another,but
rather sought to find whether by correspondence and further acquaintance a better understanding might not be arrived at,   Why the lady should make such a fuss over such
an innocent suggestion Allan has not to this day been able
to find out.   A male friend,whom Allan made his confidant,
said, "One thing was clear,the lady does not love you nor
wish to have you."   That was a rather brutal assertion;for
Allan cannot altogether admit its truth,though there may
have been some truth in it.   It has been said,that the
next best thing to being well loved is to be cordially hated;
to be regarded with indifference is a poor sort of flattery.
A young woman,not then very young,told the writer,that she
refused to marry the only man she ever truly loved.   She
could assign no reason for refusing beyond caprice or self
will; the young man seemed to love her dearly,and was all
that her heart could wish.   "I'll maybe get him yet,"she
said,but soon after,she got married to another,whom it was
to be feared she did not love.   The lady was getting old,
and her former lover may have taken her at her word.   When
Allan told his elderly lady friend how he had succeeded,or
rather not succeeded,she was surprised, "She might go farther
and fare worse.",but any more than Allan she could not clearly understand the matter.   Afterwards,Allan thought that a
third party,a mutual acquaintance,had thoughtlessly,but un-
intentionally,done mischief with her woman's loose tongue,
but he did not know,and did not try to find out.   His old
landlady,Mrs.F. a Dumfriesshire woman,big,rough spun,and in-
quisitive to a degree,somehow came to know of Allan's want
of success.   Allan had always paid his bills punctually,and

so was a favourite with Mrs.F. "Saucy hizzie,niver mine,
Allan,ther's a lassie waitin for yae,mine I'm tellin yae,
she's waitin for yae,mine what I'm sayin",and so on. Rather indistinct all this,but still not discouraging to the
poor fellow,and Mrs.F.in the long run turned out right.
She met Allan's wife years after and was highly pleased
with her. Our hero's haughty.rejector still lives;whether
she ever regretted riding the/high horse we do not know.
In any case that could not affect matters now. The lady
remains unmarried,and having now passed the three score
years is likely to remain so. In various ways Allan had,
and has reason,to regard her as a good,intelligent ,and ,
superior woman. But women for the most part allow themselves to be governed more by their feelings than by cool
and sound considerations. Better reliance can be placed
on the calm sagacity of a man,than on the passionate im-
pulses of most women. Allan waited in accordance with his
resolve,for nearly three years,writing occasional letters
to his rejector,but receiving only ambiguous answers. Then,
thinking that he had done his part fairly well,he somewhat
abruptly dropped the whole business,bade the lady goodbye,
and set himself to look for a wife in another direction.
He was now in his thirtieth year,and if a man should not
marry too soon,neither should he delay too long; if twenty
is too soon,forty is rather late,and batchelorism had no
charms for Allan.

          Years before Allan's experience as related
above,there lived in another part of the country an only
daughter of a worthy couple. In her teens the girl had
fancies,and one of them was,that if she ever changed her

name, the one name she would like above all others would
be the surname which Allan bore.   That of all names was
the prettiest in her estimation; though at that time she
knew absolutely nothing of Allan, and he knew nothing of
her.   She was not wanting in suitors, but she had to wait
for Allan.   As Mrs.F.had said, the lassie was waiting for
him, though at that time Mrs.F. knew as little of the young
woman as Allan himself.   Subsequent to Allan's sore dis-
appointment as he now and then made his way through the
public park to the news room he now and again met a young
woman who turned out to be the waiting one, though an entire stranger to him at these times.   The two by no means
looked at each other, but somehow each found out, or formed
an opinion as to what the other was like.   Of Allan's
name, character, or occupation, Mary, as we shall call her,
knew nothing.   But on consideration, apart from particulars
quite unknown to her, she arrived at the conclusion, that if
she should ever think of a husband that was the sort of man
she could like.   Allan was not quite so ignorant concerning Mary as she was concerning him, or rather he had found
out sooner than she did.   Without going into details suffice it to say, that Allan found means to get himself intro-
duced into Mary's parents house.   He spoke to Mary, and
Mary seemed pleased to speak to him.   Before long he vol-
unteered to teach Mary music, and Mary was willing to be
taught.   Going to see the old folk, as Allan pretended, one
evening he found that they were both out, but Mary was in.
"Can I ever get a better, or so good a chance" thought Allan,
and without much circumlocution he asked Mary if she would
consent to be married to him.   Not exactly that, but rather

would she agree to think and talk the matter over, say for
a few months, each side being free to make or break the engagement without offence given or taken.   In that time
they could reasonably learn enough of one another; thorough
and knowledge of one another Allan considered necessary before buckling to for life.   So far Allan had done the
speaking, Mary mostly looking at her fingers as they lay in
her lap.   He alluding to his ability to keep a wife, Mary
not unwisely asked Allan what his income was and got a satisfactory reply.   The question was regarded as encouraging,
and further when Mary said that she would not marry without
her parents' consent, he thought he had done pretty well for
one night and forthwith took his leave, cordially shaking
hands and promising to return soon.   A sensible girl thought
Allan, she should to him make a good wife: and so it eventually turned out.

In the town of Montrose, on the links, many
years ago, as the story was given to the writer by one who
professed to know the parties concerned, the incident as here
related took place.   We understand that a similar story has
been related concerning David Hume, but no matter.   On a
summer evening might be seen as stated a lady and gentleman
both clearly out of their teens, but by no means old.   Turning somewhat abruptly to his companion the gentleman said
to her, "Will you marry me?"   As promptly as Lady Jean to the
laird of Cockpen the lady said "No".   Forthwith the couple
resumed their conversation, finished their stroll, and went to
their respective abodes.   Not long after, the pair met again.
accidentally of course, and as on past occasions walked together.   By and by the lady, it was her turn this time, addres-

sed the gentleman, "Do you remember the question you put
to me the last time we were walking together?" "Yes",
was the reply. "Because I have now changed my mind on
that subject." "I have also changed mine" said the brute,
and so ended what otherwise might have been a very interesting sequel. Our informant said that neither of the
pair got married, each remaining single through life. More
sense with less sentiment would perhaps be better on both
sides than is often the case when marriage is contemplated
or desired. Perhaps men make mistakes when with the best
intentions, and regarding good motives as sufficient, they
dispense with all sentiment and ceremony, as if buying a
cow, or engaging a domestic servant. But on the other hand
when a woman is asked to marry a man, or correspond with
marriage in view, she should not give a mortifying refusal,
but rather request time for consideration. In any case
she needs not say "No" while in reality wishing to say
"Yes" without undue humility. There are however curious
phases in the feminine mind. We have known two women, and
there may be more, who concerning their husbands said, and
we believe honestly, that they never loved them, but consent-
ed to become their wives simply to get rid of their impor-
tunities. They had both reason to regret their foolish
steps, we know. When a young man and woman come to be $$$
placed so much in one another's company, and are so pleased
with one another that attachment follows as a matter of
course, they cannot well be blamed sometimes for imprudence,
even when marriage involves it. To young men who have a
tolerably free hand in the matter of marriage, our advice
grounded on Allan's experience, is to this effect. Remain

238

somewhat shy and distant,but not disagreeable,in your intercourse with the other sex.   We rather think that Allan at
times feigned an indifference to ladies which he certainly
did not feel,making his doing so a sort of armour to shield
himself against entanglements.   He liked the company of
the lasses,but steered clear of engagements.   In doing so
we think he may have been wrong.   A young man has no right
to run after a young woman merely to amuse himself,or to
pass a pleasant hour.   In doing so he may frighten away an
earnest and eligible would be suitor from a young woman who
has not many to choose from.   We have in our mind a young
man,not Allan,eager and honourable,who was too humble or
too proud to advance in the presence of another who was in
reality no suitor,nor had any intention of becoming one.
When able and willing look around,beware of thin ice,be
bluff and straight forward,and avoid long courtship.   Remember Dr.Chalmers' phrase "The expulsive power of a new affection."   All that is wanted to make wreck of an old love
is to meet one who can be loved a little better.   Write no
love letters,but be faithful to all promises,be cautious in
promising.   Do not take a refusal too much to heart,but do
not say,"I do'nt care".   Say that you are very sorry,but
hope to survive the refusal; and so try again in another
quarter.   More than likely,as Mrs.F. said to Allan,"You
will find a lassie waiting for you."   Do as Allan did and
you will do very well; barring his rashness on one occasion
when the encounter wounding left a scar,at least on his
poor ardent soul.   Fifty years ago,old Sandy Taylor,a draper at the North East corner of Market Street,Union Street,
Aberdeen,served Allan,then a boy in his teens,with a few

yards of furniture stripe to match a pattern.   Old Sandy
had produced the very thing and said to Allan, "If you're
as weel matched in gettin a wife you'll dae."   It was
very kind in the old man to say that; the boy was grateful, and always remembered the interesting observation.
Sandy was a great bather, and swimmer we presume.   Allan
remembers seeing him breasting the waves on Aberdeen sandy
beach in the bright summer mornings.   To married and unmarried alike there is given a time, a season, longer or shorter, the longest is not long.   To some, life is very short. To
others, comparatively short may in results prove very long.
But let not Allan or anyone who has lived over three score
years in good health and comfort, complain anent the short-
ness of time, or the near approach of death.   He who complains that he is growing old, in reality complains that he
has not died sooner, that the sooner he dies the better.   So
far, Allan has had his appointed time, his opportunities of
doing or not doing, of setting himself to live and die as
may be now and hereafter.   No more is given to any man,
king, commoner or outcast.   Young men should start with
their eyes open; young women should remember that life on
earth is not for ever.   But let neither man or woman unite
on earth with one they would not wish to live with in Eternity.
nity.

iv

Allan on leaving home at the age of fifteen, for the city of
Aberdeen found all the novelty anticipated by a country boy.
He soon became acquainted with other boys, and more or less

became like them.   Attending Trinity Free Church Sabbath
School (David Simpson then minister),Allan with some other lads were too many for their teacher,George Grant,Advo-
cate,not over competent,followed by others less competent.
Allan and his companions were more intent on fun on the
Sabbath evenings than eager for religious instruction.
Coming into Church as the scholars were assembling,one boy
would make it his business to open all the pew doors in
the long passage as he came along. The next comer hurrying to the class would shut every door with a bang,to the
evident amusement of his companions already in their seats,
and to the annoyance of the teacher; that is if he happened
to be forward in time to see the sport. Teachers should
aim at being first in their places,not last. When School
was dismissed Allan with Johnny,his chum,were much given to
following certain girls of their own age,and possibly the
girls liked to be followed,with a view to gallanting and idle talk. Allan knew such doings to be wrong,felt them to
be wrong,but did not promptly discontinue them,and no excuse
on Allan's behalf will here be offered. The annual soiree
of the Sabbath School came to be held in the Mechanics'Hall
Market Street,and Allan was there. The children sat in the
gallery; members of the congregation sat in the front area.
Approval or applause when expected from the audience was the
signal for the bigger,and seemingly the majority of the boys,
to start with their feet a regular tramp,tramp,thump,thump,
"like a mighty army",carrying on the movement without any apparent coming to an end. The Reverend David,good man,was
doing his best from the platform to restore order,but with
only partial success. He gave out the hymn,very popular

then, which had a refrain, "Never part again, what, never part again"? and so on, when a companion next him drew Allan's attention to the singing of certain boys who were lustily giving a rendering which we fancy drove the hymn out of practice, at least in the Free Trinity School. We never hear the hymn sung now. It may be said, why relate all this? Just to say that in organising children's meetings whether Sabbath School or others, if competent teachers cannot be obtained, and strict discipline enforced, better to discontinue the meetings. Unless this can be done, these meetings do more harm than good. When Allan and his class companions sat in the Church pew laughing and frolicking under a teacher who was ingapable of keeping them in order, or imparting instruction, though a licentiate of the Church, they, the boys, were ashamed of their conduct; but that it strangely did not mend matters till things came to such a pass, that the class had to be removed to a room outside the Church premises, and under another teacher got on much better. Indeed so much was conduct improved, that return to the old quarters was proposed and carried out. But poor Allan could not trust himself there again. Fun in his opinion was too likely to reassert itself. He would rather leave the School and go elsewhere. During the remainder of his Aberdeen experiences he attended a Sabbath morning meeting conducted by Mr. Laing, Coach Builder and will remember his kind and wise counsels while he lives. Allan's chum, John Mc. Hardie continued to attend Trinity School; he was a bit of a wag, and occasionally gave Allan scraps of information as to how things in the Sabbath School were getting on. From John's account matters did not seem

to have mended much.   "O," said John" there has been some
rows, and new rules are to be enforced as intimated by the
Superintendent from the lectern. Unruly boys are to be
dealt with thus; on first occasion of misconduct a boy will
be admonished; on second occasion he willbe more duly and
more impressively admonished; but on a third occasion he
will be kicked out with all due solemnity."   How the new
rules worked out Allan never learned.   Allan was a message
boy in Andrew Sutherland & Sons warehouse.   Boys who in
those days had to remember items, to prevent forgetting
would tie a short bit of thread round the little finger of
one hand, removing the thread when occasion for its use had
passed away.   One day Allan observing such a remember-er
on John's finger, asked him what it was for?   "O, nothing in
particular just now" replied John, "but I have so many things
to mind, that I do not think it worth while to take it off;
it will do for the next thing."   A week or two elapsed, during which time Allan had not seen John Mc.Hardie.   On Sabbath in leaving the Church, Allan asked a mutual acquaintance if he had recently seen Mc.Hardie?   The reply was, "Mc.
Hardie's dead and in his grave."   Note here the turning
point in Allan's life.   Not once, but many times, did he ask
himself the question"Why was John taken, and Allan left?"
The last time that Allan saw his chum was in Skene Terrace;
he seemed to be dull, and replying to Allan, said, "I'm not
weel at a'man, something wrang wi'my head."   His illnes
was of short duration, and ended as mentioned, in death.   The
boy was an orphan and resided with an uncle.   Dark and
gloomy were Allan's thoughts for many days.   In a Church
adjoining Belmont Street, South end, on a Sabbath evening

Allan went to the service. It was conducted by an old
minister who, it was said, had been at some time previously, confined in a lunatic asylum. His texts were in ii Chron.
xiv, 11, and xx, 12. The old man's preaching affected the
lad; he had to turn his face to the wall. On returning
to his lodgings he went to his room, and locking the door
turned his face upward and there and then became a new
boy. Beginning a new leaf, Allan became what he is to-day,
and undoubtedly will continue to be to the end of his pil-
grimage. . The change was a real one, call it what one may,
Calvinism, conversion, free will, or the new birth. The
facts of a man's inner life are not less real than the facts
of his outer.

When about twenty-four years of age Allan passed through that not unique experience among young men, when
every thing, if not every one, appeared to be against him, and
the unknown future could not be even guessed. Praying continually for direction and guidance in varied circumstances,
for a time he was inclined to regard himself as utterly forsaken as to the how, the why, and the wherefore of his goings
in life. Allan had left the Green Isle unwisely, as his
friends thought and advised, and steered his way to Glasgow.
Arthur & Co. had just started business in Miller Street and
a friend advised him to try and find a "crib" there. He
did so, and was engaged by James at forty-five pounds a year,
"to begin with". Forty-five pounds, after paying board and
lodgings and other requisites, did not leave much to assist
Mother, and virtually nothing to put in the Bank, so Allan
was anxious to obtain more. In reply to an advertisement
he called on the flourishing firm of D.& J. Mc. Donald, Sewed
Muslin Manufacturers

and was offered fifty pounds.   Thereafter, addressing Mr.
Arthur rather uncerimoniously and ~~mysteriously~~ untimeously,
he asked for an advance, got an unsatisfactory reply, and
there and then resigned.   James Arthur was very angry.
Allan had his misgivings as to the step he had taken, but
could only shift and enter the service of the Mc.Donalds.
This firm were at the time arranging for great alterations
in their mode of doing business, and in a short time Allan
was discharged.   The Mc.Donalds failed with huge liabilities, the Western Bank being principal creditors. · After
much hunting here and there for a situation, Allan entered
the retail warehouse of Kevan & Buttle, corner of Argyll
Street and St. Enoch's Square. This was a sore down come to
the man; for he was now a man, though still possessed by a
boy's feelings and vague longings.   It was eight o'clock
most nights ere he reached his lodgings, and on Saturdays
not till between ten and eleven at night.   It was sore
for a lad, for except in age he was nothing else, fond of
reading, out of town walking, and leisure for pursuits intellectual and improving.   Things in Kevan & Buttles were evidently going backwards, always an unpleasant factor in an
establishment, and Allan by invitation got a situation in
Campbell, Donald & Sellars, Candleriggs.   This Firm, like
the other, was on the "down grade".   When such is the case
there is always a tendency to blame the salesman; and before
long Allan was told to shift, and did so, but out into the
void.   In his experiences he was getting rapidly mixed; but
in time got a berth at selling machinery under the guidance
of a very "cute" American.   After some further buffetings
Allan eventually sailed into comparatively smooth waters.

and moved steadily ahead for forty years thereafter. But
now, why all this blind groping about? Why so many wise
and unwise, mostly unwise, proceedings? Why so many difficulties in finding out, or arriving at the right path? At
times Allan's thoughts were, "O to be a soldier, to do, and only
do, what one is commanded"; and so throw the entire respon-
sibility of life and conduct, so far, on her Majesty's service. But the young man had a Mother and a duty to perform
to her; moreover she was praying for him; he did not join
the army. Looking back at these hinderances, as they then
appeared, worries and discouragements, leading eventually into
the right path, Allan now can only say, that as "blind he was
brought by a way which he knew not", and was not forsaken.
The most striking fact in all this is that had Allan been
wiser and more prudent, things, so far as we can judge, would
not have gone so well with him. The most foolish things he
did went to formulate his after advancement.

Giving was always
part of Allan's religion, and when the skies began to clear a
little he gave more particular attention to the matter. In
assisting his Mother when his salary was one pound a week barely, he was giving as much as could be reasonably expected of
him; but after his Mother's death, when he was twenty-six
years old, he decided to give not less than a tenth of his income to religious and charitable purposes. Since then he
has adhered to his resolve, and now in old age, looks back with
satisfaction that he has not faltered in the matter. Apart
from any special blessing expected in so doing, there has been
to Allan much solid pleasure in the habit. Putting his
tithe into a small box, regularly as he received his wages, he

was, and is, always ready to give without a grudge to approved objects; and we are not sure but that his care and econ-
in other directions, somewhat enforced by his tithe giving,
more than compesated for all that he gave, or has given, away,
We earnestly recommend the adoption of this plan, by young
men who can afford to do so.   Acting in this manner will
not likely be regretted.   Like most good habits, in youth
the habit will be most easily learned.   Trying to get old
people to adopt the practice for the first time would be to
expect to much of fallen human nature.   Allan

                                        may be regard-
ed as quite an ordinary sort of man; for that very reason
his and similar biographies should be written.   Biographies
mostly are written of great men alone.   It is difficult to
read any other.   Very few men aim at, or expect, becoming
great as a Newton, a Milton, a Washington, a Watt, a Nelson, or
a Knox.   The examples of such men, their works, their achievements, in the way of exciting emulation, are to the great majority worthless.   But the reliable biography of a poor
struggling, half educated, ill informed boy from youth to manhood, and through it, ups and downs, downs and ups, monotonous
enough it may be, but on the whole trending upwards and upwards, till comparatively high enough as life draws to an
end, is a worthy study for all that care to read; and not
without encouragement to all anxious and pessimistic toilers
in a mingled world.

            When our friend was in his twenties he
got the idea into his head that he was a poet, or might become one.   He wrote many verses and much rhyme, but with no
clear purpose, and mostly without connected meaning.   He

thought that rhyme and poetry were synonymous terms. The rhyming however gave him much pleasure, if otherwise no profit. Not feeling very sure about his poetical genius, he tried to get his minister's opinion concerning it. His minister's opinion was of too negative a cast to give much encouragement to the aspirant. Subsequently, the poems so called, were put into the hands of an amateur critic, who in a few sentences opened Allan's eyes sufficiently to see that poetry was not his fort. He can still versify, but seldom does. Much that has been written and dubbed poetry Allan has no pleasure in reading, and aims not at remembering. From our leading poets, only a few selections find favour with matter of fact Allan. All$$ the same, if writing verses gives but a portion of the pleasure to the ambitious as composing gave to Allan, we would strongly advise becoming a poet as a delightful relaxation and harmless conceit.

What about conceited men and women? As a rule, such are not loved, at least by those who have a considerable amount of conceit themselves. Some sensible people merely laugh at the conceited ones, or regard them with compassion. But how will pride and conceit ultimately affect the possessors of them? Will the truth when fairly seen in this world, or in the next, result in depression and mortification corresponding to the pleasant illusions that previously filled the soul of the conceited one? Or, will men laugh at their previous selves as grown men laugh at their freaks in childhood? It is a question more easily asked than answered. How desirable to hear the truth, to ascertain the truth, about one's self, and to receive the truth as truth. How desirable to

to be told the truth concerning one's self by those competent to tell it, and kindly communicate it; and when the truth
tells against one, he tries to remedy the evils that the
truth reveals.   And yet Allan must be true to himself, even
true to what may be his false conceits.   Often in his opinions and in his assertions he seems to stand alone, unyield-
ing so far, yet willing to be put right if convinced that he
is wrong.   He tries to have the courage of his convictions,
but at times has felt nervous before an unsympathetic audience.   What are, or has been, Allan's faults?   Perhaps a
reader of these pages can detect not a few.   At a lecture,
where Allan was present, a number of characteristic sketches
of men were given by the speaker.   These sketches were by
no means flattering to the supposed owners; nor to any one
of them would Allan like to subscribe as being a description
of himself; but he could not avoid thinking, that there were
points in each that might have been applied to himself without injustice.   Rightly or wrongly, he has to submit to ad-
monitions from his wife and others, though rarely convinced
that he is wrong and they right.   He confesses to an eagerness to criticise, to find fault with rather than praise his
neighbours and acquaintances, and very scant in giving praise,
or esteeming others better than himself.   Some have esteem-
ed Allan, but other some have most cordially hated him.
These experiences, we suppose, fall to the lot of most men.
To know a man, one must reside with him.   Faults at the Home
fire side cannot be hid.   Allan has been, and is, fond of argument; in this he is only a true Scotchman.   In all questions
there is a right and a wrong.   It should be easier to de-
fend the right, than to make plausible the wrong.   Outspoken

utterances have sometimes made more enemies than friends.
On such occasions friends might privately pat Allan on the
back, and approve his sayings, but in the matter of giving
outspoken support they were dumb; their courage was at
fault, we suppose.   At times Allan would attack the fallac-
ious reasoning of another in a cause to which he was in
reality friendly.   It is not good when a man's falls out
with his friends, and fails to conciliate his enemies.
Anent conceit, old Captain Mc.Nab said to Allan that if the
conceit were taken out of some folk, there would be very
little left.   Whether he meant the remark for a personal
one was not very clear.   But on a subsequent occasion the
Moderator, to be, of the Free Church Assembly told Allan plaint
ly that he had his own share of conceit.   They had been ar-
guing about total abstinence, Allan being dogmatic in his assertions.   But curiously, this old Divine himself became a
total abstainer in his latter days.

                              Queen Victoria is dead.
To one who has lived during her entire reign, who remembers
her marriage, the birth of the Empress Dowager of Germany,
the birth of our reigning King, princes, and princesses, the
Queen's visits to Scotland and Ireland with State appear-
ances in England, her Reviews of Army and Navy, her recept-
ions and bestowal of honours, the Executive of a great, if
not the greatest Empire the world has ever seen, conducted
in her name, her Jubilees and length of days, length of our
Queen's reign, with the progress, discoveries, and inventions
of that reign, accompanied with the loyalty and love of her
subjects on whom the sun never sets, what is the prominent
thought in our mind on our Queen's demise?   This one cer-

tainty, that of all the world can bestow, in the most favourable circumstances, it may be slowly, but with the same certainty that the sun sets on a summer evening, these clories,
these blessings come to an end; and I as others stand on
the brink of the grave.

$$\text{\$}$$

LOVE, WHAT MEANS IT?

We love God, because he first loved us." What is exactly
meant by love? We know how a mother loves her baby. It
is perhaps, the purest form of love known to us on earth.
A young man loves a young woman, but its purity is another
question. Too often, it turns out to be love merely for
himself. An undemonstrative young man gives his poor widowed Mother, with whom he is not residing, ten shillings weekly to assist in keeping her comfortable. It is a kind of
love which his Mother appreciates highly. In India there
prevails a famine. Though not professing any special love
to these starving people, I give a donation to assist in
feeding them. My doing so may be called a love approved
by God. I admire beautiful scenery; to say that I love it
is using the wrong word. To love food may not be wrong,
but it is a selfish love. How, or in what manner, does God
love us? or in what manner ought we to love him? "God so
loved the world that he gave his only beloved son, that who-
soever believeth in him should not perish, but have everlast-

ing life." But on the other hand, "God is angry with the
wicked every day." Clearly, love and anger cannot co-exist
to the same object. "I had pity upon thee". Might not
"pity" be sometimes a better translation than "love"? God
is love, but God is not softness. "It is a fearful thing
to fall into the hands of the living God." "God is a consuming
fire." God may have pity and compassion on the
sinner; but that is a different thing from loving in its
highest and truest sense. I have pity and compassion on
a fallen woman; I love my wife. There was a difference
between our Lord's love to John and his love to Judas. We
love that which in our opinion is worth loving; where there
is nothing worth loving we can only pity. God hates sin;
but can there be sin apart from a sinner? That which in a
man is a sin is no sin in the brute. It is often said, that
while God hates the sin he loves the sinner. How can that
be? It cannot be. God may hate the sin and pity the sinner, that is all. The pity, the compassion of God is not synonymous
with salvation. It may lead to salvation, often does, without it there can be no salvation, but more is necessary. It
is not enough that God loves us, we must learn to love God.
To learn to love, to learn to hate, are things much more under
our control than we are at times willing to allow. I shall
ever remember the first Sabbath evening I spent in Limerick;
I saw some four or five little children running after and
stoning two or three of about their own age. "Why are you
stoning these children, what are they doing to hurt you?"
"Why, because they go to Church, and not to chapel, as we do."
So unreasonable is hate; so easily might love be manifested.

/////////////////

ALCOHOL.

Alcohol is the one intoxicating principle in all our intoxicating liquors.   Alcohol, is not food; it contains no nit-
rogen, and so can construct no muscle.   Chemically it might
give heat to the body, but it does not.   It in reality cools
the human frame; under its action less carbonic acid is giv-
en off, indicating less heat produced, than under normal conditions.   The thermometer shews a lower temperature in a
drunk man than in a sober man.   Dr. Richardson is our authority.   Experience amply bears out his conclusions.   How
comes it then that the drinking of alcoholics heats, or sends
heat to the face and limbs and to the skin all over?   It
paralyses the nerves that control the flow of blood to the
surface of the body, and so permits heat which is essential
to the heart and viscera, but less so to the external parts
of the body, to be used up at the expence of the former, at
times causing death owing to diminished heat where heat is
most necessary.   That pleasure is obtained by the use of
alcoholics, to many people, is undeniable.   Animal excitement gives pleasure, and alcoholics to excite is prized by
many.   But Nemesis invariably follows in the wake of alcoholic drinking.   The most miserable object we have ever
seen is the drunkard recovering from a debauch.   The passing pleasure soon subsides.   To keep up the pleasant sensation the dose must be increased and at more frequent intervals. Every one knows the rest; the victim by and by reaches
a stage when life becomes un-endurable without the accustom-
ed use of that which playing a game with him is invariably
the winner, while the drinker finds it always a losing game.

****

INSPIRATION OF THE BIBLE.

Our Bible as we have it printed, I cannot regard as verbally inspired.   I have never met one who did not admit or aver that "certain small words, clauses and passages" have been interpolated; noted first in the margin, but subsequently engrossed in the text, but "they are of no consequence."   Now, to some readers they may be of no consequence, but to believers in verbal inspiration these acknowledged faults are surely of primal importance.   Verbal inspiration, as we understand the term, must exclude them. But anent verbal inspiration it may be said, that as originally written, the books of our Bible were verbally inspired, but not insured against alterations in copying or printing. Or it may be said, they were to be, and have been, preserved from any additions or alterations that would in any way alter their meaning or intention as vehicles of instruction to men.   This latter position needs not to be objected to, if it can be logically maintained.   Apart from logic, one may accept either of these positions; but that I at one time believed in one of them, and subscribed to it, is no good reason against changing my mind, or making further inquiry anent the matter.   The Free Church of Scotland granted as much in the trial of Robertson Smith; that in removing from the Professorship they allowed him to retain his status as a Free Church Minister.

That inspiration exists in the Jewish Scriptures, the Old Testament, we cannot doubt. In such passages as the 53d chap. of Isaiah the question is in our opinion foreclosed..   The same may be said of many minor passages.   But on the other hand, the cursing of David by

of David by Shimei we can only regard as inspiration from
a totally different quarter, not Divine.   But probably in
Shimei's case it will be said, that inspiration only extends
to certification of spoken words; and only such a form of
inspiration, if it deserves the name, can be averred of many
portions of the Old Testament.   In the Bible are quotations
and insertions from previously existing M.S. where inspiration was not claimed, or even thought of,   Then, is it reasonable to expect or look for inspiration where the thing certified to does not seem to require it, nor appears to be of
paramount importance, at least to Christians of our day?   To
the Jews even, we cannot see the value, or such great value,
of much recorded in the Bible as that the ordinary channels
of history would not have sufficed to answer all that in many places is recorded.

I do not believe in the miraculous in-
tervention on the part of the Almighty except where nothing
else will suffice for the intended purpose.   We have much
difficulty anent many, if not the whole, of the Old Testament
recorded miracles; such as making an iron axe head to swim,
the restoration to life of a man brought in contact with the
dead body of Elisha, and the miraculous operation of Jacob's
rods when placed in the watering troughs of Laban's cattle.
If our Lord certifies to the reality of Old Testament miracles we must receive them as such, but except in his allusion
to Jonah, evidently for a different purpose, our Lord cannot
be said to do so.   A mere allusion to current belief is very
different from certifying to its truth.

The Jewish sacrificial
cerimonies with their numerous details, is to us a subject of

much difficulty when regarded as of Divine Appointment.   In
the 51st.Psalm,and in the 1st.and 6th.chap.of Micah,sacri-
fices and their accompanying rites are spoken of in a manner
altogether inconsistent with what we would expect in reference to God given ordinances.: Much of the Jewish cerimon-
ial law looks as of human origin.   The prophet Jeremiah 7th.
chap.disclaims the Divine origin of the sacrifices of,or at,
the Exodus,explain it as we may.

The prophecies of the Old
Testament cannot be ignored.   But even concerning prophecies it is worthy of notice,that in Deut.xviii-22 the test
of prophecy is stated to be,that the thing prophesied come
to pass.   In other words,fulfilment was to be regarded as
the proof of inspiration.

Further,in the Jewish sacred writ-
ings,our Bible,we find along with fulfilled prophecies,God-
like utterances,so far above merely human found elsewhere,
that we feel constrained to regard them as having a higher
origin than any belonging to mere man.   "I AM THAT I AM."
"As the heavens are higher than the earth,so are my ways
higher than your ways &c." "And God breathed into man's
nostrils the breath of life,and man became a living soul."
But turning to Ecclesiastes we find passages wholly at variance with the faith of Christianity and prophetical teaching in other parts of the Bible.   In Eccles. are passages
quite in accordance with our orthodox faith,but whether
they are not the words of writers who lived subsequent to
the Preacher,we cannot say.   In any case,many of the preacher's sayings cannot be regarded as inspired,inasmuch as they
run right in the face of portions that none bearing the name

of

of Christian dispute.   Much the same may be said anent portions of Esther and the Song of Solomon; taking them in
their obvious and ordinary meanings.

Turning to the New Test-
ament our faith runs in a different channel.and our difficulties are practically $non-existent.   The resurrection of
Jesus the Christ we receive as an indisputable, historical
fact; and that apart from any known or attested inspiration
of the records in which the event is made known to us.   Looking at the event of the resurrection in all its aspects,we
are shut up to receive it as a fact conclusive and final,and
so accept it,with all the corallaries that are involved in
it; the Divinity of Christ,his miracles and his teaching.
To the New Testament writers inspiration may have been given;
but whether or not,my faith in their narrations is not thereby affected.   The writings are evidently the productions of
sincere and honest men,neither ignorant nor the victims of
superstition.   I receive their stories as I receive Boswell's
life of Johnson; and in like manner welcome any honest crit-
icism that tends to throw light upon them.   I meet with difficulties in both gospels and epistles,but to assure me of
their verbal inspiration would do little or nothing in the
way of clearing up said difficulties.   And after all,these
difficulties are of minor importance; while their presence
precludes any supposed collusions among the several writers
as if intending to deceive; while supposing deception,flaws
here and there would have inevitably indicated fraud in such
manner as would have prevented these writings being received
as by millions they have been.

Between the miracles of Jesus

recorded in the New Testament and the miracles of the Old
Testament we see and urge a difference clear and explicit.
The miracles ascribed to our Lord's agency, and his resurrection are intended to prove his Divinity, which could not
be proved by any better means, or other means so good.
Hence, with their beneficence and open performance we see
the reasonableness of their being wrought.   But then, NOLENS
VOLENS this very position keeps us from accepting any other
pretended miracles outside of this one purpose manifested
in the miracles of Christ and of some of his immediate disciples.   Old Testament miracleswithout exception, may be
said to be lacking conjointly in great purpose, beneficence
in action and trustworthy evidence.   For the miracles performed by our Lord we have ample evidence which in old Testament miracles is non-existent; unless we admit a theory of
inspiration which is the very matter in dispute.

It may be
well to note here, that although we in our day regard miracles
as a proof of Divinity, or of a Divine mission, the Jews in
the time of our Lord do not seem to have done so; at least
many of them did not.   While acknowledging the reality of
our Lord's miracles some Jews ascribed them to the agency of
    the Devil.

        I am a disciple of Jesus the Christ, God incar-
nate.   I am a Calvinist as the term is currently understood.
I am evangelical in my faith, and a daily reader of my Bible,
believing that God reveals himself there to all who care to
readit.   But I think I can be, and do, all that quite consistently without accepting the Bible as verbally inspired in
all, or even in most of its parts.   In holding this position

I feel clear of many difficulties, doubts, and fears, that continually assault me in the verbal inspiration theory.

****

In connection with what has been said above, the question may be put, "What will become of the Christian Religion if we do not recognise an inspired Bible, as hitherto received by Christians in all countries and in all ages?" The question is a pertinent one, though logic may have no part in it. The religion of the patriarchs existed before any inspired record, was in supposed existence. There was a God fearing number among the Hebrews before the prophets, whose writings we possess, were in existence. And the early Christian Church was a flourishing one before either gospels or epistles were known, or written. So called Christianity existed in the dark ages before the invention of printing, but mostly in a very corrupt form. But even then we must not forget the Waldenses and the Albigenses co-existent in the darkest times. Even our Bible, granting inspiration, fails in securing that attention from the indifferent which earnest souls give to it apart from inspiration. Verbal inspiration of itself will neither make nor unmake true Christians. At the Reformation the Reformers had to altogether reject the great mass of legendary matter existent and believed in by the then existing Christian world. The only available rule of faith remaining to them, as to us, was the Bible, the whole Bible, and nothing but the Bible. As the Church had hitherto accepted the Bible as wholly inspired, it suited the Reformers to accept controversy on these understood terms, and at the

time it answered the purpose.   But subsequently, it would
have been better to have given more careful attention to
this article of their faith, and to have distinguished between portions that must ever be received by Christians as
of Divine authority and portions of which we can only say,
that they never were inspired, nor ever made any claim to
inspiration.   The words of our Lord in the gospels stand
first as inspired; the transcriptions from heathen records
as in Daniel and in Ezra can in no proper sense be inspired;
the most that can be said about them is that they were inserted by Divine direction.   But that they were so, we have
no proof.   It is a mistake to regard the Bible as only one
book; doing so has resulted in not a little evil in, and outside our Churches.   The ill informed, inexperienced, and
careless are prone to jump to the conclusion, that in find-
one Bible passage unworthy of credence, the whole collection
should be rejected.   To do so is foolish, but there is here
a manifest stumbling block our Churches should be at pains
to remove.   The truth of Christianity is not proved by the
inspiration of the Bible, but by the resurrection of our
Lord the Christ.   Prove the resurrection, as it can be proved,
and the rest is easy; but failing this , our cause is a lost
one.   "I AND THE FATHER ARE ONE."
                        There are men, conscientious
men, who when they have once signed to a creed or formula, consider themselves bound ever after, to adhere to their first
confession under all circumstances; to depart from it , they
think is criminal, or indicative of a weak mind.   It may be
forgotten that in so thinking they are in danger of arrogat-
ing to themselves an infallibility which does not belong to

them.   There are other men who quite honest in their action, consider in a general way what is the current opinion
anent certain parts of the formula, sign with that understanding, but are ready to listen to any new suggestions
that may be presented to them.   Each of these classes may
be right from his own point of view.   Sometimes the first
class may be intolerant of the second; sometimes the second
may regard the first as bigotted or weak minded.   Both may
be wrong in their surmisings.   On both sides there may be
a want of candour.   The one jealous for the truth, and af-
fraid as to where the notions of the other may lead to, does
not confess when he in reality sympathises; and more from
timidity than any clear conviction.   Antagonism may at
times be more apparent than real.   In the case of Robertson Smith, we think he would have relieved the minds of many,
had he taken occasion to clearly express his faith in Christ
as the Divine Saviour as publicly as he submitted his crit-
icisms to all who cared to read.   In all persuasions there
are certain points that may not be regarded as open questions.   Roman Catholics must acknowledge the supremacy of
the Pope.   The Reformed Churches maintain the right of private judgment.   So long as Evangelical Churches are clear
in adhering to evangelical truth, we do not think that the
question of verbal inspiration should cause a want of har-
mony among the members.   Nor do we think that any effort
should be made to remove the Bible as we possess it from
the position it has hitherto held in our Churches as our
only guide and rule in faith and practice.   It has come to
us in God's providence; and in his good way will achieve
the completion of his work.
****

TOBACCO

The last time I smoked tobacco it made me sick. I was
achild at the time,and have not smoked since; but I feel
confident that were I to start smoking tobacco to-day it
would affect me in a similar manner. Tobacco is a narcotic,and tends to lower the action of the heart. Hence
the sickness and faintness caused on first using it. I
knew a young man who in trying to accustom himself to the
use of the weed was often sick,but persevered I presume
successfully. I was not aware of any reason why this
young ploughman was anxious to acquire the habit,beyond
this,that his companions,or the most of them,smoked and
he thought the right thing was to be like them. We now
and again hear of death caused by the excessive use of tobacco; and generally of boys. It may be difficult to speak
positively on the subject; but there can be little doubt
that the use of tobacco seldom,if ever,does good to the
smoker while it often does harm. I knew a boy of seventeen whose death was in my opinion caused by excessive
smoking. He was at farm service,and evidently smoked to
his heart's content. One day he suddenly fainted away,
but by degrees came round and went about his work as usual,
resuming his smoking as before. In about a week or ten
days thereafter,he fainted again; but on this occasion did
not come round; he died. The use of tobacco by young
boys has seemed in my experience to stunt the growth and
due development of the body. That excessive ,or heavy,
smoking hurts the general system of adults there can in
my opinion be no doubt; I have been too close an observer
of its effects to come to any other conclusion. Smoking

in many cases seems to do little harm to the smoker; it
yields pleasure if not importance, and more may not be expected of it.   Tobacco is a poison to begin with; but
as in the case of some other poisons, the human body learns
to accommodate itself to the presence of the drug till it
can with comparative impunity absorb more than enough to
kill a constitution unaccustomed to its use.   The penalty
however has to be paid in this fashion; discomfort, if not
utter wretchedness, becomes the condition of the person
without the usual stimulant, or narcotic, while all the time
nothing is in reality gained, but a general lowering of vit-
tality is the result; slowly it may be, but none the less
surely.   I was acquainted with John Rolf; he was a private
in the Royal Artillery, and had been for a time far too free
in his use of not merely tobacco but of beer and whiskey as
well.   When I knew him he had become an abstainer from
alcoholics, and he also tried to give up using tobacco, but
the effort, he said, was too much for him.   When taking his
turn in the stable, and attending to the horses, without his
customary smoke he said he could do nothing.   To give up
both beer and tobacco at the same time by the copious user
of them, seems to be too much for most men.   This is never
the case with ordinary wholesome food.   I am very fond of
oatmeal porridge, but I could quite well live without them.
And so with most men, I presume, give them wholesome food
and it soon becomes a matter of indifference whatever the
food may be.   Certainly good food never produces that ever present unnatural craving between meals, and at all times
which seems to possess the much to be pitied abject slave
to tobacco.   I have known a man, a Superintendent of an In-

dustrial School who seemed to smoke continually, morning,
noon and night.   To stand within ten yards of that man
was a nuisance to me; the rancid smell of fetid tobacco
smoke ever present with that man to me was abominable.
His wife was more to be pitied than I however.   On the
other hand, my employer at one time, a respectable farmer
took daily one smoke in the evening; I never saw him smoke
at any other time, and I do not suppose that his habit was
offensive to any body, nor did material hurt to himself.
I had an intimate friend who at the age of fifty-five died
of nervous exhaustion, brought on by anxieties in his work
as the Superindendent of a large Reformatory.   Up to a
year or two before his death he had never smoked; but when
his nerves were giving way he became an ardent smoker.   I
asked him what was the cause of his turning to the pipe?
He said it was to satisfy a craving for tobacco which had
recently come over him.   I fancy what he meant was that
he had a craving for something to quiet his restless nerves,
it is not easy to see how it could be tobacco, an article about
which he personally knew nothing as to its effect on the
body.   The truth seemed to be, that the poor man wanted
something and he tried tobacco, which whatever temporary relief it may have given, could not avert the final issue.
But after ＄＄ ＆＆＄ all, it may be said, why object to smoking
which yields so much pleasure to the smoker, and if an evil,
one that only hurts himself? But is smoking an evil only
to the smoker himself?   To me it is a nuisance almost
wherever I go out of my own house; unless I restrict myself
to a lone walk in the country.   On the steam boat I am annoyed by it in spite of all strict orders to the contrary.

On the rail how often am I asked, "Do you object to smoking?"
Of course I object to it but am unwilling to say so out of
pity to the poor wretch who seemingly cannot go the length
of his own shadow without having recourse to what is a nuisance
ance to every one except his own darling self.   Well, if
his wife is with him ,she will likely say how much she likes
smoking though she herself does not smoke.   Just so, but
note this.   As I was on a pretty long journey by rail years
ago, I met a gentleman with whom I was slightly acquainted.
Being at the time stepping about in the station he invited
me to come into the compartment where he seemed to be alone.
Almost immediately he set about lighting his pipe.   I made
no objection beyond remarking that I did not think that we
were in a smoking compartment.   "O" said the gentleman "I
prefer to smoke where no one else is smoking, and in any case
not in a smoking compartment."   I could appreciate the gentleman's reasons, but not much his utterly selfish practice.
Apart from inside a railway carriage ,how often have I been
annoyed on the top of a bus or on an open brake with the
fumes of an inconsiderate smoker puffing away on the windy
side of my face, and the inhalation of the thing I detest
forced upon me "nolens volens".   How often in my experience has an otherwise pleasant acquaintance "really wished
to be excused on account of pressing engagement", when it
was quite evident that he only wanted to have a smoke, with
possibly something to moisten it.   How humbling to me
when I think how often my company, my conversation, my information and all that I am in any way vain about, has been
hustled aside and considered by my not unlikeable companion, for the time being, as not worth "a smoke".

$$$$$$$$$$$$$$$$$$$$

THE RESURRECTION OF CHRIST

Among intelligent and thoughtful men, it may be ignorant of
truth as revealed in the Bible, conforming more or less to,
the popular religious rites of their fellow men around
them, though without any deep seated faith, or firm convictions regarding religion, it must always be a question pressing itself upon them, but without a satisfactory answer, "Do
men in any form live hereafter, when dead to their fellow
men and all which concerneth this present world?"   To this
question even our Old Testament by no means gives the clear
and definite answer which, without presumption, we might expect it to yield.   We know that among the Jews there was
not that uniformity of belief in a resurrection which a
clear intimation in their holy writings would have presumedly secured.   The Pharisees believed in a future life, the
Sadducees did not.   And yet it does not appear that these
latter were ostracised on account of heterodoxy, although
continually disputing with the Pharisees anent the doctrine.
We think, however, that the question of a resurrection was
more one concerning the future existence of man under any
conditions, than a question of details regard-ing the nature
or conformation of a risen man after ordinary death.   Paul's
words in i Corinth.xv-35 and following verses, imply as much
when speaking of his own conception of the risen man.   Paul
was a Pharisee, and continued a Pharisee so far as the resurrection of the dead was concerned.

Passing from these general
considerations, let us consider the recorded resurrection of

Jesus of Nazareth, to us the Christ of God.   Appearing to
men as a man, though God incarnate, and performing deeds
transcending any power possessed by mere man, the, his, resurrection so far eclipses these miracles, and stands in such
a central position in the whole body of both Old and New
Testament truth, that all other recorded miracles may safely be dropped out of sight, and our Christian faith be allowed to stand or fall with this the keystone, the foundation
of vital Christianity.   We do not entertain the question,
"Did Christ rise from the dead?"   We say boldly, he must
have risen.   The existence of Christianity proves that its
founder arose from the grave.   Had there been no resurrection there would have been no Christianity.   The name of
Jesus of Nazareth would have perished from the earth in such
case, or if remembered for a brief time, it would only have
been so as the name of an impostor little thought of, or seriously, and unknown except to a small number while he lived.
Let us remember, that had there been no resurrection, we could
have possessed no writings of Matthew, Mark, Luke, John or Paul,
no writings of the Fathers, no martyrs for Christ's sake, no
falling away in the middle ages, nor a Reformation in later
days.   Had there been no resurrection of Jesus of Nazareth
we, the British Nations, the inhabitants of Continental Europe,
the civilised parts of America, Africa, Australia, and the Islands of the Sea would have remained in heathen darkness, as
in the days of ancient Greece and Rome.

                        The Christian religion
rests on the records as contained in our New Testament, and
supported by the prophetical writings of the Jewish nation.
But the New Testament records rest on the reality of the re-

surrection, and the reality of the resurrection is known to
us by the testimony of trust worthy witnesses, the authors
of the various writings that go to make up our accepted
canon.   The most determined opponents to the truth of the
resurrection are the Jews.   But so far as we know, the Jews
never call in question the fact that Jesus lived, a Jew in
Judea, and taught as described in our New Testament.   They
may deny the reality of his miracles, but with the exception
of his resurrection, not the main facts of his life.   They
call him deceiver, impostor, and what not; and others, not
Jews, may call him enthusiast, fanatic, or the best of men, but
only a man.   But no one worth listening to nowadays, ever
denies the fact that Jesus lived, taught, and was the founder
of Christianity.   All Christians accept the truth of the
resurrection, and that he who rose was God manifest in the
flesh, God incarnate.   Unitarians, so called, may designate
themselves Christians; their only bond of union being , that
Jesus did not rise; a negative bond which cannot be a strong
one.   But clearly to be seen in these days in some of our
Churches, there is a continual tendency among certain leaders
of thought, ministers and professors among the number, to min-
imise the importance of the resurrection as a fact, or ########
that it necessarily proves the Divinity of him who rose.   To
establish the reality of the resurrection, and the truth of
Christianity we must go back to its inception.   We believe
in the resurrection of Christ because the Apostles and their
contemporaries, followers of Christ, believed in it.   The
question now is, are we right in receiving the relation as
presented to us on the testimony of these men? or in the
face of said testimony is any man justified in rejecting

their evidence, and writing them down as deceivers, fanatics,
or fools? We have never heard it asserted that our New
Testament was an afterthought, a product of the middle ages,
or of times corresponding to any other than those immediately after the life and death of Jesus as represented to us;
nor would we make the suggestion but only to complete as
far as possible a logical chain of argument. It lies with
those who deny the resurrection, not merely to account for
the universal belief in its reality among Christians, but also for the very existence of Christianity and its marvellous expansion in the first century. Either it was the result of mere superstition and fanaticism, or it was promulgated by deceit and imposture if the resurrection was not a
reality. But first as to superstition; the followers of
Christ were Jews. Their superstitions lay altogether in a
different direction. Had their expectations and a reported resurrection tallied with a warlike king victorious in
Jerusalem, then indeed superstition might have led them to
believe in any upstart leader, and in anything he professed
in the lines of their fanaticism. But of all things the
crucifixion of their hoped for leader was the one event
calculated to dash their expectations in the dust, and hurl
their national pride to the lowest depths of degradation.
Jesus had warned his disciples of his coming death and rising again, but not one of them regarded the intimations as
anything else than a parable, that meant something altogether different from the apparent meaning of his words. His
death, when he was crucified, they regarded as an irremediab-
le disaster to their enthusiastic hopes; and even when the
Christ arose it was with much difficulty that they could

be brought to think of a resurrection, a thing unexpected,
not to say unthought of, or barely believed in as a possi-
bitity.   True, Christ had raised others; but if he failed
to save himself from death, rising from the dead was out
of the question.   The women who went to the grave on the
third day, went to embalm his body.   Peter and John visited the grave, but not till after hearing the women's story.
The two disciples going to Emmaus, so little thought of a
resurrection that at first they failed to recognise Jesus
though walking in his company, and though that in the morning they had been apprised of an empty grave.   Thomas
point blank refused to believe in such a thing on less
than indubitable froof; and of the five hundred who saw Jesus on the Galilean hill after his resurrection, even some
of them, we are told, doubted.   The meaning of the resurrection they at first failed to comprehend.   Some of them,
notably Peter and the sons of Zebedee, returned to their former occupations as fishermen; and had not Jesus told them
to hold together for a time, we cannot but think that Jesus
and his rising from the dead would soon have passed out of
mind as it had out of sight, and the knowledge of them and
belief in them have died with our Lord's immediate followers.

When the day of Pentecost arrived six weeks after the
resurrection, the followers of Christ met, as did other Jews,
to celebrate the feast.   One hundred were present, and twenty
the twelve included.   We can only suppose, that the majority
of these could say very little anent the resurrection.   At
the crucifixion, or shortly before, we are informed that "all
the disciples forsook him and fled." and at the special meetings of the twelve

ings of the twelve the disciples are not mentioned as being
present. These were evidently inquiring disciples if not
decided followers of our Lord. About the miraculous outpouring of the Holy Spirit we need say little beyond this,
that from this date, or rather at this date, the witnesses to
the resurrection received an altogether new idea as to its
meaning and purpose. Hitherto the whole had been to them
an inexplicable riddle. "Wilt thou at this time restore
the kingdom to Israel?" they had inquired at the risen master, but had received an answer which had left them as much
in the dark as ever anent our Lord's real work and mission
in the world. But now, recognising the Christ's spiritual
kingdom and vicarious mission as the Saviour of men, all the
facts of his life, his words, his communications, his miracles,
and even his crucifixion, all combined to shew them that the
resurrection was their reasonable, necessary, and appointed
outcome. To the Apostles these things, now, did not indicate
the restoration of the kingdom to Israel, but the salvation
of the world. Henceforth the resurrection was to the followers of Christ the foundation stone of their faith, and
their hope in time and for Eternity. These we regard as
incontrovertible facts shewn by the New Testament narratives.

Still, it may be said, that failing superstition, imposture
was concerned in the Christian's belief in the resurrection
of their founder; that "the disciples stole away the body
while the guards slept", or in some unknown way promulgated
the story of the resurrection, knowing all the time that
their testimony was false. But men do not tell lies except for a purpose; to get gain or glory, to escape pains

or penalties,or for mere mischief or amusement..   The followers of Jesus did certainly preach and proclaim the resurrection of their Master. · It was the one thing above
all others that they did preach.   But then at the inception
of Christianity it was the one thing which they were forbidden to preach,under the severest pains and penalties for
disobedience.   Preach anything,but not that which implied
that the Jewish leaders, the Sadducees,were murderers.   Per-
sistence in proclaiming that truth brought no gain,no glory;
nor was it a light matter to be persecuted,cast into prison,
deprived even of life.   The Apostles safety lay not in retailing a lie,if a lie it had been,but in saying nothing,or
refraining from saying,that Jesus the son of Mary had risen
from the dead.   But all through the Apostolic writings the
resurrection is brought to the front as the one fact by
which Christianity must stand; or if not a fact must fall.
The eleven Apostles were the leading,but not the only witnesses to the resurrection of Christ.   There were in Jerusalem many other Jews who became Christians,as detailed in
the opening chapters of Acts,who had ample opportunity to
test in many ways the truth of what the Apostles averred,
and who could hardly be imposed upon,far less become the
victims of a superstition which could yield them no benefit
but only expose them to confiscation, imprisonment and death.
Superstition may act on many minds in devising magical methods of procuring salvation with little trouble or self denial to themselves,but read the epistles of the first preachers of Christianity in the New Testament,and what do we find?
Never ending commands,injunctions and entreaties to lead holy lives and practice good works; and to such an extent as

might lead one to believe, what indeed is stated in positive terms, that "without holiness no man can see the Lord". These early Christians would know and remember many circumstances connected with the life of our Lord, and in ways not available to those not contemporary with the Apostles; such as the darkness at the crucifixion and the commotions in Jerusalem at that time: Paul says to Agrippa, "These things were not done in a corner." Many of the first Christians had seen Jesus, heard him speak, and witnessed, at least some of his miracles, and were likely enough acquainted with Joseph of Arimathea, or even with the Roman soldiers that guarded the sepulchre. These first believers had means of inquiry not available to later Christians, or to us. We do not here press the fact that the Apostles exercised miraculous power, or knowledge; we would regard our doing so as unnecessary. But we cannot account for the rise and spread of Christianity in those early days of its existence in any other way than by granting the existence of an evidence which to the first Christians was irresistible. No doubt, when Paul and others preached to the heathen, the truth was received in virtue of evidence against which they had no animus. The same may be said regarding later and present day accepters of Christianity. But the resurrection as presented to us in the New Testament is a historical fact in our world's existence, available for all people and for all times.

To conclude, there is in reality nothing more strange in the resurrection of Jesus the Christ than in the first creation of man. Divine power or agency is regarded as necessary in both cases; as exceptional, we may

believe, in the Creation as in the Resurrection; and as indubitable in the one case as in the other.

Much has been
said anent the authenticity of our New Testament records,
their origin and age.　A point we have never heard urged
in this connection we shall try to explain.　It is conced-
ed on all hands that the first Christians, the Apostles included, had very sanguine views regarding the reappearance
of Jesus the Christ on an early day, and at latest within
the lives of many then living.　In this they were mistak-
en; and before the end of the life of Peter and others a-
mong the first Christians, they evidently began to see as
much, Peter reminding them that with the Lord "One day is
as a thousand years, and a thousand years as one day."　Is
it then conceivable that any later fictitious writer, or
writers, would have put into the mouths of the averred Apostolic writers the expression of a faith and hope which every one knew had not been realised, nor could be, the time
for realisation as understood by the Apostles being long
past.　This mark of authenticity confines us to a period
not later than the end of the first century, or the beginning of the second.

$\phi\phi\phi\phi\phi\phi\phi\phi\phi\phi\phi\phi\phi\phi\phi\phi\phi\phi\phi\phi\phi$

From James's Note Book.

"July 31st.　Came home.　I was not much better of my holiday, if any.　I am still losing flesh, but otherwise, I think,
I am improving, but I don't know.　I have left myself in
God's hands, and I know he will do what is for the best; and
when I bring myself to think of it, it is not a fearful thing

to die; yet when I put up a little blood it gives me a
start,I suppose that is natural.   Dying grace is for dying moments."

    In Memoriam.   James A.--------Died 22nd.Dec.1885
O,James,beloved brother,   In days not long by,James,
James,whether have you gone?We saw thee growing wan,
Athwart the vale of shadows,But could not think as near to the
So chilly,dark,and lone.   The common lot of man.

We stood around your death bed, We saw thee very quiet,James,
Saw sweet life ebb away;   But making no complaint;
A final ,dismal midnight   God's hand may make us thoughtful,
Preceding Heaven's day.   But shall it make us faint?

We saw quiet resignation   We hoped in God for thee,James,
Bow down to Heaven there;   That health you might regain;
We saw thy pale lips quiver For what is life on earth to us
And heard thy final prayer. In weakness joined with pain?

O,can it be you've left us, Vain,vain,our hopes for thee,James
Not here to reappear?   Thy shortened race was run,
We cannot think thee far away,Stopped in the blush of manhood,
Art thou not very near?   Ere life was well begun.

When shall we meet again,James, Thy love for us,thy yearning,
To grasp thy hand arise,   Thy look into the gloom,
Hear welcome in thy whisper,Thy joy,and hope for morning,
See soul glance in thine eyes? To dawn beyond the tomb,

Are graved upon our memory; So farewell, brother, dear one,
Our dearest wish to be   James, in our dying hours,
All gathered in the evening   May thy calm trust in Jesus,
At home with Christ and thee. Thy love to God be ours.

                    ****

                        Jeanie
                    Born 15th. Jan.1879.
                    Died 20th. Jan.1882

We have wept for Jeanie, darling,   There are those who will
As we never wept before;   thee welcome
The sword has pierced our tender   As a branchlet of our tree,
                    hearts   Partakers of a glory,
And touched the very core.   We"long and pant to see".

O loved and loving dear one,   There may be work before
To know thee was to love,   us
But our faithful God has ta'en   Still on this weeping
                    thee   earth;
To his heavenly home. above.   But we'll sorely, sadly
                                             miss thee
                                    Around our family hearth.

                    We loved our little sunbeam,
                    All vied her friend to be;
                    But our Saviour said, "I love her,
                    Wee Jeanie, come to me."

            ****